DOSTOEVSKY:

Child and Man in His Works

DOSTOEVSKY Child and Man in His Works

by William Woodin Rowe

New York: New York University Press

London: University of London Press Limited

1968

© 1968 by New York University
Library of Congress Catalog Card Number 68 — 29852
Manufactured in the United States of America

Contents

Introduction   vii

PART I.   THE GENESIS OF FEELINGS

ONE   The Child as Victim   3
TWO   The Child as Adult   41

PART II.   THE CHILD AS MENTAL IMAGE

THREE   The Child in Memory   75
FOUR   The Child in Dreams, Visions,
       Hallucinations, and Illusions   93
FIVE   The Child as Religious Ideal   119
SIX   The Child in Hypothesis   139

PART III.   THE CHILD AS MODIFIER

SEVEN   The Adult as Child   161
EIGHT   The Child in Descriptive Devices   205
       Conclusion   229
       Index   239

Introduction

The child in Dostoevsky is an essential vehicle for conveying the author's deepest and most acute feelings. Moreover, Dostoevsky's little children often lead to his biggest ideas. Indeed, Vyacheslav Ivanov has asserted that the child in Dostoevsky "is the central point of his doctrine concerning the world and concerning man." [1]

Significant children are not merely abundant in Dostoevsky's works; these works continually evince signal mental images of children; and within nearly every Dostoevskian adult, there hides exceeding much of the child. The present study seeks to reveal, examine, and evaluate these diverse children — and a few others as well.

André Gide has observed that

> In Dostoevsky's works children are numerous, and it is worth noting that the majority of his characters — and of these the most important — are still young, hardly set. It seems to be the genesis of feelings that interests him chiefly, for he depicts them as indistinct, in their larval state, so to speak.[2]

So intensively was Dostoevsky preoccupied with this "genesis of feelings" that the concept affords an incisive criterion for his children's categorization. Nor does it exclude many of his adults. Just as Dostoevsky's children are either naturally (through prematurely awakened sensibility) or artificially (through victimization) adult-like, so are nearly all of his adults in varying degrees childlike.

Many of the adult personages in Dostoevsky's works readily assign to one of two significantly contrasting categories: those who somehow wrong children and are subsequently pursued by this in dreams, memories, hallucinations, visions, delirium, etc.; and those who are meek, innocent, and childlike and who were often themselves wronged in childhood, the effects of which are still significant and are more patently apparent in memories, dreams, etc.

Thus, three themes are inherent in the present study: "genesis of feelings," the child as mental image, and the childlikeness of adults. These themes correspond roughly to the general divisions: real children, imagined children, and children utilized in descriptive devices.

As one examines the children who experience a "genesis of feelings," two distinct but by no means mutually exclusive criteria for analysis appear: (1) the circumstances forcing a child to develop and make use of his capacity for adult thoughts and emotions, and (2) this capacity itself. Hence, the two subdivisions of Part One of this study: the child as victim and the child as adult. The "child-adult" is often (but not necessarily) precocious and grows through a painful awakening to the adult world. The "child-victim" is subjected, primarily as a passive sacrifice, to the adult world's cruelty and injustice.

There is nearly factitious pathos, if not bathos, about many of Dostoevsky's children. They suffer. They often apprehend and even ponder their own sickliness and helplessness — an ordeal that, one is occasionally tempted to suspect, their author experiences, vicariously and perhaps even masochistically. If so, the reasons for this are no doubt manifold. As Leonid Grossman has pointed out, Dostoevsky's own life experience constantly exposed him to the "highest concentration of human suffering." He had no need to imagine, Grossman continues,

> the grief of a father losing a young child, nor to employ fantasy in describing the death of little Ilyusha . . . There were times when he was ready to undergo the tortures of the Cross in order to bring his daughter back to life.[3]

Perhaps more significant than Dostoevsky's life experience, however, was his acute sensitivity to suffering.[4] Especially in *The Diary of a Writer*, one is impressed by the pity that relentlessly besets him for the children he indefatigably describes and discusses. Konstantin Mochulsky dubs *The Diary* "a laboratory for *The Brothers Karamazov*,"[5] and in a well-known letter to N. A. Lyubimov,[6] Dostoevsky insists that Ivan's grisly pictures of child victims are rooted in fact.[7] He implores his editor not to delete the word "excrement" in Ivan's account of a child of five who was besmeared with her own excrement by her mother for soiling her bed at night. Dostoevsky's aesthetic election for lurid detail in such cases is typical, as is his insistence that the incident actually occurred. Indeed, it is not uncommon for him to add: "and such instances happen by the hundreds, I assure you."[8]

But such scenes in Dostoevsky should not be summarily dismissed as unsavory sensationalism. The author's sympathy and empathy do perhaps lead him to condemn the generic from the particular. But he is sincere — and convincing, if one accepts the perspective subsisting within his analyses. Dostoevsky was a master of prolepsis, however, and it behooves the reader to be chary of such *a posteriori* pessimism.

There is, anent pathos, yet another contributing factor deserving but curiously resisting analysis: Dostoevsky's alleged pedophilia.[9] Whether or not one gives credence to Strakhov's accusations (that Dostoevsky himself had once raped a young girl), his "sexual perception" of children is unmistakable, although he scrupulously eschewed scatology. One feels, for example, an itchy prurience about the scheming gentleman in *The Fir Tree and the Wedding* which perhaps reflects Dostoevsky's own agitation but surely intensifies the uneasiness and near revulsion felt by the young girl and thereby heightens the dramatic tension inherent in the genesis of her feelings — the startling awakening of her sensibilities.

That the child in Dostoevsky often assumes the form of "mental image" is quite understandable. Indeed, he was so imbued with a nearly phenomenological outlook that his work fairly predicates a tenuous relationship between illusion and reality. Many of his heroes seem constantly to be in a strange psychic state of quasi-unaccountability for their actions. They are febrile. They are often desperate to a degree of nightmarish detachment, and they are occasionally distorted

by the shadow of a looming epileptic fit. In *The Diary* of 1877, Dostoevsky somewhat equivocally asserted:

> . . . and not just miracles alone are miraculous. Exceedingly
> often, that which occurs in reality is the most miraculous of
> all. We apprehend reality always, almost, as *we wish,* as we
> *pre-conceivedly* wish to interpret it. If, however, we some-
> times suddenly discern not what we wished but what *really
> is,* then we directly take what we have perceived to be a
> miracle, and this happens quite often, and sometimes, I
> avow, we are more inclined to believe a miracle and an im-
> possibility than reality, than the truth, *which we do not wish
> to see.* And it always happens thus in the world; in this is
> the entire history of mankind.[10]

Despite the Gogolian usage of "almost," which I have attempted to
preserve by inserting Donne-like commas, Dostoevsky's message seems
clear: that reality is potentially in the eye of the beholder.

In the case of Kornilova, who threw her six-year-old stepdaughter
from a fourth-story window — discussed no less than five times in *The
Diary,* to comprise an aggregate exceeding fifty pages — Dostoevsky
constantly stresses the fact that Kornilova was pregnant at the time, a
factor which he construes as a valid extenuation for, if not a vin-
dication of, her admittedly heinous deed. This is not to say that Dostoevsky imperiously pardoned all crimes committed by persons in
unusual psychic states; he continually appears to be suggesting,
however, that in many instances, such as the murders perpetrated by
Raskolnikov, what actually happened could well have been averted
under other, relatively normal conditions.

There is a theme in Dostoevsky of the uncanny vividness of detail
perceived in various unusual psychic states,[11] and the "genesis of
feelings" often occurs therein. This theme often redounds concom-
itantly, if not derivatively, from various manifestations of the Dostoevskian child as mental image.

One function of the child in descriptive devices is significant
throughout this study and thus deserves mention here. Dostoevsky
often manipulates age (or apparent age) for dramatic effect. Typically, a child is suddenly described as younger when undergoing victimization by the adult world. But more than mere age manipulation

is involved. The Russian word *"rebyonok,"* for instance, has the overlapping denotations of "baby" and "child" which in themselves can imply or signify a genesis of feelings, especially in certain applications. Whatever pathos is evoked by "the child decided to avenge his father's death" is yet more intense in "the *rebyonok* decided. . . ." (Such strategic usages of the word *rebyonok* are often indicated below before the device is more fully examined in Chapter Eight.) The same is true of the countless diminutives in Russian, which can render a description of a child's adult-like feelings exceedingly poignant. Such linguistic considerations must be examined if one is fully to appreciate the intensity of the Dostoevskian child's early emotional experiencing of sex, murder, suicide, etc., as well as the normal thoughts and feelings of the Dostoevskian childlike adult. As will be shown, this technique of age gradation increases pathos of victimization with little or no damage to the child's potential for apprehending his plight.

Notwithstanding the significance of children in Dostoevsky's journalistic works (*The Diary* of 1876 is richest in this regard: 32 per cent of its pages deal primarily if not exclusively with children and childhood), the ten volumes of his *Collected Works* (Moscow, 1956–1958) are the principal area examined in this study.

As for the transliteration of Russian words found below, scholarship defers to readability and accepted usage.

I would like to thank emphatically for all their help Professors Robert Magidoff, Leonid Rzhevsky, and Zoya Yurieff of New York University, where this study was accepted as a doctoral dissertation in a somewhat different form. Also Professor Wladimir Weidlé, for his numerous helpful remarks. And also my wife Eleanor, whose critical power patiently parted the book's hair, brushed down its cowlicks, and even washed behind its ears.

Notes

[1] Vyacheslav Ivanov, *Freedom and the Tragic Life: A Study in Dostoevsky,* trans. Norman Cameron (New York, 1960), p. 95.

[2] André Gide, *Dostoevsky* (Norfolk, Conn., 1961), p. 109.

[3] Leonid Grossman, "Problema realizma u Dostoevskogo," *Vestnik Evropy* (February, 1917), p. 68. Unless specified otherwise, all translations from the Russian are my own.

[4] In the words of David Magarshack, "Dostoevsky was extremely sensitive about the suffering of children. . . ." (David Magarshack, *Dostoevsky* [London, 1962], p. 28.)

[5] K. Mochulsky, *Dostoevsky: zhizn: tvorchestvo* (Paris, 1947), p. 459.

[6] F. M. Dostoevsky, *Letters,* ed. A. S. Dolinin (Moscow, 1928–1959), IV, 52–54.

[7] As Ernest J. Simmons, among others, has noted. See Ernest J. Simmons, *Dostoevsky: The Making of a Novelist* (New York, 1962), p. 348.

[8] See, for example, the Kroneberg, Kornilova, and Dzhunkovsky Cases, amply discussed in *The Diary,* 1876–1877 (F. M. Dostoevsky, *The Diary of a Writer:* 1873, 1876, 1877 [Paris, YMCA-Press]).

[9] The reader is referred to Mark Slonim, *Tri lyubvi Dostoevskogo* (New York, 1953), pp. 197–201 and to Avrahm Yarmolinsky, *Dostoevsky: His Life and Art* (New York, 1960), pp. 298–303. See also Simmons, p. 39; Ralph E. Matlaw, "Recurrent Imagery in Dostoevskij," *Harvard Slavic Studies,* III (1957), 201–202; and Dominique Arban, *Dostoïevski "Le Coupable"* (Paris, 1953), p. 97.

[10] Dostoevsky, *The Diary* of 1877, pp. 170–71.

[11] As Gide has noted. See Gide, p. 122.

DOSTOEVSKY:

Child and Man in His Works

PART I

The Genesis of Feelings

CHAPTER ONE

The Child as Victim

Probably no child victims in Dostoevsky engage one's pity and indignation more profoundly than those in the "pictures" propounded by Ivan in the chapter entitled "Rebellion" of *The Brothers Karamazov*.[1] Each seems unforgivably true. Such victims urge *ipso facto* the arraignment of their very potentiality. Moreover, each seems insidiously typical.[2] To imagine that these children are not imaginary is virtually to obscure the possibility of their obscureness.

An inquiry into the mechanics effecting these pictures' plausibility necessitates a cursory examination of the preceding chapter. Entitled "The Brothers Get Acquainted," it serves as a most important prelude to the depiction of Ivan's child victims.

"I've figured something out about you," says Alyosha to Ivan, and, when asked what it is, replies:

> That you are exactly the same sort of young person as all other twenty-three-year-olds, just as young and callow a boy, just as fine, just as green, well — a boy.[3]

Not only does Ivan concur, five pages later he abruptly declares: "Alyosha, look at me: I really am just the same sort of little boy as you. . . ." The two brothers then proceeded to discuss "Russian boys" for three pages,[4] whereupon the chapter ends with Ivan smiling. Smiling, we are informed, "exactly like a timid little boy. Never before had Alyosha seen him smile in this manner." This most uncharacteristic, childlike smile, set against the uncharacteristic background of Ivan-as-little-boy, is thus the cue for his child victims to enter. But, one should note, Dostoevsky has already allied Ivan with the children he is to describe, thereby subtly intensifying Ivan's, and consequently, the reader's emotional involvement.[5] This sudden, barely noticeable transformation of callous intellect into callow emotion serves two essential purposes. It is conducive to convincing us both of Ivan's sincerity and of the "naturalness" inherent in his disturbingly plausibly un-unique pictures.

But here Dostoevsky effects what is even for him a forensic tour de force. Purporting to explain why he cannot "love his neighbor," Ivan twists the argument in quite a different direction. He had wanted to speak of the suffering of mankind, he says, but "it is better to limit the discussion to the sufferings of children," though this "reduces my argument by nine tenths" and "weakens my case." But what argument? And what case? It must be remembered that Ivan is soon to conclude: "I return my ticket" (since the world's aggregate goodness and joy can never counterbalance the suffering of one innocent child).

It is difficult to envision how the sufferings of children weaken Ivan's case when without them he should never have had one.[6] Under close scrutiny, the above progression admits of two agile fallacies. First, Ivan's introducing "the suffering of mankind" induces the reader to presume: "Still, no matter how my fellow man suffers, I cannot love him." Secondly, his focusing on children's sufferings suggests: "Yes, when innocent children suffer, it is yet more difficult not to love them." Actually, however, Ivan's whole case for returning his ticket rests on his love for these children and, *a posteriori*, for his fellow man!

Nevertheless, an eerie, Dostoevskian consistency pervades this entire chapter: "The man who tortures an innocent child is potentially my fellow man; therefore, I cannot blanketly claim to love him." This, it should be noted, is the same mode of reasoning utilized in Ivan's ensuing argument, though both are clothed in showy sophistry. Here, in essence, one bad neighbor spoils all good ones; there, one suffering child poisons life itself.

But then, the description of Ivan's children is not without further internal Dostoevskian contradictions — always psychologically
persuasive and subtly sophistical. Apparently, Ivan is sometimes
aware of them and sometimes not. He objects, for example, to the term
"bestial cruelty" as "a grossly unfair insult to beasts: a beast can
never be as cruel as a person, as artistically, aesthetically cruel."[7]
Four pages later, dilating on man's "love for torturing children,"
Ivan declares:

> In every man, of course, there lurks a beast, the beast of
> wrath, the beast of voluptuous heat at the screams of tor
> tured victims, the uncurbed beast, released from its chains,
> the beast of diseases begot of depravity, of gout, of kidney
> ailments, and so on.

Presumably, both Ivan and Alyosha are unaware of this partial *non-
sequitur*, so hypnotized do they appear by the disturbing truth in the
latter assertion. Ivan probably was cognizant, however, of painting
the motivations (and reactions) of child torturers in most unharmonious and contradictory colors. He says that some people "love exceedingly to torture children; in that sense, they even love the children themselves."[8]

Ivan's children are perhaps sufficiently famous to pall even in
succinct recapitulation. It is necessary to recall the three principal
instances in some detail, however, in order to correlate them with
those described in *The Diary*.

First, Ivan turns to the Turks, who "torture children with a
voluptuous pleasure,

> . . . cutting unborn babies with daggers from their mothers'
> wombs and throwing infants in the air to catch them on
> bayonet points before the mothers' eyes. It is in the mothers'
> eyes that they find the essence of sweetness. . . . Imagine a
> baby in its mother's trembling arms, surrounded by Turks.
> They've hit upon something hilarious: they pet the baby and
> laugh to make it laugh. They are successful, and the baby
> laughs. At that instant a Turk points his pistol at the in
> fant's face, four inches away. As the baby boy reaches out
> with his little hands to grasp the pistol and giggles with joy,

the artist suddenly pulls the trigger right in his face and disintegrates his little head . . . Artistic, is it not? By the way, they say the Turks love sweet things.''[9]

To receive the full impact of this passage, one must notice that ''sweet things'' echo ''sweetness'' and that ''artist'' and ''artistic'' echo the above-described uniquely human cruelty: ''artistic, aesthetic.'' The words ''hilarious'' and ''successful,'' of course, reflect the feelings of all present at first, and then, as the ''something'' is abruptly consummated, only those of the Turks. And yet there is a typically uncanny Dostoevskian consistency in what the mother must feel: it is somehow a short step from her tense, hopeful, *pleading* laughter at first to the chilling hysterics which undoubtedly follow.

Second, ''intelligent, educated, and highly respected'' parents subject their ''five-year-old little daughter'' to ''beatings and all possible tortures.'' Finally, they devise ''the highest of refinements'': because the girl is not yet night-toilet-trained, her mother smears this child's face with her own excrement, forces her to eat the same, and then locks her for the night in their freezing latrine.[10] (The word ''little'' in ''little daughter'' does not quite do justice to the affection implied by the Russian diminutive, ''*devochka*,'' the light irony of which subtly sets up the more obvious irony of ''refinements.'')

Third, a boy of eight who accidentally injured a general's favorite hound's paw with a stone is stripped naked ''before his mother's eyes'' and instructed to run. The general sets his hunting dogs upon the boy, and they ''tear him to fragments.''[11] (Dostoevsky's choice of emotionally charged words plays its usual role: when the lad is called out, he is referred to as ''the guilty boy''; when he stands naked, trembling, and numb from fright — ''*rebyonochek*,'' the diminutive of ''*rebyonok*.'' The victim thus seems perhaps even younger than part ''child,'' part ''baby,'' the word's two basic meanings. This strategic usage of *rebyonok*, which tends to render the victim ''even younger'' at the very climax of victimization, is typically Dostoevskian.)

In addition to the devices discussed above, Dostoevsky employs here an interesting technique to arouse our extreme pity. This is a sort of ''dual assault'' upon the reader's emotions that Dostoevsky often uses to attain surprisingly persuasive melodramatic, sensationalistic effects. In two of the three pictures, it was not enough that the child was brutally slaughtered: The mother was forced to watch. The reader is thus induced vicariously to experience the mother's suffering both for the child and for herself. (Ironically, Ivan is not supporting the point he shall ultimately make — returning his ticket because of one innocent child's suffering — as much as another: it is *the mother's* suffering that is so deep and unbearable. Further irony derives from the fact that these mothers are, in effect, the neighbor Ivan finds it so difficult to love.) Nor is this technique absent from the third picture. Locked in the cold latrine, the five-year-old girl "beats her agonized breast with a tiny fist and meekly weeps convulsive, unresentful tears to 'dear, kind God' to protect her." [12] Again, the reader can experience the little girl's emotional pain *as well as* indignantly pity her brave helplessness. One easily feels that both the child's parents and her God have let her down.

Dostoevsky often employs this device of dual assault. For example, there are themes in his works of epileptic fits and of pretending to be asleep. Fits of epilepsy often occur in precarious places (on staircases, and once, even on a roof), rendering the falling a double one. Dostoevsky's characters often feign sleep when a potential murderer is present, thus doubling the suspense (will the one kill, and will the other awake?). In *The Village of Stepanchikovo and Its Inhabitants* the fifteen-year-old Sasha experiences what might be termed a doubly motivated genesis of feelings. As the rogue Foma Fomich abuses her father on the one hand and her eight-year-old brother on the other, Sasha's dual indignation breaks out — the "open rebellion . . . of a little girl who is not even permitted to speak loudly in her grandmother's presence." [13]

Circumstances similar to those in which Ivan's children find themselves are discussed and developed at great length in *The Diary of a Writer*. There, by indicating the effects of such abuse, Dostoevsky yet more vigorously solicits our pity and indignation. Both the Dzhunkovsky and Kroneberg Cases are developed in this manner.

The Dzhunkovskys were tried for extreme cruelty to their own children, Nicholas, age thirteen, Olga, twelve, and Aleksandr, eleven. Dostoevsky is quick to stress repeatedly that the parents were acquitted and that such cases are "typical" to the point of being a "multitude" in contemporary Russian life.[14] In addition to being "beaten continually with whatever was handy," including firewood and horsewhips, the Dzhunkovsky children were sometimes locked in the latrine overnight.

Dostoevsky proceeds to adduce egoism as a significant source of the vicious evil such parents feel for their own children. "Children," he declares, "are precisely the predetermined victims of this capricious egoism." [15] He continues,

> Be not astonished that this hatred for one's own children can at last turn into genuine revenge, and, with the encouragement and fillip of impunity — even into bestiality.

Ivan has suggested that such parents "love" their children in the sense of loving to victimize them. We now see revealed another fulsome facet of this relationship: the parents cannot forgive these children for being their victims — for "allowing" them to perpetrate such crimes! Dostoevsky had a genius for wielding emotions that perversely prey upon themselves, feeding and growing as desperate as the nature of such food suggests. But the reader can become so appalled at the verisimilitude of such individual possibilities that he fails to notice Dostoevsky dressing them up as universal probabilities. Truly, the following description (of a case repeatedly said to be "typical" and "everyday" and issuing from the above generalized psychological motivations) is nearly hypnotic:

> . . . this lady finally springs from her bed, seizes some kindling wood and beats, beats her own child relentlessly, insatiably, evil-gladly, so that "it was frightful to look at," as a servant testified. And for what, why? Because the boy had brought his hungry little sister (suffering from epilepsy) a bit of potato from the kitchen — that is, she was beating him for his own goodness, for the fact that the child's [rebyonok's] heart had not yet become callous and corrupt.[16]

The fallacy that spanking is usually brutal is inevitably lost in the terrible glitter of such a description. Fortunately, such sensationalistic journalism is rare in the Collected Works.

From here, Dostoevsky proceeds to pursue the incident still fur-

ther — to describe its reaction upon the children. During these pro-
longed corporeal punishments or while locked in the latrine, "the
little Dzhunkovskys could learn to see strange fantasies . . ."[17]
Having speculated as to the nature of these escape dreams, Dostoevsky
"swears" that the little children "perhaps" deeply repented, within
a few days, having testified to their mother's wickedness: "Children's hearts are soft." To prove this point, Dostoevsky propounds
the "little instance" of a seven- or eight-year-old girl who started
sobbing "horribly" at seeing her dead mother. A "stupid old
woman" attempted to mitigate the child's anguish by reminding her
that the mother had once made her stand in a corner and hence, had
not loved her. It worked: The little girl "suddenly stopped crying."

> Not only that, the next day, and at the funeral, she was
> somehow affectedly cold and offended: "Then she didn't love
> me." She liked the idea that she was abused, unwanted, un-
> loved. As God is my judge, this happened with a child
> [rebyonok] of about seven or eight. But this child's "fantas-
> ticalness" did not last long: in a few days, the child once
> more missed her mother so deeply that she became ill, and
> never again in her whole life could this child remember her
> mother without a feeling of reverence.

The emotions evoked here are of such forceful stuff as to obfuscate the
fact that Dostoevsky has in effect sworn to us by God that he could see
into this *real* child's heart for the remainder of her life.

In discussing the Kroneberg Case (in which a father was tried
for cruelly beating his seven-year-old daughter), Dostoevsky again
speculates about the victim's reactions:

> My God, such little children are impressionable and percep-
> tive so early![18]

> Do you know what it is to wrong a child? Their hearts are
> full of innocent love . . . Have you seen how a child [rebyo-
> nok] retreats into a corner to avoid being seen and cries
> there, wringing his little hands (yes, wringing his hands,
> I've seen it myself) — and *beating his little breast with his
> tiny fist,* not knowing himself what he is doing, not under-

standing just how he is guilty or why he is tortured but feeling only too well that he is not loved? [19]

Dostoevsky declares that God sees all this, completing the parallel with Ivan's second child who, when locked in the cold latrine, beats her little breast with her tiny fist, crying timid tears to her "dear God." [20]

If the Dzhunkovsky and Kroneberg Cases approximate the circumstances of Ivan's little girl described above, there are several instances in *The Diary* which perhaps *surpass* Ivan's little boy and baby as to sheer cruelty of victimization.[21]

Even when he treats of topics quite removed from childhood, Dostoevsky fairly dwells on such child victims. Consider the chapter in *The Diary* of 1877 where he discusses Tolstoy's Levin: Whole paragraphs are devoted to how the Turks "voluptuously gouge out a child's eyes" while the boy's seven-year-old sister shouts and "rushes madly to tear him from the Turk." [22] Levin is left behind for a time as this leads to a general description of the Turks, who slaughter their prisoners after "unheard-of tortures in the nature of cutting off noses and other members.

> They have specialists at destroying tiny infants, experts who, having seized a little baby between two knives, slice it instantly in half for the pleasure and amusement of their comrades . . ." [23]

Scarcely has Levin forced his way back into Dostoevsky's discussion of him, when child victims seem to crowd him out by the hundreds. The argument turns to

> . . . children with crushed heads crawling beside the dead bodies of their mothers, raped and with their breasts cut off. That is what happened in a Bulgarian church, where two hundred such bodies were found . . .[24]

But if the Turks had a large repertoire of lurid tortures, Dostoevsky had a still larger one of grisly incidents gleaned from Russian life. With these particulars he threaded *The Diary* until its fabric of child victims shows virtually opaque.

Consider the following "anecdote." A twelve- or fourteen-month-old baby who was cutting teeth "got on its mother's nerves with its crying and constant suffering." Dostoevsky's word choice heightens the irony here by slightly implying that the mother felt little or no compassion. He proceeds to describe protractedly what a "pity" it would be to beat the "helpless" baby. This hypothetical and hypnotic (the reader cannot help but feel that the beating has at least partially occurred) bathos culminates as follows:

> . . . his little tears would flow in streams, he'd cling to you with his little arms, sometimes trying to kiss you and crying, crying. But she did not beat him: a samovar was boiling in the room. . . . She held his little hand under the boiling water for about ten seconds.[25]

This dual assault upon the reader's emotions gains added force from the word "but" (so often employed by Dostoevsky to insinuate that the preceding narration at least partially transpired in a character's mind) which here implies that the mother carefully considered beating the baby before scalding it. However, be this as it may: only an unfeeling reader could approach the samovar without already reproaching the mother simply because she *might* have thought of beating her baby. Such is the subtle power of Dostoevsky's factitious sensationalism. It should be noted that the impact of these separate incidents is especially cumulative in context because Dostoevsky constantly refers to *The Diary's* previously described victims while preparing to present new ones.

In his purely literary compositions, Dostoevsky often employs at least minimal restraint and, sometimes, even humor. There is mention in *Crime and Punishment,* for example, of a forty-year-old hypochondriac who, unable to endure the daily ridicule at dinner of an eight-year-old boy, cut the child's throat.[26] No further details are given, and in context the incident is cited with reference to hypochondria rather than child victimization.

Perhaps the most lurid story of child victimization in all Dostoevsky occurs in *The Idiot* and is similarly rendered less horrible in context, this time through its emphasis of hunger and subtly humorous treatment. Lebedev tells of a man who, after a long famine in the twelfth century, freely admitted to having

> . . . killed and eaten personally and most secretively sixty monks and several secular infants — six or so, but no more, that is, unusually few compared to the quantity of clergy consumed.[27]

The anecdote is further drained of pathos by several rather humorous Gogol-like touches, the most obvious of which being the use of "unusually few" concerning cannibalism. The incident is discussed for five pages, Lebedev continuing and ever emboldening his humor, which soon springs from arguments similar to those utilized in *A Modest Proposal*, the difference being that Lebedev mockingly endeavors to mitigate the crime, whereas Swift attempts to effect its mock sublimation. The anthropophagist's ratio of six to one is cited by Lebedev as evidence of occupational penitence. But the rub, he admits, is that while an occasional preference of infants to clergy does soften the crime's harsh "quality," it increases its "quantity," because children are "too small, that is, not substantial," and for any given period, three times as many infants would be needed. (A conservative estimate indeed!) Besides, infants are "not nourishing" and even perhaps somewhat sweet and insipid, so that instead of satisfying requirements they might merely induce "gnawings of conscience." (He mentions the cannibal's "gnawings of conscience" three times.) At last, Lebedev abruptly concludes by suggesting that a snack be served, which fact, Dostoevsky informs us, pacified those present whose sensibilities his words had offended.

    Although child victimization in Dostoevsky's purely literary creations is not always softened by such isolation and humor, even pictures such as Ivan's are less relentlessly sensationalistic than those in *The Diary*. There, Dostoevsky fairly harps on the effects of such scenes upon little children. Their memories, it seems, become permanent mirrors of the experience, hauntingly prolonging both the cruelty of the deed and its crippling consequences. The two tortures most often discussed in this manner are eye-gouging and skin-removing.

One vivid account is of an eight- or nine-year-old girl who "faints from the memory" of how she had recently seen her father skinned alive "and skinned completely." [28] Dostoevsky employs the above-described device (of intensification through cumulous impact) to introduce what is perhaps the most compounded incident of child victimization to be found in *The Diary*. Having mentioned an orphanage for Bulgarian children who survived the "havoc there" and were brought to Russia, he mentions, as if in passing, a sick little girl in the orphanage traumatically similar to the girl who "faints from the memory . . ." This one also cannot forget having seen the Turks skin her father alive. "Well, in this orphanage," continues Dostoevsky (having re-evoked horror in the previously conditioned reader) "there is another sick Bulgarian girl, also about ten . . ." This girl has "a strange disease." She grows constantly weaker and needs more and more sleep; perversely, however, sleep seems to weaken her still further.

> She also has a certain memory which she is unable to bear. The Turks took her little brother, age two or three, gouged out his eyes with a needle, and then impaled him on a stake. The tiny child, while dying, cried long and wildly — this fact is absolutely true. Well, that is what the little girl is unable to forget: they did all of it in front of her, right before her eyes. Perhaps nature sends sleep to such emotionally afflicted victims because they cannot long remain awake with the memory of such a thing constantly before them.[29]

Thus, through a series of superimposed incidents, this story's emotional impact is chillingly distilled to an essence of unreal concentration. It is difficult to extract from the final child's emotional suffering her brother's physical suffering, the other girl's emotional suffering, and even previous children's sufferings. Even though the experience is thus subtly magnified beyond the bounds of a single human being's ability to endure pain, the lonely, desperate nature of this child's escape paradoxically intensifies her suffering.

Unquestionably *The Diary's* most discussed incident of child victimization is the Kornilova Case. As mentioned above, Kornilova threw her six-year-old stepdaughter from a fourth-story window, and the child "by some miracle" remained unhurt.[30] Despite the attention he grants the case, Dostoevsky says little about the girl's reaction, confining himself to comments on the order of: Does the child's survival in any way lessen the crime's cruelty, and, Was this not a harrowing experience for the little girl?[31] In terms of physical suffering, the girl is scarcely a victim; what interests Dostoevsky virtually to the exclusion of all else is that Kornilova was in the last stages of pregnancy. Yes, she hated her husband and took it out on *his* daughter, Dostoevsky seems to say, but had she not been pregnant, she might well not have committed the crime at all.[32] He harps on this possibility until it becomes an annoying probability[33] and even emphasizes the apparently unrelated fact of pregnancy in other cases.[34]

Dostoevsky's main point is undoubtedly that crimes committed in unusual psychic states are "different," much as he often renders the vivid detail perceived therein "different." One is tempted to compare Kornilova with Raskolnikov, since this feverish hero often acts in an abnormal condition, and especially since both criminals give themselves up voluntarily, Kornilova immediately.[35] The latter, it seems, lured her stepdaughter onto a window ledge to see something below, seized the girl's legs, and heaved. Dostoevsky comments in italics that her deed was "too strange by far," suggesting that a close analysis of the case could well extenuate the crime.[36] According to Yarmolinsky, Dostoevsky was instrumental in obtaining Kornilova's retrial and acquittal on the grounds of temporary insanity.[37]

Perhaps the most frightening child victim in all of Dostoevsky's works is Liza in *The Eternal Husband*. A nearly nightmarish eerieness is somehow sustained throughout her portrayal. And little wonder: the initial four sections of this story are a continuous shading in and out of memory, fantasy, and reality[38] rare even for Dostoevsky. All that follows is thus tinged with a mordant bad-dream atmosphere, and the characters' emotions seem somehow justified in flouting the notion of objective correlative.

Our first glimpse of Liza is through Velchaninov's nightmare-lensed eyes. Dostoevsky effects this vicarious impression with carefully controlled vagueness: her "father" is quieting her with

. . . cries, gesticulations, and *perhaps (or so it seemed to Velchaninov)* even kicks. . . . She, *it seemed,* was in utter hysterics . . . and was stretching out her arms towards

Pavel Pavlovich *as if* she wanted to take hold of him, to embrace him, to beg him, to implore him to do something.[39]

This descriptive technique is typically Dostoevskian. Vague narrational expressions strangely mute intense emotions, nearly forcing the reader to suspend his disbelief at being overtold. The sequence, "to take hold of, to embrace," subtly effects a sensationalistic bathos (in both senses of the word) reminiscent of Ilyusha's kissing the hand that was abusing his father in *The Brothers.*

Even when we first see Liza clearly, it is through the eyes of Velchaninov:

> There was in her look the childlike importance of children who are left alone with strangers and back into a corner, from where they untrustingly and importantly survey the newcomer, the guest they have never seen before; but there was *perhaps* another, *seemingly* altogether unchildlike thought — *or so it seemed to Velchaninov.*[40]

The controlled vagueness employed here by Dostoevsky to convey a relatively small genesis of feeling to the reader is most important: This device soon suggests sadism and perhaps pedophilia.

The above description is strikingly similar to the meeting of Nellie and Prince Volkovsky in Vanya's apartment in *The Injured and the Insulted.*[41] In both instances, neither the fathers nor the daughters seem to be aware of their true relationship, but their emotional reactions are manifoldly similar to those of their counterparts. Both daughters hide in a corner, become most distrustful, and experience a disturbing near-dislike for the fathers (who, it turns out, have both abandoned them). The fathers seem to share a strange fascination for — that is, seem to be drawn uncannily towards — the girls and appear to experience a somewhat inordinate initial involvement in the girls' emotions. One can speculate that Dostoevsky intended to insinuate similar mutual subconscious recognitions. If so, it seems consistent that a sense of being abandoned takes the form of vindictive distrust, while a sense of guilt surfaces as compensational sympathy. A further factor uniting the circumstances of Liza and Nellie is that each girl lives in close quarters with a man who is not her father. Dostoevsky's apparent interest in such a situation can be construed to reflect the agitation typical of his more overt treatments of pedophilia.

At the meeting of Liza and Velchaninov, Trusotsky explains ''with aggrieved solicitude'' to Velchaninov and *in front of Liza* that she is ''a strange child, nervous anyway,'' but that after her mother's death, she became ill for two weeks, hysterical.

> She was crying that way just now, when you came in — hear me, Liza, hear me? . . . I don't love her anymore like I did while her mother was alive — that's what she accuses me of. And such a fantasy gets into the head of a little child [*rebyonok*], who should only be playing with toys.⁴²

Trusotsky's supposedly salutary admonishments are poisoned by traumatic reminders of the girl's emotional crisis. Moreover, the phrase ''like I did while her mother was alive'' can be seen to carry disquieting insinuations about Trusotsky's attitude towards the young girl.

Yarmolinsky remarks that the sensualities of Trusotsky and Svidrigailov (*Crime and Punishment*) are similarly ''aroused by innocence and immaturity.'' ⁴³ The critic here refers to Trusotsky's shadowy plans for ''marriage to a schoolgirl,'' but the man's earlier attitude towards Liza, as perceived by Velchaninov, is perhaps not entirely inimical to adduction as a similar symptom.

As Velchaninov leaves with Liza, the old woman who seems to haunt the hallways of the building in which Trusotsky lives accuses the latter by asking: ''Is it proper for a little child [*rebyonok*] *who understands* to witness such shameful goings on?'' ⁴⁴ Only later does one apprehend the full import of this question. Velchaninov returns, and the old woman expands upon Trusotsky's unsavory behavior:

> And isn't it a sin, he brought a slut home at night when there was a little rebyonok here *who understands*. He shouted: ''This'll be your mother if I choose!'' Would you believe it, she was a coarse slut, but she spit right in his face then. He shouted: ''You're not my daughter, you're a b . . tard.'' ⁴⁵

Trusotsky, the woman continues, has badgered Liza with suicide threats and "used to fashion a noose" before her eyes. After Liza's death, Dostoevsky employs a controlled descriptive vagueness to hint at something more than sadism. Velchaninov ponders Trusotsky's strange attitude towards the girl:

> How, how could that scoundrel be so cruel to a child he loved, and is it probable? But each time he would hastily drop the question, as if trying to wave it away; there was something horrible in that question, something unbearable, something he could not quite decide.[46]

Nadezhda Fedoseevna, the high school girl Trusotsky plans to marry, is an obvious object of his unwholesome desire. This girl undergoes typical Dostoevskian, rationalized age stretching. "She's fifteen!" exclaims Velchaninov. "Fifteen now; but in nine months she'll be sixteen, sixteen years and three months . . ."[47] (This is strikingly similar to Svidrigailov's rationalized lie about a girl he considers marrying: ". . . well, what of it, that I'm fifty, and she's only sixteen."[48] He has just said that she will be sixteen in a month.)

It is interesting that Nadezhda's smile is "charming, although often evil"[49] (one wonders how much of the evil is induced by Trusotsky's presence). She is a perfect victim for the aspirations of pedophilia:

> . . . fairly well shaped, with incipient thoughtfulness in her impulsive face, which was at the same time still almost entirely childlike.[50]

Velchaninov feels a familiar vague revulsion as Trusotsky persuades[51] him to meet his young bride to be.

> But Velchaninov was still refusing, the more stubbornly because he sensed in himself some kind of depressing, wicked idea. This evil thought had long been stirring in him, from the very first, as soon as Pavel Pavlovich had told him of his

fiancée: whether it was merely curiosity or some kind of still entirely unclear attraction, something was inducing him — to agree.[52]

The salacious Trusotsky, however, was sure he would agree. And as they drive off to inspect the young girl, Velchaninov's "thought" remains vague as to articulation but turns disturbingly clear by substitutional inference:

"And Liza?" — wondered Velchaninov and immediately dropped the thought, as if fearful of some sort of blasphemy. And suddenly it seemed to him that he himself was at that minute petty and worthless; it seemed that the thought which had been seducing him was such a small, vile idea.[53]

The potential substitution of Liza for the young girl of Trusotsky's disturbing aspirations is sustained even by the language itself. Recall, for example, the above-cited phrase "dropped the question." In both instances, the Russian reads "*brosal*" — literally, "threw." [54]

Then, Trusotsky hoists his true colors. "Innocence loves little presents," [55] he says to Velchaninov, "smiling happily and slyly."

Innocence is my cup of tea, Aleksey Ivanovich; it's not so much beauty — as innocence. . . . Here you've got the pungency of a ripe apple!

"Can it be that he's one of those?" wonders Velchaninov.

These persistent inferences of pedophilia in Trusotsky are the more brought out by a background of implied sexuality in children or, rather, in childlike adults. Indeed, the entire story is laced with sexual ironies.

The "youngish little officer," who is to take over, after Velchaninov's departure, as Trusotsky's wife's lover, is described by Dostoevsky as a boy: "Natalya Vasilevna received the boy graciously but she treated him like a boy." [56] Later we learn that about twenty years before, Klavdia Petrovna "nearly married Velchaninov, then still almost a boy, still a student." [57]

The Eternal Husband contains several ironic references to Velchaninov's being "like Liza's father" and Trusotsky's "loving but abandoning his daughter."[58]

Even the young man whom Trusotsky seeks to displace in Nadezhda Fedoseevna's heart is called "a youth" by Dostoevsky and a "little urchin" by Trusotsky.[59] And when "the youth" remarks that in nine months, Trusotsky may look rather foolish marrying Nadezhda, the latter finds "dirty insinuations" in his words, whereupon "the youth" replies:

> Dirty insinuations? What do you mean by that? You yourself are dirty if you're thinking such thoughts.[60]

Also not without ironic overtones is the burly Velchaninov's condition after seeing Nadezhda Fedoseevna: "He grew weak as a child."[61] The doctor prescribes food for him "as for a babe in arms."[62] When Trusotsky visits the sick Velchaninov and makes a frenzied fuss over the latter, whose throat he will soon attempt to cut:

> . . . Pavel Pavlovich, God knows why, was nearly beside himself, as if it was a matter of saving the life of his own son.[63]

Nellie (*The Injured and The Insulted*) seems both an adult and a child victim. Perhaps no single child in Dostoevsky is so deeply affected by diverse painful exposure to the adult world.

Nellie is strangely flexible as to factual age. Her slight, pathetic physical appearance somehow belies the fact of her years — even before this fact undergoes subtle manipulation. Indeed, Vanya, the protagonist, describes Nellie initially in such a way that she seems indelibly to remain an emaciated baby throughout her subsequent spate of struggles with adult thoughts and emotions. Ironically, the child's sudden weird appearance in the darkened room of her deceased grandfather frightens Vanya sufficiently to intensify her harmlessness and helplessness in direct proportion to the insufficiency of justification for his fear.

> To my extreme horror, I saw that it was a rebyonok, a tiny
> girl . . . I looked at her more closely. It was a tiny girl of
> about twelve or thirteen, slight, frail, and with the pallor of
> someone recovering from a cruel illness.[64]

Thus does Dostoevsky render the child physically young enough to
suffer with a vivid innocence and yet factually old enough to undergo
the throes of mature mental and emotional torture.

At the second meeting between Nellie and Vanya, an interesting
descriptive technique further establishes this twofold potential for
suffering. Vanya remarks that it was hard to imagine a more strange
and distinctive creature, "at least in appearance." [65] But, having
earned the reader's trust with such relative narrational reserve, he
somewhat presumptively proceeds to read a most precocious characterization into Nellie's appearance :

> Her eyes were especially striking : they flashed with intelli-
> gence, together with a kind of inquisitor-like distrust and
> even suspicion.

Dostoevskian pathos is demanding. Nellie's intelligence shines cou-
rageously through her suffering, and beauty timidly subsists within
her sickliness :

> . . . despite all the ugliness of squalor and sickness, she was
> even quite pretty.[66]

This Dostoevskian technique of utilizing emotionally two nearly
antinomical facets of a given situation (childlikeness — maturity;
sickliness — strength; unattractiveness — beauty) derives a dual
effectiveness from versatile construction and strange reconciliation.
Nellie is physically childlike but forced to be mentally and emotionally mature (although her factual age helps further to reconcile these
would-be opposites) ; she is physically sickly but emotionally strong
(the fact of her continuous struggle against life saps her strength
without denying it) ; and her outer shabbiness and sickliness are in
sharp contrast to an inner richness and health (the spirit of which,

one may infer, actually enhances Nellie's physical appearance). The method extends to and attends even Nellie's smile:

. . . [Nellie] somehow strangely distorted her mouth, as if she wanted to smile distrustfully. But the impulse to smile vanished, replaced instantly by her former severe and mysterious expression.[67]

The antinomical attitudes of friendliness and hostility are partially reconciled by the velleity to smile: She does smile and yet she does not. But more: had she smiled, it would have been "distrustfully" — a suggestion which subtly effects two alignments of opposing emotions: not only would the smile, had it happened, have been less inappropriate to her reticence; the very fact that she did not smile becomes more likely, since the motives for withholding a smile are undoubtedly similar to those for muting it with distrust.

Nellie's pride is to play an important role in the novel's dénouement; as Vanya informs her of the death of her grandfather (who, she "involuntarily" whispers, did not love her), he notices that "she was expending *horrible* efforts to suppress her agitation, as if out of pride in his presence." [68] Here, the word "horrible" (*uzhasnye*) reflects all the tortures of Nellie's emotions: It is horrible that he did not love her, but, perhaps, *why he did not* is more horrible still.

When Vanya has followed Nellie "home," the reader's pity is engaged by a device employed in the description of Ivan's children. (It will be remembered that the general had his hunting dogs tear viciously apart "the guilty" boy.) The furious Madame Bubnova has just thrown herself upon the "poor little girl" when, noticing another woman watching, she

. . . suddenly stopped and, addressing her, began to screech even louder than before, wildly waving her hands, as if calling upon her to witness the *monstrous* crime of her poor victim.[69]

(The "monstrous crime" [70] was to procrastinate when sent for some cucumbers.) In a fury, Madame Bubnova hurls Nellie down by her hair, breaking the container of cucumbers: "This intensified still more the fury of the drunken termagant."[71] The implication, of course, is that the little girl perpetrated another "monstrous crime" by dropping the cucumbers as she was hurled down. In Vanya's words, "she beat her victim on the face, on the head."

As Vanya attempts to intercede, Nellie is the victim of an epileptic seizure, which compounds her plight. But all this is perhaps surpassed by the scene which soon reveals the reasons for Bubnova's "bringing up" Nellie. As Masloboev informs Vanya, the woman prettifies little orphan girls to satisfy her customers' lustful desires. "How old is the little girl?" he adds.

> By her face, about thirteen.
> But by her size, less. Well, she'll do it to her too. If she has to, she'll say eleven, if not, fifteen.[72]

It will be remembered that Nellie was initially described as "about twelve or thirteen." Here, her age is manipulated in both directions: Masloboev implies that Nellie can be passed off for eleven or fifteen, presumably, according to necessity and perhaps even taste. The fact that fifteen is still startlingly young for a prostitute evokes the reader's indignation, while the implication that "eleven would do" hints at Dostoevskian pedophilia.

As Nellie's misfortunes unfold, her age seems to diminish, which somehow underlines more darkly the genesis of her feelings. She "is a tiny little girl of about twelve or eleven," says Masloboev later in the novel.[73]

But this does not prevent Dostoevsky from subtly raising Nellie's age when he intends to emphasize an emotional awakening nearly beyond her years. "You know what, Vanya?" says Natasha, "I think she loves you."

> "What . . . how could — " I asked in amazement.
> "Yes, it's the beginning of love, of a woman's love . . ."
> "That's ridiculous, Natasha! Why, she's a rebyonok!"
> "A rebyonok who will soon be fourteen."[74]

Nellie's sorrows come not single spies; Dostoevsky pursues her with dual disasters. Bubnova's cucumber abuse was followed by epilepsy; the incident predicted by Masloboev now brings on a fever and delirium.[75] As usual, descriptive extremes work hand in hand: Nellie is a shocking combination of pretty little girl and disheveled victim. Dostoevsky achieves this especially by having Vanya notice that "little pink bows had somehow survived in some places on her dress," survived enough, it seems, to evoke the image of this victim's outrageously intended prettiness *without detracting from* (and perhaps even intensifying by contrast) the ravaged results. Symbolically, these stubborn, delicate bows seem to signify Nellie's successfully defended innocence. The mere memory of this incident later causes "her cheeks to flare up suddenly and glow,"[76] and helps explain why she becomes "horribly [*uzhasno*] ashamed"[77] when Vanya gives her a new dress. And Nellie's face seems barely to have ceased burning when Vanya assures Ikhmenev that "one can speak freely in her presence because she is a child."[78] This irony, however, is but tributorial to the novel's central tide: the two men proceed to discuss the very adult problem into which Nellie is later to display such devastating insight.

When Vanya tells Nellie of the tension between Natasha and her father, concluding, "Do you understand me, Nellie?" — "Eyes flashing," she answers, "I understand."[79] (She has already evinced a rather thorough and deeply felt understanding of the situation.[80])

All this is the sort of irony in description discussed below as Dostoevskian rather than Dickensian. Dickens seems to have reserved irony rather for exposing hypocrisy in adults, although his works are often structurally ironic, as are some of Dostoevsky's. It smacks of *Great Expectations,* for example, that only deep in *The Injured and The Insulted's* epilogue[81] is Nellie proved Volkovsky's lawful daughter.[82]

Dostoevsky has Vanya paraphrase Nellie's first story of her past, and he stresses how much she *understood*[83] of what befell her:

It was the story of a woman led to desperation, walking the cold, filthy streets of St. Petersburg to ask alms with her little girl, *whom she still considered a rebyonok* . . . It was a strange story of the mysterious, even hardly understandable relationship between a half-crazy old man and his tiny granddaughter, *who was already able to understand him and who, though a child, was able to understand much of what others do not grasp during entire years of their smooth, secure lives.*[84]

Emphasized as it is, Nellie's early understanding of the adult world
is laid in a narrationally safe vagueness. Dostoevsky effects this by
having Vanya stress Nellie's insight at the nearly perplexing expense
of just what it was that she understood so early and so well ("mysterious, even hardly understandable . . ."). Paradoxically, this para-
leipsis calls attention to the circumstances conducive to Nellie's genesis of feelings without delineating them to the degree of incurring
the reader's disbelief.

Dostoevsky achieves a dual pathos by having Nellie recall her
violent past near the novel's end, against the background, as it were, of
her violent present throughout the book. For example, her pathetic
begging for money to replace a cup she has broken at Vanya's [85]
coalesces with all the indignities of her previous begging both with
and for her moribund mother.[86] But further: Dostoevsky has already, at the outset of the novel, had Vanya describe in sensationalistic
detail a "tiny, thin little girl of seven or eight, not more," who
stretched out her "tiny trembling hand" to Vanya and Ikhmenev, timidly looking at them "with a kind of submissive fear of refusal." [87]

Another example is Nellie's repeated shouting in Ikhmenev's
face that he is "evil." [88] (This aligns vividly with the recollected
episode of throwing money in her grandfather's face.[89] The money
was to her mother's life, perhaps,[90] what Ikhmenev's proposed adoption is to Nellie's, but both men have damned their daughters.) When
Nellie accuses Ikhmenev, her words contain a rather touching Dostoevskian contradiction: "Yes, evil, evil . . . I'm evil myself, more evil
than anybody, but you're even more evil than I am!" [91] Truly,
Nellie does possess a particle of Lise Kokhlakova's perverseness. Consider, for example, her disturbing antics with the doctor's medicine:
"Something cruel and evil flashed across her face." [92] Consider also
her smashing of Vanya's cup "with a look of challenging triumph,"
which follows another emphatic pretension to being more evil than
anyone else.[93]

As Nellie finally recalls her past, Dostoevsky again has Vanya
stress the astonishing potential of this child for full experience. "One
could see," says Vanya, "that her 'mommy' had often talked with
little Nellie about their former happy days,

> . . . crying over her and at the same time not even suspect-
> ing that her stories would so forcefully resound in the hyper-

sensitively impressionable and precociously developed heart of the sick child.[94]

The novel's epilogue is filled with Nellie's fatal illness and with a nearly bewildering Dostoevskian blending of illusion and reality. Typically, Dostoevsky endows the details of her delirious recollections with a somewhat tendentious vividness.[95]

Nor is Nellie's versatility (now babe, now little adult) without tendentious overtones: her potential for adult experience is never questioned, only emphasized. Indeed, the epilogue affords cause for wonder, who is more the child — Nellie or Ikhmenev:

> The sick girl was happy as a rebyonok; she flirted with the old man, ridiculed him, told him her dreams, always inventing something, and made him tell stories too . . .[96]

But it should be noted that this description does not really deny the concept of Nellie's being a child, despite all the implications of adult behavior ("flirted," "ridiculed," "made him") and even false contrast ("as a child").

Nellie's manipulation of the old man can be found oddly suggestive of something more than purely childish affection — especially so, it seems, following her victimization by Madame Bubnova. And if one scrutinizes Nellie's attitude towards Vanya, it, too, can be seen to suggest, in the words of Natasha, "a woman's love." But Nellie's attitude towards the doctor is the most unchildlike of all. Whether she attempts to live with him intending, as she suggests, to marry him eventually, or whether she feels unable to remain with Vanya for other reasons — her motivations are clearly somewhat sexual.

As seen above, the new dress Vanya gives Nellie reminds her of the one in which she had been victimized. "Will you sew me many dresses," she abruptly asks the doctor, "after I marry you?"[97] Her symbolic suggestion is unmistakable. Even the doctor, who, of course, did not witness the first two dress episodes, exclaims "What an idea!" and "frowns involuntarily."

We have observed that The Diary is perhaps without peer as to lurid details of child victimization in Dostoevsky. The same can be said regarding pedophilia and, as shown below, child suicides. Typically, sensationalistic descriptive techniques intensify *The Diary's* depictions of lust for young girls.

Dostoevsky devotes thirteen pages of *The Diary* of 1873 to discussing a new play by Kishensky and fairly dwells on the fate of two young girls. "Here," says Dostoevsky, "is a little girl (Matryosha)

> an unfortunate, victimized creature, and, what is most horrible, you feel that she is not alone, that we have as many as you want of such "unfortunates" in Russia, all the villages are full, masses.[98]

(One should note that Dostoevsky surrounds the reader with such "creatures" even before describing them.) "The poor little girl!" he continues,

> She has been debauching, perhaps, since she was twelve and —she herself is almost unaware that she is debauched.[99]

The reader's pity, as was his credence, is thus reserved in advance. Matryosha is, surely, a poor little girl, but Dostoevsky somehow manages to capitalize on two somewhat contradictory aspects of pathos: her pathetic ignorance of morality and the implied painfulness *inherent in the realization* that she has little choice but to be corrupt.

If Matryosha therefore suffers less than Nellie, who apparently *realizes* more fully the horrors of her victimization, the girl Masha combines both plights: she both realizes and is victimized. Matryosha is "sincerely astonished" that Masha prefers her "honor" to the rewards of a merchant scoundrel. "And when the unfortunate Matryosha" drugs "poor innocent Masha" so that the vile merchant can rape her, unconscious,

> . . . and later, when she crawls up on the stove to see if the victim is asleep — she does all this evil . . . completely convinced that she is doing her former friend Masha a good and charitable deed for which, afterwards, she will thank her.[100]

When Masha regains consciousness, she wants at first to kill herself but later flaunts the facts before her mother "out of evil-gladness, *for the torture of it.*"[101]

In *The Diary* of 1876, Dostoevsky typically tells of an incident he read in the papers. "Torturers" came and burned an old man,

> . . . raped a little girl, carried off another, a beauty, and gouged open the bellies of all the little babies with sabers . . .[102]

It is fortunate that Dostoevsky employed some artistic restraint in depicting such incidents in his creative works; only in *The Diary* does such unadulterated sensationalism abound.

Nikolai Trubitsyn briefly discusses four types of "pensive" children in Dostoevsky.[103] The following four, he feels, exemplify various degrees of early awareness, in increasing intensity, of victimization by the adult world. The range is vast.

Trubitsyn begins with little Lena and Kolya (*Crime and Punishment*), who are captive witnesses of their mother's grotesque,[104] deranged degradation on the streets of St. Petersburg. "Such little tots," he concludes, "have hardly started to become pensive." This seems quite accurate: Marmeladov's accounts of his own unconscionable weaknesses [105] direct most of the impact upon his wife and thirteen-year-old thrust-into-prostitution daughter. Indeed, Dostoevsky strangely refrains from developing character and cognition in the three little Marmeladovs. Although we first see them as typical Dostoevskian child victims, trembling, whimpering, and huddling in corners, there is little or no evidence of their having appraised the sordid circumstances which surround them. Despite all the pathos inherent in these victims' depiction (in a single sentence, the nine-year-old Polenka is described as "tallish and spindly like a match" and as embracing her little brother with her "long arm, emaciated like a match") — still, the "fear" in this girl's "dark, large, large eyes" suggests sheer shock rather than incipient indignation.[106] Even when the masochistic, maudlin Marmeladov "cries out" to Raskolnikov that he derives "great pleasure" from his family's plight, the children's reaction, though violently emotional, is strangely devoid of mental suffering.[107] Theirs is the fear of frightened animals, with just enough sense to cling together, which they repeatedly do.[108] There *is*, however, a flicker of understanding in Polenka as Dostoevsky (typically) manipulates her age [109] to intensify the genesis of her feelings. But only a flicker, probably because her character and personality have hitherto been virtually undeveloped:

> . . . the ten-year-old Polenka, who, although she still understood little, understood quite well just what her mother needed and therefore always followed her with large intelligent eyes, striving with all her might to dissemble understanding.[110]

The children's reaction to their father's accident ("Crushed on the street! Drunk!") is limited to yet another terrified huddle.[111] Finally, Marmeladov's death does little, it seems, to penetrate the protective numbness of terror encasing his children. Even when Polenka, sent by Sonya to thank Raskolnikov, exclaims, "I'm so sad about dear papa!" — her words are somehow minimally moving, partially because of her smiles of gratitude [112] and partially because she speaks "with that especially solemn look which children forcibly assume when they suddenly try to talk like 'big people.'"[113]

The Marmeladov children's outburst of sobbing (when Luzhin later abuses Sonya) is structurally important in the novel: it evokes Lebezyatnikov's speech exposing Luzhin. But still, the children feel, rather than comprehend, their sister's degradation. As if miming their mother, they embrace Sonya; even the eldest, Polenka, appears to be motivated empathetically — by a sort of emotional osmosis. When she "seems to drown in tears" and "sobs convulsively," Dostoevsky renders her reaction largely irrational: "She did not quite understand, however, what was happening."[114]

At last, during her mother's mad charade,[115] Polenka understands something of the situation: she "kept hiding her tears, guessing at her mother's insanity and looking around uneasily."[116] Dostoevsky adds a mordant touch of irony [117] at this juncture: Katerina Ivanovna tells Sonya (who keeps trying to persuade her to return home): "You're just like a child! You yourself don't know what you're asking!" (The mother's object, of course, is to show the world that "noble, well-bred children" are reduced to begging.)

As the children witness their mother's death, Dostoevsky again renders the youngest two children's reactions purely emotional:

Kolya and Lena, who still did not understand what had happened, but foreseeing something very terrifying . . . began to scream.[118]

One may well inquire why the author had Kolya and Lena, in the words of Trubitsyn, "hardly start to become pensive"; surely, there is adequate justification for them to suffer mentally, even though they are only about seven and six, respectively.[119] Considering what vast potentials Dostoevsky presumed to exist in little children (described here early in Chapter Two), one is nearly forced to conclude that he intended to show how accurately, *how articulately* tiny children can *feel* the complex suffering inherent in the adult world and supposedly beyond the reach of their understanding. This perhaps explains why Kolya and Lena constantly seem to feel deeply the family's misfortunes by a sort of emotional telepathy rather than through conscious thought. This makes them at once both younger and older than their years: mentally younger and emotionally older. Dostoevsky, considering the completeness of these children's feelings, may well be suggesting that very young children "reason emotionally" in a manner displaced by subsequently developed patterns of thought. Moreover, it is interesting that although the Marmeladov children's begging is paralleled by the same technique examined above concerning Nellie, this time Raskolnikov encounters a woman and child begging on the street *after* all the Marmeladovs' troubles, and this child's mental reactions are not even suggested.[120]

The second "pensive" child discussed by Trubitsyn is the governess's son who attends a children's party (*The Fir Tree and The Wedding*). This spindly boy of about nine, it seems, received "only one little book" and . . .

Having received his little book, he walked for a long time near the other toys; he horribly felt like playing with the other children, but he did not dare; one could see that he already felt and understood his position.[121]

Subtle techniques effect this boy's pathetic humiliation. There is nothing to indicate that the other children had ignored or avoided him. Although this may well have happened, the mere fact of his inferior

Christmas present seems enough to make the child feel inferior as a person: the material world seems to infect the spiritual, causing the lad to inflict unfairness upon himself. This pathetic self-restraint (he is dying to play but afraid to, and must exercise great control, knowing that at least he could *try* to bring about a state of fairness) — this restraint is Dostoevskianly reflected in the ironic tension evoked by the words "horribly felt like." After all, "felt like" is hardly a strong enough form of volition to warrant "horribly," and, perhaps, the child's best efforts are barely enough both to contain his impulse to play and also to grasp *as a fact* the unfairness of his situation. There is here, of course, a dual application of "horribly" [*uzhasno*] which reconciles strangely (and typically) this tension: one feels the horror inherent in the boy's very restraint.

When he finally does play, a bully pummels him, and "the rebyonok does not dare to cry." Told by his own mother not to bother the other children, he enters the next room — the stage upon which the drama of pedophilia is soon played. "I love to observe children," says the story's protagonist. "The first independence they display in life is exceedingly interesting." [122] Although the scene which follows owes most of its interest to the calculating man who fondles an eleven-year-old girl, the children's reactions reveal much of Dostoevsky's descriptive technique at work. The terrified children embrace each other, and their sense of disgust is vividly conveyed by the frowns with which they react to the "gentleman's" saccharine attack. The girl's outburst — half angry resentment, half distasteful fright — which follows suddenly upon two passive frowns, is eloquent testimony to her inner sense of what lies behind the man's affections — half salaciousness, half financial calculation.

The third thinker treated by Trubitsyn is a little girl whom the protagonist of *Winter Notes about Summer Impressions* encounters in Haymarket, London. Although this child is introduced by a statement about twelve-year-old girls, she is only "about six, no more." [123] (More accurately, she is introduced first, two pages earlier, by a description of general chaos in London: On Saturday nights, the people "with their children" engage in "morbid" revelry; the wives "get drunk together with their husbands as the children crawl among them." [124]) The girl walks along, "rocking her head from side to side as if meditating about something," and "as if in a trance." She has

. . . such a look of grief, such hopeless despair on her face that it was even somehow unnaturally and horribly painful to see this little creature, who already bore so many curses and despair.

The reader feels this victim's pensiveness only by inference: her thoughts are virtually undescribed. Still, Dostoevsky's descriptive technique is so effective that the reader is led to imagine considerably more than is in fact stated. When the protagonist gives this girl a coin, she regards him with wild amazement and suddenly runs away as fast as possible, "as if afraid I would take the money back."

As Trubitsyn concludes, such children usually choose one of two paths: sin or suicide.[125] Nevertheless, the fact remains that these children appear pensive primarily because Dostoevsky vividly describes their victimization — so vividly that the reader himself unwittingly fills in the details of their attending mental anguish.

The path of suicide leads to Trubitsyn's last example of the Dostoevskian pensive child. This is the fourteen-year-old girl who drowns herself after Svidrigailov rapes her (*Crime and Punishment*). Suicide thus renders her a dual victim; she too is pensive only by inference. This child is treated here in Chapter Four.

Curiously enough, there are several child suicides in Dostoevsky, and surely they are among the most pathetic of his callow victims. These child suicides are mostly girls, especially girls who have been sexually molested or at least indecently pursued.[126]

Luzhin tells of another fourteen-year-old girl suicide whom Svidrigailov had allegedly raped.[127] Besides Matryosha (*Stavrogin's Confession*), there is Olya (*A Raw Youth*) — not actually molested, but thrice threatened.[128] (In the words of L. P. Grossman, "driven to the noose by a whole hoard of callous corrupters."[129]) "And such was the fate," adds Grossman, "of 'A Gentle Creature.'" As noted above, the drugged and raped Masha wanted to commit suicide when she first regained consciousness.

Other child suicides in Dostoevsky are the little boy who drowns himself in Makar Ivanovich's story (discussed here in Chapter Four), the boy of twelve or thirteen in *The Diary* of 1877 (analyzed by Dostoevsky with reference to a boy who considers suicide in Tolstoy's *Childhood and Youth* [130]), and the seventeen-year-old girl who left a fascinating note requesting, among other things, that everyone assemble to celebrate her resuscitation (should the suicide attempt prove unsuccessful) with goblets of wine.[131] Grushenka (discussed in Chapter Seven below) implies that she may kill herself as a result of being seduced five years before.

Probably the most lurid child victim of another's suicide is the tiny girl who, upon seeing her mother hanging herself, keeps walking around her crying, "Mommy, why are you choking?"[132]

Perhaps the most unique instance of a young girl's suicide is the deeply suggestive image utilized by Dostoevsky early in *The Brothers Karamazov*. First, the narrator digresses to discuss the curious case of a young girl he knew who perversely preferred drowning herself in a raging river to marrying her lover.[133] He proceeds to compare whatever charm this choice may have had with Fyodor Pavlovich's first wife's delight in preferring elopement to marriage (the inference being plangently clear, given the disharmony inherent in the comparison, that eloping with such a man is perhaps tantamount to suicide). *Then,* after this woman's death, when the orphan who becomes Fyodor Pavlovich's second wife agrees to elope with him, the narrator placidly remarks: ". . . besides, what could a little sixteen-year-old girl understand, except that *even the river* would be better than remaining with her benefactress."[134] Thus, the reader shudders at a *second* implication that marriage to this man is a kind of suicide.

Finally, Ippolit (*The Idiot*) undoubtedly merits honorable mention on the roster of child suicides: he endeavors, however unsuccessfully, to meet both qualifications. He is probably the youngest major figure in the works of Dostoevsky not treated by this study as a child.

Ippolit is first described as a "very young person of about seventeen, perhaps eighteen";[135] immediately after his "Essential Explanation," he is called an "eighteen-year-old boy."[136] There are several passive child victims in his "Explanation," which fact possibly brings out more of the victim in Ippolit himself, thinker though the young man is. Besides the frozen child (whose eldest sister poverty has made a prostitute) who seems to haunt the apartment above Ippolit,[137] there are the two tiny children (one, three, and the other, three weeks, whining in expectation of its sick mother's emaciated breast) to whose father Ippolit returns a lost wallet[138] and the unnamed children so traumatically (if one recalls what the Turks did to

Ivan's children) juxtaposed in the story of the senile "general." [139]
This man, it seems, spent his life visiting prisoners in Siberian camps
and loved to caress and tickle exiled women's babies until they
laughed. He made such an impression upon the prisoners that he
would suddenly be fondly remembered, perhaps after a hiatus of
twenty years,

> . . . by any one of the "unfortunates" who had killed some
> twelve persons — who had slaughtered six children or so ex-
> pressly for his personal pleasure (there were such people,
> they say).[140]

It should be noted that (typically) the universality of these slaugh-
ters' occurrence is twice stressed ("any one" and "such people").
The fact that Ippolit's "Explanation" is studded with such glittering victims somehow adds to the eloquence of this young, consumptive, would-be-suicide's conclusion: would that I had had the power
not to be born.[141]

Notes

1 As mentioned above, it is well known that these pictures were drawn from real accounts Dostoevsky had culled from the newspapers; *The Diary* abounds in parallel and perhaps still more grisly passages.

2 Indeed, Rimvydas Silbajoris explicitly assumes that these victims are representational in nature.

> Ivan's tortured children are not isolated individuals; they are instead the concrete manifestation of Dmitrij's metaphysical "babe," who is suffering for us all and with whom we are all to suffer if there is to be salvation (Rimvydas Silbajoris, "The Children in *The Brothers Karamazov*," *The Slavic and East European Journal*, VII [Spring, 1963], No. 1, 34).

3 F. M. Dostoevsky, *Collected Works* (Moscow, 1956–1958), IX, 288.

4 At one point, Ivan states: "I am convinced like a baby . . ." (*ibid.*, p. 295).

5 Silbajoris remarks that "as Ivan begins to talk about the tortures of children, . . . he seems to identify himself with the children, to become, as it were, a suffering child himself" (Silbajoris, p. 30).

6 Maxim Gorky perceived this basic fallacy but apparently remained insensitive to the rhetorical subtleties comprising its mechanism. He was content, it seems, to point out that "one's neighbor is — a child, a person . . ." and to conclude that everything Ivan says here is — "a sentimental lie" (Maxim Gorky, "Eshchyo o 'Karamazovshchine,'" *F. M. Dostoevsky v russkoi kritike*, ed. A. A. Belkin [Moscow, 1956], p. 396). In sharp contrast to Gorky, Mochulsky deems Ivan's argument "brilliant" (K. Mochulsky, *Dostoevsky: zhizn: tvorchestvo* [Paris, 1947], p. 506). Gus finds it "theoretically fallacious" but "psychologically powerful" (M. Gus, *Idei i obrazy F. M. Dostoevskogo* [Moscow, 1962], p. 453).

7 Dostoevsky, *C. W.*, IX, 299.

8 *Ibid.*, p. 303.

9 *Ibid.*, p. 299.

10 *Ibid.*, p. 303.

11 *Ibid.*, pp. 304–05.

12 *Ibid.*, p. 303.

13 Dostoevsky, *C. W.*, II, 486.

14 See pp. 250–52 of *The Diary*, 1877 (F. M. Dostoevsky, *The Diary of a Writer:* 1873, 1876, 1877 [Paris, YMCA-Press]).

15 *Ibid.*, p. 256.

16 *Ibid.*, p. 257.

17 *Ibid.*, p. 259.

18 Dostoevsky, *The Diary* of 1876, p. 91.

[19] *Ibid.,* p. 96.

[20] Dostoevsky, *C. W.,* IX, 303.

[21] Even in the present study, it is possible only to examine *The Diary's* most typical and colorful episodes. Actually, the indignities to which little children in *The Diary* are subjected are exceedingly numerous and varied, ranging from exposure to vulgar language (1873, 327) to indulgence in smoking (1877, 245) and drinking (1873, 307) to subjection to strange crusades (1876, 412), fleeing terrorism (1877, 292), and starvation (1876, 39–40) to indulgence, by little boys and little girls of ten, in "licentiousness unknown to Sodom" (1876, 323). Dostoevsky continually insists that such instances are countless. For example:

> Are there not many children who in the past twenty or twenty-five years have grown up under these vile selfish people who live on the last money from their pawned possessions, leaving their children to poverty and the call of corruption — are there not many such families? (1877, 180).

See also 1876, 412.

[22] Dostoevsky, *The Diary* of 1877, p. 307. See also p. 308.

[23] *Ibid.,* p. 309.

[24] *Ibid.,* p. 311.

[25] Dostoevsky, *The Diary* of 1873, p. 207.

[26] Dostoevsky, *C. W.,* V, 220.

[27] Dostoevsky, *C. W.,* VI, 426.

[28] Dostoevsky, *The Diary* of 1877, p. 54. See also p. 55.

[29] *Ibid.,* p. 236.

[30] Dostoevsky, *The Diary* of 1876, p. 375.

[31] *Ibid.,* p. 213.

[32] *Ibid.,* p. 376.

[33] See ibid., pp. 376–81, 458–67; see also Dostoevsky, *The Diary* of 1877, pp. 162–64, 440, 442–43, 445–46, 449, 457, 461–62, 467.

[34] Dostoevsky, *The Diary* of 1873, p. 205; Dostoevsky, *The Diary* of 1876, p. 193.

[35] Dostoevsky, *The Diary* of 1876, p. 376.

[36] *Ibid.,* p. 376. See especially Dostoevsky, *The Diary* of 1877, pp. 445–46.

In a letter to K. I. Maslennikov dated November 5, 1876, Dostoevsky relates a conversation he had with Kornilova herself which seems to confirm his theories.

> Without mentioning her *pregnant condition* I asked: how could she have done it? In a thin, breaking voice she answered: I myself do not know, "it was as if a strange force had taken hold of me." Another factor: "When I got dressed, I did not want to go to the police station; yet somehow I walked out to the street, and I really have no idea how I got to the station" (F. M. Dostoevsky, *Letters,* ed. A. S. Dolinin [Moscow, 1928–1959], III, 250).

[37] Avrahm Yarmolinsky, *Dostoevsky: His Life and Art* (New York, 1960), p. 340.

[38] The above-discussed theme of vivid detail perceived in unusual psychic states is also richly represented.

[39] Dostoevsky, *C. W.*, IV, 468. My italics.

[40] *Ibid.*, p. 472. My italics.

[41] Dostoevsky, *C. W.*, III, 241–42.

[42] Dostoevsky, *C. W.*, IV, 473.

[43] Yarmolinsky, p. 302.

[44] Dostoevsky, *C. W.*, IV, 476–77. My italics.

[45] *Ibid.*, p. 495. My italics. As usual, Dostoevsky stresses the child's genesis of feeling: She "understands."

[46] *Ibid.*, p. 512.

[47] *Ibid.*, p. 518.

[48] Dostoevsky, *C. W.*, V, 501.

[49] Dostoevsky, *C. W.*, IV, 524.

[50] *Ibid.*, p. 524.

[51] In the words of Velchaninov, "insists horribly." As often happens in Dostoevsky, the word *"uzhasno"* (horribly) can be seen to modify the effect of an action (as well as its mode of execution).

[52] *Ibid.*, p. 519.

[53] *Ibid.*, p. 521.

[54] Dostoevsky conveys similar hints in *The Landlady*. Consider the implications, in the context of what Ordynov knows or might imagine, of the following: "I'm tainted, I've been tainted, I'm ruined!" exclaims Katerina, and Ordynov stares at her in astonishment. "Some kind of ugly thought flashed across his mind" (Dostoevsky, *C. W.*, I, 462). And later: "Some kind of ugly thought started to torture him more and more" (*Ibid.*, p. 499).

[55] Dostoevsky, *C. W.*, IV, 522.

[56] *Ibid.*, p. 466.

[57] *Ibid.*, p. 480.

[58] See, for example, *ibid.*, pp. 475, 476, 479, 482, 495, 497, and 508.

[59] *Ibid.*, pp. 555 and 556.

[60] *Ibid.*, p. 555.

[61] *Ibid.*, p. 557.

[62] *Ibid.*, p. 558.

[63] *Ibid.*, p. 558.

[64] Dostoevsky, *C. W.*, III, 61.

[65] *Ibid.*, p. 122.

[66] *Ibid.*, p. 123.

[67] *Ibid.*, p. 123.

[68] *Ibid.*, p. 124. My italics.

[69] *Ibid.*, p. 129. My italics.

[70] A similarly effective use of calculated descriptive irony can be found in the concluding episode of Ilya Erenburg's story, "Trubka kommunara." A French Captain is amusing his fiancée by letting her try to shoot a little pipe out of the mouth of "a four-year-old insurgent." When the frivolous young woman shoots, Erenburg remarks that "since it was the first time she had ever shot, her miss was entirely excusable." The reader soon learns that her "miss" killed the boy (*Rasskazy russkikh sovetskikh pisatelei*, ed. N. S. Atarov and V. A. Kovalevsky [Moscow, 1957], p. 521).

[71] Dostoevsky, *C. W.*, III, 130.

[72] *Ibid.*, p. 149.

[73] *Ibid.*, p. 232.

[74] *Ibid.*, p. 308.

[75] *Ibid.*, p. 153.

[76] *Ibid.*, p. 157.

[77] *Ibid.*, pp. 165–66.

[78] *Ibid.*, p. 171.

[79] *Ibid.*, p. 334.

[80] *Ibid.*, pp. 302–03.

[81] *Ibid.*, p. 376.

[82] Liza (*The Eternal Husband*) and *The Landlady* are similar cases. So are two hoaxes (though both are short-lived): Burdovsky (*The Idiot*, Dostoevsky, *C. W.*, VII, 310–13) and "Versilov's child by Lidia Akhmakova" (*A Raw Youth*, Dostoevsky, *C. W.*, VIII, 162, 179, 185, 508–09). Humor ensues from the revelation (Dostoevsky, *C. W.*, I, 389) that perhaps Evgeni Nikolaich (*A Novel in Nine Letters*) is the father of the baby mentioned earlier (*ibid.*, p. 379). Pathos redounds from Shatov's rapturous insistence that he is the father of his wife's child by Stavrogin (Dostoevsky, *C. W.*, VII, 517) and from Netochka's double shock: She was long deceived into thinking her stepfather to be her real one (Dostoevsky, *C. W.*, II, 84); then, when she finally feels a great love for the man even though knowing him to be her stepfather, he viciously denies being and wanting to be her father (*ibid.*, p. 109). The fact that he actually is not, as will be shown, ironically deprives her of what she never really possessed.

[83] One is reminded of Liza (*The Eternal Husband*), who repeatedly "understands . . ."

[84] Dostoevsky, *C. W.*, III, 185–86. My italics.

[85] *Ibid.*, p. 307.

[86] *Ibid.*, p. 350.

[87] *Ibid.*, p. 66.

[88] *Ibid.*, p. 302.

[89] *Ibid.*, p. 350. See also p. 353, where she shouts that he is "cruel and evil."

[90] *Ibid.*, p. 348.

[91] *Ibid.*, p. 302.

[92] *Ibid.*, p. 289.

[93] *Ibid.*, p. 303.

[94] *Ibid.*, p. 340.

[95] See especially *ibid.*, p. 371.

[96] *Ibid.*, p. 368.

[97] *Ibid.*, p. 295.

[98] Dostoevsky, *The Diary* of 1873, p. 312. The Gogol-like phrase, "as many as you want," drives the guilt home.

[99] In *The Diary* of 1876, Dostoevsky describes a ten-year-old boy who steals "mechanically" (p. 25).

[100] Dostoevsky, *The Diary* of 1873, p. 313.

[101] *Ibid.*, p. 320. The italics are Dostoevsky's. He even quotes their conversation.

[102] Dostoevsky, *The Diary* of 1876, pp. 326–27.

[103] Nikolai Trubitsyn, *Dostoevsky i deti* (Kronshtadt, 1903), pp. 7–13.

[104] The adjective is Donald Fanger's (*Dostoevsky and Romantic Realism* [Cambridge, Mass., 1965], p. 238).

[105] Dostoevsky, *C. W.*, V, 19–27.

[106] *Ibid.*, p. 29.

[107] *Ibid.*, p. 30.

[108] *Ibid.*, pp. 29, 30, 185, 186–87, 414, 423, 454.

[109] On page 29, she is "about nine." Here, on page 185, she is "ten."

[110] *Ibid.*, p. 185.

[111] *Ibid.*, pp. 186–87.

[112] Polenka's smile sets the tone for this abrupt transformation from happy gratitude to nearly unnatural seriousness. First, her smile becomes "still more joyful"; then, *just prior to* expressing pity for her father, Polenka's smile becomes "suddenly more serious." Immediately after, she continues speaking, "very seriously and not smiling" (all, *ibid.*, p. 196).

[113] *Ibid.*, p. 196.

[114] *Ibid.*, p. 414.

[115] Lebezyatnikov reports that she is "beating all the children" (*ibid.*, p. 442). In Dostoevsky's notes for the novel, she immediately beats the children whenever they begin to cry, "whether from sickness or from hunger." (F. M. Dostoevsky, *The Notebooks for Crime and Punishment*, ed. and trans., Edward Wasiolek [Chicago, 1967], p. 33.)

[116] Dostoevsky, *C. W.*, V, 447.

[117] This irony, however, is perhaps less trenchant than that which underlies Katerina's remark about her deceased husband: "Imagine, Rodion Romano-

vich, they found a little cookie chicken in his pocket: Dead drunk he was, and still he remembered the children" (*ibid.*, p. 401).

[118] *Ibid.*, pp. 454–55.

[119] *Ibid.*, p. 29. Dostoevsky apparently foresaw no difficulty here, because he raised all the children's ages from his original plan. In *The Notebooks*, Kolya is six and Lena, five; the nine- or ten-year-old Polechka, "about [*sic*] seven" (Dostoevsky, *The Notebooks for Crime and Punishment*, p. 41).

[120] Dostoevsky, *C. W.*, V, 549.

[121] Dostoevsky, *C. W.*, I, 581.

[122] *Ibid.*, p. 581.

[123] Dostoevsky, *C. W.*, IV, 97.

[124] *Ibid.*, pp. 94–95.

[125] Trubitsyn, p. 12.

[126] The two crimes seem to have been strangely allied in Dostoevsky's mind. "Suicide," says Makar Ivanovich in *A Raw Youth*, "is the greatest human sin . . ." (Dostoevsky, *C. W.*, VIII, 424). Father Tikhon tells Stavrogin:

> It says in The Book: "And whosoever shall offend one of these little ones," you remember. According to the Gospel there is no greater crime . . . (F. M. Dostoevsky, *Stavrogin's Confession*, trans. Virginia Woolf and S. S. Koteliansky [New York, 1947], pp. 80–81).

It is intriguing to suppose that a raped young girl's suicide signifies Dostoevsky's own Lise-Khokhlakova-like delight in ruining a situation as perfectly as possible, plus a faint touch of satisfaction that the victim he narratively wrongs is herself guilty of a crime. In this respect, the psychological need to find one's victim guilty is more obviously consummated in Svidrigailov's dream of the five-year-old temptress.

[127] Dostoevsky, *C. W.*, V, 309, 495.

[128] Dostoevsky, *C. W.*, VIII, 192–99.

[129] L. P. Grossman, "Dostoevsky — khudozhnik," *Tvorchestvo F. M. Dostoevskogo*, ed. N. L. Stepanov (Moscow, 1959), p. 400.

Grossman lists here eight "abused girls" in Dostoevsky, among whom are Varenka Dobroselova (*Poor People*) and Grushenka (*The Brothers Karamazov*).

[130] Dostoevsky, *The Diary* of 1877, pp. 38–43.

[131] Dostoevsky, *The Diary* of 1876, pp. 480–83.

[132] Dostoevsky, *The Diary* of 1873, p. 206.

[133] Dostoevsky, *C. W.*, IX, 12. He concludes with the usual Dostoevskian dual assertion: (1) this is a true fact, and (2) there have recently been many "such facts." Thus, the "digression" subtly becomes more than a digression — a sort of background atmosphere — even before it is further brought out as shown below. The passage is the more remarkable, however, in view of what Simmons terms the novel's initial "concise exposition" (Ernest J. Simmons, *Dostoevsky: The Making of a Novelist* [New York, 1962], p. 329).

[134] Dostoevsky, *C. W.*, IX, 19. My italics.
[135] Dostoevsky, *C. W.*, VI, 293.
[136] *Ibid.*, p. 472.
[137] *Ibid.*, pp. 446, 449, 450.
[138] *Ibid.*, pp. 451, 455.
[139] *Ibid.*, pp. 458–59.
[140] *Ibid.*, p. 459.
[141] *Ibid.*, p. 471.

CHAPTER TWO

The Child as Adult

Ernest J. Simmons has evinced wary reservations concerning the characterization of Dostoevskian children: they "may appear to be too grown-up, too mature for their age."[1] He has also referred to the "exaggerated sophistication of Dostoevsky's 'thinking children.'"[2] Simmons stresses that Dostoevsky believed in "the innate wisdom, the intuitive comprehension of children" and notes that his child personages are often "victims of the sadder and more mature experiences of life." These two factors are undoubtedly vital in the adult child's depiction.

"A child's imagination," wrote Dostoevsky in 1877, "by its very nature alone, and especially at a certain age, is exceedingly susceptible to perception and inclined to the fantastic."[3] Expatiating upon a twelve-year-old girl's running away from home, he remarks that "this age (twelve or thirteen) is extremely interesting, in a little girl even more so than in a boy."[4] "Here," he concludes,

is a most interesting age, an age which still completely retains the most baby-like, touching innocence and immaturity on the one hand and yet, on the other — which has already acquired a quick, even greedy perceptual ability and a capacity for quick acquaintance with ideas and concepts that — according to the firm convictions of an exceedingly large number of parents and pedagogues — this age is supposed to be as yet incapable even of imagining.

But even a cursory examination of *The Diary* reveals that Dostoevsky endowed almost any callow age with nearly numinous potentials. "A five- or six-year-old child," he avers,

> sometimes knows about God or about good and evil such astonishing things in such unexpected depth that one involuntarily concludes that this babe was endowed by nature with some other means of acquiring knowledge — a means not only unknown to us but which we, on the basis of pedagogy, should rather have had nearly to repudiate.[5]

At still another place in *The Diary,* Dostoevsky descends even to age three:

> It is curious to observe how the most complex concepts develop almost unnoticed in a child — how the child, still unable to connect two thoughts, sometimes splendidly understands the deepest things in life. A certain German scholar said that any child, upon attaining the age of three, has already acquired an entire third of the ideas and concepts which he will take with him, as an old man, to the grave.[6]

Since Dostoevsky attributed vast potentials to children of almost any age, it is not surprising that he was most interested, in the words of Gide, by the genesis of their feelings — the awakening of their sensibilities in confrontation with the adult world. It is presumably in this confrontation that Simmons finds the children possibly "too mature for their age." Since Professor Simmons concludes that "psychologically" Dostoevsky's "treatment is exceptionally sound and wonderfully penetrating," one is tempted to ask: are Dostoevskian children "psychologically sound" even though "too mature for their age," or are, perhaps, their ages elusive and even deceptive? But what sort of elusiveness and deception could evoke such incompatible designations as "exaggerated sophistication" and "psychologically exceptionally sound"? Is age manipulation, perhaps, still more decisive in the characterization of Dostoevskian adult-like children than in the depiction of his child victims?

Of all Dostoevskian children, Kolya Krasotkin in *The Brothers Karamazov* seems the most deliberately adult. The word "deliberately" suggests itself because Kolya strives desperately to appear mature. Although he often succeeds, one continually discerns the child in Kolya through the chinks of his armor — his daringly dissembled adulthood.

Leonid Grossman suggests that Kolya was born of Dostoevsky's plan, in the middle seventies, to compose a novel exclusively about children.[7] Grossman points out that Kolya is "manifestly an embryonic revolutionary who proclaims himself a socialist." He considers himself, continues Grossman, "an expert on the common man, quotes Belinsky and Voltaire, and asserts that 'the Christian faith has served only the rich and the ruling, stultifying the lower classes in slavery.' " Simmons finds that Kolya's "trenchant observations on life and psychological wizardry exaggerate nature's most extravagant gifts to her fourteen-year-old sons" but acknowledges that "in general, Dostoevsky's treatment of the whole group of children is remarkably effective."[8]

Especially impressive is the resourceful — albeit somewhat unfounded — self-assurance with which Kolya flaunts his philosophies and even flouts Fate itself. Alyosha appropriately mentions a German's evaluation of the "contemporary" Russian schoolboy: show him a map of the heavens with all the stars and constellations, about which he has no knowledge at all, and the next day he'll return the map — corrected.[9] Kolya, one feels, might well correct the corrections. Consider his handling of the peasant Matvey,[10] whom he mendaciously assures that his teachers flog him in school, lest the peasant wax uneasy or dissatisfied since, as Kolya puts it, "peasants believe that schoolboys are flogged."

Understandably, Soviet critics have also accorded Kolya his ideological due.[11]

In order to examine and evaluate Kolya's brazen affectations, one must first seek out the machinery behind their depiction. Perhaps the most salient aspect of Kolya's psychological portrayal is his age: he is constantly concerned about how old he appears to others. (Lest the reader doubt the importance to Dostoevsky of the following passages dealing with Kolya's age, he is referred to correspondence between

N. A. Lyubimov and Dostoevsky [12] wherein the latter pays meticulous attention to the matter of age in many of these passages. Moreover, Dostoevsky elsewhere discusses with emphatic deference the potential deception redounding from such age manipulation.[13])

Although the reader quickly receives the impression that Kolya is fourteen,[14] the truth is revealed considerably later:

> "Are you thirteen?" asked Alyosha.
> "I'm really fourteen, fourteen in two weeks, in no time at all." [15]

Indeed, to trace Kolya's intense concern about how mature he appears to others is to inquire deeply into the motivations behind his singular exploits. For example, Dostoevsky explains Kolya's decision to lie between the rails under a speeding train as follows:

> The main thing was that these *fifteen-year-olds* were looking down on him too much; and at first, they chose not to have anything to do with him, "a little kid," which was really an intolerable insult.[16]

Having passed off the fact of his fainting (beneath the train) with characteristic resourcefulness, as a ruse to fool the others, the "manly" Kolya later "repented" and "sobbed," Dostoevsky informs us, "giving in to his feelings like a six-year-old boy." [17] (The phrase "six-year-old" here seems almost to suggest Kolya's subsequent shame at such unadult behavior.)

We are told that in looking after little Nastya and Kostya, Kolya "condescended" to play soldiers with them. When his classroom was rife with rumors to this effect, Kolya

> . . . proudly parried the accusation, pointing out that with his peers, with thirteen-year-olds, it really would be despicable to play soldiers "at their advanced age," but that he was doing it because he loved the "little tykes," and besides, no one should dare demand an accounting of his motivations.[18]

Although Kolya professes to disapprove of Alyosha's empathy with little boys,[19] he curries Alyosha's approval with all the "manliness" he can muster and masquerade. About to meet Alyosha for the first time, Kolya prepares to "display his independence:

> 'Or else he might think I'm thirteen years old and take me for the same sort of despicable little boy as these others.' "[20]

Similarly, Kolya emphasizes his perspective on "little tykes" like Ilyusha, two classes below the school.[21]

Preparing to detonate the emotion-charged Zhuchka deception, Kolya disingenuously disapproves of Ilyusha's new puppy "in order not to burst out crying like a 'little one.' "[22] Dostoevsky vividly describes Ilyusha's genesis of feelings as Kolya puts into play his carefully prepared ruse:

> As for Ilyusha, he was unable to speak. He stared at Kolya with his large, somehow horribly bulging eyes, with gaping mouth, and pale as a sheet. And if only the unsuspecting Krasotkin had known that such a moment could so agonizingly and murderously affect the sick boy's health, he should never even have considered his bizarre prank.[23]

Typically, the word "horribly" (*uzhasno*) can be seen to serve a dual function. It subtly applies not only to Ilyusha's eyes but also to what they beheld and thus, even to his intense reaction. Moreover, the word "somehow" affords the reader just sufficient freedom for such a process of, as it were, Dostoevsky-controlled reader's discernment.

There is a nearly uncanny symmetry of age metamorphosis inherent in the above scene. Kolya is first called "Kolya" and then, suddenly, when the psychological devastation is described, "Krasotkin," almost as if in mock deference to the wisdom of his resourceful remedy. Kolya has just called Ilyusha "old man" three times (to bolster the lad's spirits) and now — Dostoevsky refers to him as "the sick boy." Finally, we see that Ilyusha's aging father ". . . was somehow completely transformed into the smallest boy possible." All these metamorphoses contribute to both the pathos and the irony of this scene, the latter perhaps redeemingly mitigating the former. Such an effect, it should be noted, is quite unlike Dickens' relatively unqualified pathos, although it is a commonplace of Dickens criticism to compare the death of little Nell (*The Old Curiosity Shop*) with this deathbed drama.

Aldous Huxley asks why Ilyusha's suffering and death are "so agonizingly moving" compared to Dickens' treatment of Little Nell, which "leaves us not merely cold but derisive." [24] Huxley's attempt to answer suggests that in Dostoevsky's account there is an "incomparably greater richness in factual detail" and implies that Dickens' own emotions prevented him from "seeing." George H. Ford, who twice mentions Huxley's comparison, finds the question "unnecessarily difficult" because Dostoevsky's most mature novel is used for the comparison.

> If he had referred, instead, to *The Insulted and The Injured* [*sic*] (1862), there would be less special pleading. The life and death of the young girl, Nellie Valkovsky, as critics have recognized, is modelled directly upon *The Old Curiosity Shop*, and Dostoevsky's sentimentality is often as excruciatingly gauche as that of his model. [25]

In an article entitled "Dostoevsky and Dickens," Michael H. Futrell compares Little Nell with Dostoevsky's Nellie and concludes that

> . . . Dostoevsky saw in Nell by no means a now unfashionable excess of sentiment, but rather a haunting ideal of innocence. [26]

Futrell seems somewhat off the mark: the innocence of Dostoevskian children is characteristically spiced with sophisticating ironies not to be found in Dickens' plentitude of pure sentiment, as a close comparison of Nellie and Nell reveals.

Ernest J. Simmons sees a "vast difference" between Nellie and Nell; Dickens, he explains, "is more intent upon wringing our hearts and draining the last tear of pity for his abused minors," and "his creations can hardly be called 'thinking' children.'' Dostoevsky's Nellie, he feels, may be somewhat too sentimentally painted, but,

> against an unusual background her puzzling nature and strange actions seem true to the experiences of life, and the characterization remains convincing and altogether absorbing.[27]

It is a pity that Simmons failed to take yet another step forward, instead of drifting off into vague and easy praise. Actually, Dostoevsky's "factual detail" derives its "richness," in Huxley's phrase, from two touches of irony which Simmons seems almost to note and then strangely to ignore.

Yes, Nellie's "puzzling nature and strange actions" — at times, as has been seen, thoroughly perverse — do render her "true to life." there *is* a shocking seed of evil in this little angel. Nor should one forget that the sweet little Ilyusha — admittedly, under the crude tutelage of Smerdyakov — amused himself by feeding Zhuchka pin-poisoned bread, subsequent remorse notwithstanding. Rather ironically, Dostoevsky's sweetest little beings seem capable of exceedingly perverse behavior, but this at least partially saves them from monotonous mawkishness. Polzinsky suggests that the sicknesses of Nellie, Netochka, and Ilyusha are perhaps more psychically than physiologically induced.[28] He finds in Dostoevsky's children a "cruelty" unique for two reasons. Not only, writes Polzinsky, is this cruelty sometimes spontaneous and devoid of vengefulness; it also appears in children whose natures are generally incompatible with such a feeling. He cites as examples Varenka's continual baiting of Pokrovsky and Ilyusha's cruelty to Zhuchka.[29]

Second, yes, as Simmons writes, Dostoevsky's are the more "thinking children." Their awareness of their own suffering serves to engage more deeply the reader's interest, sympathy, and credence. Here too, the sobering powers of irony at least partially redeem an otherwise somewhat contrived and extreme victimization. The more adultly the child feels its helplessness at the mercy of the adult world, the more vivid is the reader's vicarious involvement. This irony is especially trenchant because of the fact that Ilyusha and Nellie, among others, "stand," in Trubitsyn's words, "for the family honor." As these apparently helpless child victims attempt to defend *adults* against the adult world, the reader experiences a synergistic blend of pity *and indignation* that no purely passive preys could ever evoke. As has been seen and shall be further developed, Dostoevsky's mode of depiction utilizes a pathos-tempering irony of which Dickens surely never dreamed. Dostoevsky similarly employed the grotesque and the absurd. There is, for example, a feeling of comic relief about the floppy-pawed, slobbering dog's bounding in towards Ilyusha's deathbed — a feeling that somehow serves both to redeem and to intensify the scene's obvious impact. All these factors — but especially Dostoevsky's "good" children's capacity for bad and for an acute apprehension of their own suffering — make for shades of depiction (however roily) beside which Dickens' art shows (however brilliantly) poster-painted.

Upon leaving Ilyusha's bedside, Kolya repeats to Alyosha his recent rationalization about being fourteen almost word for word [30] and then perseveres: "Good heavens! You seem to be taking me for the boy Smurov!" [31]

Then Dostoevsky allows the reader a glimpse behind Kolya's towering attempts to appear old: "Well, perhaps I was fibbing, I agree," he tells Alyosha, "sometimes I am a terrible rebyonok . . ." [32] (It should be noted, however, that this attempt at perspective can be construed as a further attempt to appear mature; moreover, Kolya's use of the word "sometimes" partially belies his confession: to admit of occasional weakness is to presuppose prevailing strength.)

There is yet another significant child in this section of *The Brothers* — a hypothetical one; Ilyusha speaks:

"Papa, don't cry! But if I die, find yourself a good boy, another one — choose him yourself, choose a good one from all the others, call him Ilyusha, and love him instead of me — "
"Quiet, old man, you'll get well!" Krasotkin suddenly shouted, as if in anger.

Dostoevsky may have intended to intensify the pathos here by having Ilyusha nearly imply that "a good boy" and "another one" are to some extent mutually inclusive: "I'm no good; I'm dying." [33] Surely, the dying boy's concern for his father's future is touching, as is his wish that his father have the best, as is his selfless relinquishing of his own father's love and favor, even to his very name. The light irony of "old man" (Ilyusha has indeed just displayed the emotional stoicism of an old man, and yet the image is hardly inimical with impending death) echoes, of course, the usage treated above, suggesting, as it were, a similar, if not more drastic dénouement. The author's opting for "Krasotkin" also has hauntingly familiar connotations, casting the shadow of doubt upon Kolya's conviction that Ilyusha will recover.

Such is the machinery that produces pathos in Dostoevsky. It is little wonder that his techniques have been termed both brilliant and cruel — powerful and sensationalistic. Perhaps the most eloquent epithet to this effect is the title of N. K. Mikhailovsky's article, "Cruel Talent." [34] In the words of Vyacheslav Ivanov, Dostoevsky's is a " 'cruel' Muse." [35]

Apparently uncharacteristic or otherwise strange (twisted, tortured, malicious, masochistic, and even ambiguous) smiles play an important role in the depiction of Dostoevsky's various children. Such unusual smiles sometimes serve the purpose, among others, of conveying genesis of feeling. For example, when Perezvon plays dead before the still shocked Ilyusha: "Ilyusha kept staring with his former agonizing smile." [36]

It has been difficult, in discussing Kolya Krasotkin, to exclude the genesis of feeling undergone by Ilyusha Snegiryov. There is yet much more. Indeed, this pale, emaciated boy seems endowed by Dostoevsky with a Hamlet-like capacity for apprehending his dilemma. This dilemma — a deep and bitterly helpless suffering induced by the plight of one's parents — is experienced, in varying degrees, by many of Dostoevsky's children. And what is more purely pathetic? If the reader's suffering for child victims is cathartically mitigated by indignation at their oppressors, it is only aggravated — for the deeply thinking child who pities a wronged parent — by the nobility implicit in this pity.

In this sense, Ilyusha exemplifies an important type in Dostoevsky; Trubitsyn classifies him with Kolya Ivolgin (*The Idiot*) and Nellie (*The Injured and the Insulted*) as "children who stand for the family honor." [37] Sasha (*The Village of Stepanchikovo and Its In-*

habitants) [38] should not be omitted here; nor should, to a certain extent, Netochka and The Raw Youth, all of whom think deeply and suffer both with and for their parents. Similar feelings are experienced by The Little Hero, who suffers *for another*, as does the little girl in *The House of The Dead*, who blushes and feels compelled to give the imprisoned protagonist a little coin he "kept long afterwards." [39]

Early in Part Two of *The Brothers Karamazov*, Alyosha comes upon a group of schoolboys, aged nine to eleven, six against one in a stone-throwing fight. Dostoevsky immediately remarks that "although he [Alyosha] loved three-year-olds most of all, he was greatly fond of school children, aged ten or eleven." [40] Alyosha accosts one of the six with a straightforward, matter-of-fact remark about how the boy is carrying his schoolbag, whereupon the narrator intrudes as follows:

> Alyosha began simply and openly with this businesslike remark; in fact an adult cannot begin otherwise if he is to gain a rebyonok's confidence directly, and especially that of a whole group of children. One must begin seriously, in a businesslike manner, and act so as to keep things on a level of mutual understanding; Alyosha knew this instinctively.

One must admire Dostoevsky's convincing insights into child psychology and agree with Ernest J. Simmons, who finds that the sections dealing with "Kolya, Iliusha, and the gang of boys provide brilliant proof of Dostoevsky's acute understanding of child behaviour." [41]

As Alyosha approaches Ilyusha, Dostoevsky typically manipulates the latter's apparent age for dramatic effect:

> The boy awaited him without giving ground. When he got there, Alyosha found before him a rebyonok of no more than nine, weak, slight, with a pale, long thin little face, regarding him maliciously with large dark eyes.

Almost imperceptibly, the boy who was fighting six others is transformed, as Alyosha reaches him, into a "rebyonok" — a word which not only intensifies the boy's loneliness but stresses the unfairness of the fight's odds. This is the "baby" who recently plunged a penknife into Krasotkin and is imminently to bite Alyosha's finger.

Withholding, for the moment, what drove the boy to these actions, Dostoevsky ruthlessly pursues Ilyusha's painfully awakening emotions. Presumably unable to face Alyosha's question, "What did I ever do to you?" (he has just hit Alyosha in the back with a stone) — Ilyusha turns and flees, leaving the reader to imagine what bitter convictions could cause such complete and agonizing isolation.

But the boy's father, who wears odd trousers he appears to be "outgrowing like a little boy," is soon to speak at length on the righteous wrath pent up within Ilyusha:

> "Anger, sir!" declared the captain, "I'll say, anger. In a tiny being, but a great anger. . . . And what he went through then, when he kissed your brother's hand and cried 'Forgive my dear papa, forgive my dear papa' — only God knows, and I too, sir. . . . our little children . . . find out the truth on earth at only nine years of age."

As the proud Ilyusha implores his father not to make humble peace, Dostoevsky again evokes sympathy through word choice:

> "Papa," he said, "papa, don't ever make peace: I'll grow up, challenge him to a duel and kill him myself!" His little eyes flashed and burned.

The diminutive of "eyes" (glazyonki) and the appended emphatic particle, -to, graphically intensify the contrast between the child's sentiments and his years. The captain continues his description:

> You know, if little children are silent and proud, and hold back tears long enough, then, if a great misfortune hits, their tears burst out and flow like a rushing stream.

Finally, just before Ilyusha is to die, he asks his father to bury him in a favorite spot of theirs, "to go there in the evening with Krasotkin, Perezvon . . . And I'll be waiting for you . . . Papa, papa!" Thus a nine-year-old boy raises a question of the dead's perception of the living — the note on which The Brothers Karamazov is to end. Moreover, Ilyusha projects his deep concern for his father, which has caused him such suffering, even beyond the grave.

Kolya Ivolgin (*The Idiot*) — whom, as seen above, Trubitsyn classifies with Ilyusha as "standing for the family honor" — Polzinsky classifies with Kolya Krasotkin, as an "early thinker," but stresses that the former lacks the latter's "affected seriousness." [42] This seems true enough. Indeed, the thirteen-year-old Kolya Ivolgin is first described by Dostoevsky as "a boy with a cheerful and rather dear face, with a trusting and open-hearted manner." [43]

This and other characterizations are undoubtedly conducive to convincing the reader of the embarrassment felt by Kolya as he dedicatedly *"watches after* his father." [44] One can easily imagine the genesis of Kolya's feelings as he is continually forced to witness the derision virtually solicited by this prodigious fibber.

Consider the "Indépendance incident," in which Nastasya Filippovna literally goads the gullible general into the arena of his own greedy fantasy. As the fun progresses, Kolya desperately tugs at Myshkin's sleeve:

"Oh, can't you lead him away somewhere! Can't you? Please!" Even tears of indignation burned in the poor lad's eyes. [45]

And, when the general's wild story is irrevocably exposed:

The general turned horribly red; Kolya also turned red and clenched his head between his hands. [46]

And later, as Rogozhin insults the general:

"Oh, how vile!" cried Kolya, streaming tears of shame and vexation. [47]

The child's intense suffering for his father thus presses him into participation in these typically Dostoevskian scenes of woefully unrestrained confrontation.

We have observed the importance of age to Kolya Krasotkin. One wonders whether Dostoevsky was aware of transforming the thirteen-year-old Kolya Ivolgin [48] into a fifteen-year-old.[49] At this juncture, Kolya is being denied "the slightest friendly attention" by his "twenty-seven-year-old brother Ganya," and this, says Dostoevsky, "led Kolya beyond the last boundaries of human patience." These last words are enclosed in parentheses, presumably to acknowledge the phrase as born of Kolya's own umbrage. Age transformation — whether or not a conscious consideration of the author — thus serves once more the purpose of stressing awakened sensibility in a sensitive, thinking adolescent.

Entrusted by Myshkin to transmit a note to Aglaya, Kolya is deeply hurt when she "insultingly" declares, "Still, it's humorous to trust such a little kid."[50] Dostoevsky reinforces the word, "insultingly," by adding that she marched by him "scornfully." This, we read, "was too much for Kolya to take . . . He took offence cruelly."[51]

Doubtless, the most striking example of Kolya's genesis of feeling is his drastic discovery that he has been instrumental in slandering his friend Myshkin — that the article he has just read aloud about the alleged "son of Pavlishchev" is both spurious and of a rather despicable cast. "Without a word," Kolya

> threw himself into a corner, jammed himself forcefully into it, and covered his face with his hands. He felt unbearable shame, and his childlike impressionableness — as yet unaccustomed to dirt — was muddied beyond measure.[52]

As is typical in Dostoevsky, the combined impact of "unbearable" and "beyond measure" is mimetically intensified by physical action. Both the corner and the face-covering are easily construed as symbolic of the inner recesses to which Kolya retreats.

Notwithstanding his predilection for convoluted brooding, Dostoevsky's depiction of Lise Khokhlakova is nearly *sui generis*. This fourteen-year-old child is surely one of his most mature masochists. "Alyosha was right," remarks Yantarevoy, "in calling her a martyr."[53] Although she flouts Faith with a vengeance, there *is* something deeply religious about Lise, perhaps because she occasionally pauses, while berating Alyosha, to speak the excruciating truth *about herself* and, perhaps, because she suffers with such a savage honesty.

In fact, there are strange parallels between Lise and Alyosha, despite their apparent dissimilarity, and it is probably not fortuitous that Dostoevsky first shows them to us at the monastery. Consider what befalls their fingers, the dream they both have, Lise's nearly identical references to both of them as "the tiniest of children" (discussed below), and the somewhat unsettling way Alyosha agrees with part of her extreme pessimism (also discussed below).

Instructed by her mother to thank the elder for having healed her, Lise becomes serious for a moment but then bursts out laughing. She immediately claims, however, "childishly vexed at herself for giving in and laughing," [54] that she was laughing at Alyosha. It should be noted that Alyosha then approaches Lise, hand out-stretched, and "somehow strangely and awkwardly smiling."

Whether or not one may infer that Alyosha exists not independently, in space, but rather lives in the emotions of those around him — as, writes Mochulsky, does Prince Myshkin [55] — this odd smile strangely allies him with Lise. Indeed, her intense, romantic attitude towards Alyosha often appears to balance uneasily upon the brink of derision. "She had long before observed," we are told, "that Alyosha was embarrassed and tried not to look at her, and this had begun to amuse her horribly [*uzhasno*]." [56] Once more the word "horribly" works overtime. Lise is *horribly* amused precisely because she finds it horrible that Alyosha is embarrassed; and, more subtly, because she finds it horrible (once the hero image is shattered) that this really does amuse her. Such is the fiber of her twisted inner honesty.

Dostoevsky soon illustrates this. Asked by the elder why she keeps deriding Alyosha, "Lise suddenly, most unexpectedly turned red, her eyes flashed, her face became horribly [*uzhasno*] serious." Explaining, in effect, that Alyosha has not courted her in a manly enough manner, she adds, quite symbolically: "Why have you put that flowing gown on him? If he runs, he'll fall . . ." [57] Literally, the Russian reads: "He will run . . . he will fall." (The future, as well as the imperative, may serve as the conditional.) Thus, Lise can be seen to imply that Alyosha *will run*, i.e., will at times act unbefitting his religious role, with comic consequence. Alyosha is, after all, a Karamazov, and even if this is wishful thinking on Lise's part, the very plausibility of her insight allies the two of them more closely.

And suddenly she hid her face in her hands and gave in,
laughing horribly [*uzhasno*] and uncontrollably, to her pro-
longed, nervous, devastating and inaudible laughter.

Such laughter, one feels, is "horribly" akin to tears. Indeed, three
lines later she weeps, begs forgiveness, and calls herself a fool.

Despite its masochism and perverse anticipations, Lise's letter to
Alyosha contains traces of surprisingly delicate articulation. She
deeply feels and suffers for the helpless, compelling impropriety of
her position.

Paper, they say, does not blush. This, I promise you, is un-
true: It is blushing all over now, just as I am. Dear Alyosha,
I love you, I have loved you since childhood, . . . and I shall
love you always.[58]

Just as Lise was (above) "childishly vexed," so this fourteen-year-
old is here allegedly separated from "childhood." Dostoevsky thus
subtly reintensifies the adolescent's pain through the implicit assumption that she is as mature as her dilemma.

A somewhat frightening symmetry develops as her confession
progresses: Just as Alyosha dared not look at her before (when she
"waited with all her might," caught his look, and mercilessly de-
rided him), she now implores him "if he has any pity for her" not
to look upon her when next they meet, lest she burst out laughing.
"Besides," she rationalizes, "you'll be wearing that long dress
. . ." But her real message is clear: "Please, oh please, prevent me
from ruining things!" Dostoevsky achieves maximum effect here by
illuminating, with Lise's childlike honesty, her mature insight into
her own immaturity. "Goodbye until we meet," she concludes, "until
we *horribly* meet." (The italics of *"uzhasno"* are Lise's.)

Alyosha reads this letter carefully and then "suddenly, quietly,
sweetly" bursts out laughing.

He started to shudder: this laughter seemed sinful to him.
But a moment later he again burst out laughing, just as
quietly and just as happily.

Thus Dostoevsky further establishes a symmetrical reciprocity between Lise and Alyosha. There is perhaps a touch of her infernal fire in his lambent, warm-hearted laughter, just as she, at times, can nearly surpass him as to candor. As mentioned above, Alyosha *is* a Karamazov,[59] and consequently, it is not surprising to discover minute horns poking through his nimbus.[60]

The thus anticipated meeting between Alyosha and Lise opens by echoing the unexpected way she laughed instead of thanking the elder, and her mother again sets the scene for the surprise. "Why," she greets Alyosha, "is Lise in hysterics?" "Mama, it's you who are in hysterics, not I," declares Lise, her voice "nearly hysterical, as if she wanted *horribly* to burst out laughing but was holding back the laughter with all her might."[61] The word "horribly" (*uzhasno*) can be seen to have a typical twofold function. Recalling Lise's letter, in which she so belabored the agony of this impending laughter, one can easily imagine how horrible it is now to want to laugh, and how horrible the consequences.[62]

The meeting soon comes to a climax — one which echoes a familiar theme. ". . . how can you," angrily cries Lise,

> associate with little urchins, and in that long dress besides!
> . . . Why after that you yourself are a little boy, the very smallest boy possible![63]

This instance is most significant here in terms of the symmetry we have been tracing. Lise soon says:

> But you can't possibly consider me a little girl — a tiny little girl — after my letter with such a stupid joke!

When she proceeds to ask Alyosha if he laughed at her "very much," he replies, "Not a bit." As we have observed, he laughed twice. The reader is left to wonder what portion of this laughter was "at her" and consequently, to what extent he is sometimes less candid than she.

Alyosha then speaks seriously of marriage, whereupon Lise exclaims: "But I'm a cripple!"[64] And she both blushes and bursts out laughing — eloquent external testimony to what she is experiencing inside.

Lise's reaction to Alyosha's proposal of marriage, as it is developed, suggests the mutual incompatibility of childlikeness and of sex. For not only do wheelchair and monastery loom in Lise's mind between reality and marriage to Alyosha. He is, she fears, a child.

> "Imagine, mama, on the way here he fought with urchins on the street. An urchin bit his finger. Isn't he little then, isn't he a little person too, and is it possible for him to get married after that, mama . . . Imagine him married — wouldn't it be funny, wouldn't it be uzhasno?"
>
> And Lise kept laughing her thin nervous giggle, slyly eying Alyosha.[65]

This could be said of Myshkin by any one of several women in *The Idiot;* surely it is no coincidence that Dostoevsky's two most "positively good men" are both childlike and exceedingly fond of children. Apparently, these capacities give rise to a disquieting ambivalence in the women Myshkin and Alyosha attract. (Perhaps they sense that each of these two men is, in the words of Vyacheslav Ivanov, "a child when he is among children."[66]) The urge to mother anticipates success, while the desire to submit foresees defeat.[67]

Dostoevsky has Lise subtly reveal her ambivalence towards Alyosha as she tells him, late in the novel:

> "I've just been considering again, for the thirtieth time, how good it is that I refused you and won't be your wife."[68]

Obviously, such repetition and protraction ("considering") belie assurance. "You'd never do," she continues,

> "as a husband: I'd marry you and then suddenly give you a love-note to take to the man I'd love next; you'd take it, deliver it without fail, and even bring the answer back. Even at age forty, you'd still be carrying my love-notes."[69]
>
> She suddenly laughed.

Lise loves Alyosha, perhaps, but she longs for a man who will give her a child, not be one; and, most important, she realizes all this and reacts to her own attitude with *a secondary ambivalence*. The laugh is, as usual, both at him and at herself. Furthermore, the strange symmetry between Lise and Alyosha continues as his ambivalence echoes hers: "There's something spiteful and yet open-hearted about you," Alyosha smiled. Finally, Lise's masochism and ambivalence coalesce in what is perhaps the epitome of all Dostoevskian penetrating rationalizations: "I shall love you horribly because you let me unlove you so soon."

At this juncture, Dostoevsky allows us a glimpse of Lise's mental world. Beneath her remarks to Alyosha about Kalganov lurk some lurid inferences.

"Why live life," he [Kalganov] says, "it's better to dream. One can dream up delightful things, but real life is boring and sad."

Not only does Lise seek in fantasy to escape from sadness and boredom; she finds evil satisfaction in what she imagines.

"I want horribly to burn a house, Alyosha, our house. You don't believe it, do you?"
"Why not? There are even children about twelve years old who want very much to burn things, and they do."

In her imagination's sadistic domain, Lise mercilessly pursues her own perverseness: "Sometimes I think of doing horribly much evil." Nor does she exclude others. Regarding the idea that Dmitri killed his father, she perversely proclaims:

"They love it, they all love it! Everyone says it's horrible, but inwardly they all love it. I love it most of all."
"There is some truth in your words about everyone," Alyosha softly declared.[70]

It is actually in the world of dreams, however, that Lise and Alyosha become the most disturbingly similar. They both have the very same dream — about devils, who keep creeping up but retreat as the dreamer makes the sign of the cross. In Lise's words, the dream ends as follows:

And suddenly I feel horribly like profaning God. I do, and the devils crowd towards me again, delighted. They start to seize me again, again I suddenly cross myself: they retreat. It's horribly funny; I gasp for breath.[71]

When Alyosha remarks that he has had the very same dream, Lise is quick to find philosophical implications in this fact.

. . . Alyosha, don't laugh, it's horribly important: Can it really be that two different people have one and the same dream?

"It's not the dream that's important," she explains, "it's the fact that you could see exactly the same dream as I."[72] Clearly, this fourteen-year-old is considering other dimensions of reality. "Lise was horribly startled by something and grew silent for half a minute."

She then hits at the essential question of the nature of reality. Having asked Alyosha whether it is true that Jews steal children on Easter and "cut them up," she tells him of reading once that a Jew cut off all of a four-year-old boy's fingers, crucified him on the wall with nails, and later testified in court that

"the boy had died quickly, in four hours. That's quickly! He groaned, and the man stood and relished the sight. How good!"
"Good?"
"Good. *I sometimes think that it was I myself who crucified him.* He hangs there groaning while I sit opposite him eating pineapple compote."[73]

The inference is that intense emotional experience can induce a psychic state in which reality appears to be altered, or actually *is altered,* if one concedes the phenomenological concept that human perception is interaction rather than reaction. Even in her escape world, Lise must block out the too painful "reality" of the child's suffering by creating her own compote fixation:

> I imagine the child screaming and groaning (four-year-olds *understand*, you know), and I can't get the compote out of my mind.

When Alyosha leaves, still vividly hearing, perhaps, Lise's exclamations [74] that the idea of a boy with cut-off fingers is a "good" one, Lise immediately opens a door. Inserting her finger, she crushes it, thereby weirdly aligning herself with Alyosha *and* the four-year-old. Her masochism is now doubly satisfied: She has avenged herself both for telling Alyosha a partial lie (how "good" she deemed the story of the boy) and for the fact that it was only a partial one. Admitting that she has evil feelings is perhaps even more painful than is the feigning of them, with masochistic perverseness, before the person whose respect she probably values most in all the world. It is just as well that Dostoevsky leaves us in doubt as to whether or not Lise characteristically proceeds to imagine that Alyosha has correctly interpreted her conduct, i.e., has perceived the face-to-face-mirrors-like quality of her masochism. There is more than enough of the adult in Lise as it is. This childs expands her own suffering with a rare maturity indeed.

There are some similarities in the characters of Lise and the orphan peasant girl Masha (in a story of that name by Mark Vovchok which is discussed for thirteen pages by Dostoevsky in *The Diary* of 1883).[75] Masha, it seems, "received the conviction that she had the right to think, to question, and to object."[76] Forced to reap for a female landowner, little Masha purposely slashes her arm with a sickle, causing the blood to spurt.[77] Frightened, the landowner produces her handkerchief, ordering that the wound be bound and the child sent home. But,

> Masha failed to appreciate the lady's favor: once home, she immediately tore the landowner's handkerchief from her arm and flung it far away . . .[78]

It is difficult to ignore the many similarities between Lise Khokhlakova and Princess Katya (*Netochka Nezvanova*). Yantarevoy
groups the two as "nervous children"; Polzinsky, as "persistent,
proud, and despotic." [79]

It is yet more difficult, perhaps, not to focus one's attention upon
Netochka, for whose awakening sensibilities the willful princess often
seems merely an emotional foil. The love affair of these two children is
sharply characteristic of an unmistakable theme in Dostoevsky: the
eroticism felt by and for young girls.

Netochka herself can be considered an epitomical focal point from
which several parallels emanate.[80] The awakening of her erotic feelings, as well as Katya's, suggest The Little Hero and Lise Khokhlakova; Netochka's feelings for her stepfather remind one slightly of
Nellie's for Vanya and for the doctor (*The Injured and The Insulted*) and even, perhaps, of the five-year-old prostitute of whom
Svidrigailov dreams (*Crime and Punishment*). Such feelings are re-
quited not infrequently; there are faint suggestions of pedophilia in
both Netochka's stepfather and in Vanya. Adult lust for young girls,
of course, comes rather more to the fore in the calculating gentleman
(*The Fir Tree and The Wedding*), the customers of Madame Bubnova
(*The Injured and The Insulted*), Svidrigailov's molestation of a
fourteen-year-old girl, certain sections (discussed above) of *The
Eternal Husband, The Landlady, A Gentle Creature, Poor People*,
instances of raping young girls discussed in *The Diary*, and in the
curious *Stavrogin's Confession*. Mark Spilka attributes great significance to this theme in Dostoevsky:

> His recognition that little girls can appeal to innocent love
> and furtive lust, and, more appallingly, can *respond* to both
> appeals, reflects insightfully on the little girl theme in
> Dickens, Eliot, Carroll, Dowson, Barrie, Spyri and others.[81]

But possibly of equal or even greater import than sexual feeling
in Netochka is the imagination. As Mochulsky points out, it is the
genesis of her feelings which opens up her other world, and here, one
is tempted to group Netochka with Lise Khokhlakova.

The enmity between her parents had a devastating effect
upon the child's imagination. "My heart was wounded from

the first instant,'' she says, ''and my development began
with an inconceivable, enervating swiftness.''[82]

Lise Khokhlakova touches upon the question of perception's essence; Dostoevsky develops the problem still further in Netochka by
examining the possibly unique nature of child perception. He seems to
suggest that for the child — as yet little conditioned by previous experience to perceive partially through automatic assumptions —
imagination emerges as an exceedingly vital altering force in the perceptional process. Mochulsky quotes Netochka herself as saying it was
''little wonder,'' considering what strange people surrounded her
when she was so young, that she became a ''fantastical child.'' ''The
innocent Netochka,'' he continues, ''experienced a complex feeling for
her stepfather — maternal sympathy, child attachment, and adult passion.''[83]

Examples of Netochka's genesis of feeling are a legion, as are her
precarious journeys across the borderland between illusion and reality. She describes at length a strangely vivid and mature awareness
that invaded the process of her perception when she was eight and a
half: ''I developed quickly, unexpectedly, and many entirely unchildlike impressions became frighteningly accessible.[84] She then stresses a
forced awakening of her own feelings: She ''understood'' the turbu-
lence between her mother and stepfather, and this affected and developed her imagination.[85] One should observe that Netochka is rendered
adult-like in childhood not by precocious love alone. It is her suffering
and, more precisely, her awareness of this suffering (the text abounds
with passages beginning ''I understood'') that especially effects her
early maturity.

Netochka felt at this time a new love for her stepfather, a ''somehow boundless but wonderful love, as if not a child's at all.''[86] She
''even sometimes flirted with him.''

Truly, this wondrous attachment of mine somewhat resembled an affair . . .[87]

One can but shudder, then, at the tumult within Netochka when he
''disowns'' her, she having refused to continue furnishing him with
her mother's funds. The result is ironical: In league with her step-

father against her real mother, the child now reverses her emotions, seeking what she had abused and being spurned by what she had preferred.

I'm not your father any more, do you hear? . . . I don't want to know you![88]

"I understood," says Netochka, "what this money meant to my poor mother . . ."

But he . . . considered me a three-year-old rebyonok, when I understood everything.[89]

Interestingly enough, the child has such a mature grasp of her step-father's situation that he nearly becomes, as Ikhmenev before Nellie, a child in her eyes.

He himself definitely resembled a rebyonok when he started telling me about his enemies.[90]

Netochka mentions the same unique process of perception in strange psychic states discussed above with reference to Lise Khokhla-kova.

There are minutes when one's consciousness experiences far more than during whole years.[91]

She proceeds to describe one of these experiences — her early under-standing that she was being falsely advised to take her mother's money. Another such experience is the process of comprehending that the body beneath a blanket is her dead mother. Netochka withdraws from this into a long series of half-fantasies — strange Dostoevskian syntheses of the real and the imagined or dreamed. "I kept thinking I was dreaming,"[92] says Netochka. Later, recovering at Princess Katya's:

There were minutes when I thought I was dreaming, and, I remember, I kept wishing that what was happening really would turn into a dream![93]

Finally, Netochka comes to grips with the idea that she is now an orphan. But Katya's father, pitying Netochka, exclaims, "Poor orphan!" whereupon the child's emotional reaction actually appears to alter her apprehension of reality:

"No, no, not orphan, no!" . . .
"Where is my mama? Where is my mama?" I cried, loudly sobbing, . . . "Where is my mama?"[94]

Dostoevsky often stresses, as will be shown, the reality dead people, especially dead children, have for those who were close to them — a reality which, in moments of intense emotion, nearly appears to outshine normal reality and render it unreal by contrast.[95]

In this half-real world of recuperation, Netochka first sees Princess Katya. Netochka's nearly instant love for this girl, it seems, carries her deeply back into illusion:

I started to dream about her. Awake, in her absence, I would compose whole conversations with her; I, her friend, played pranks, was naughty, and cried with her when we were reprimanded for something — in a word, I dreamed about her like a girl in love.[96]

It should be noted that this world of fancy is both factually resourceful and emotionally self-sufficient. "My fantasy," says Netochka, "developed so widely that, it seemed, I could feel myself becoming oblivious to the world that had previously surrounded me."[97] Later, Netochka stresses the fact that when the two became separated, Katya never left her mind: It was as if she still lived with her. Especially in her dreams and "fantastic adventures," they "always walked together, hand in hand."[98]

The Little Hero is replete with references to sexual awakening, and the scope of its symbolism is far greater than that in Netochka.[99]

The protagonist is a boy almost eleven years old, whose constant fondling by beautiful young women has the following consequences:

> . . . some kind of sensation I myself could not fathom had already taken possession of me; something as yet unknown and alien to my heart was already stirring there . . . a sudden blush often covered my face. At times I was somehow ashamed of and even offended by my various child's privileges.[100]

At last, a "sly blonde" leads "The Little Hero" to believe himself in love, and here, Dostoevsky employs one of his more effective descriptive techniques:

> . . . in a word, I was in love, that is, let's suppose this is nonsense: it could not have been; but then why, of all those around me, did I notice only one person?[101]

A favorite device of Dostoevsky's is to describe something "by being wrong." Such a description begins with a bald exaggeration, the absurdity of which is instantly conceded, as if to an imaginary objector. Then follows, however, an irrefutable hint that the opening words were indeed not far off the mark. (An alternative to this procedure is Dostoevsky's technique that opens with an obvious understatement. Then, once his descriptive foot is in the door, the describer easily slips in through controlled vagueness. The important thing to notice is that neither device begins describing exactly where it intends to end. But both plant viable descriptive seeds.[102])

As noted above, both Alyosha Karamazov and Prince Myshkin lose much of their attraction to women because they are childlike. Conversely, one could infer, sexual awareness and attraction mark the margins of childhood.[103] The kiss which ends *The Little Hero* (in perhaps, then, more than one sense) is surely the first to afford him such pyrotechnical pleasure. The protagonist culminates his description of this kiss: "My first childhood ended at this moment."[104] In this sense, Arkadi's revulsion at seeing the naked whore (*A Raw Youth*) tends to emphasize his childlikeness, as does Alyosha's apparent lack of stimulation at sitting upon Grushenka's lap.

Julius Meier-Graefe effusively claims that Dostoevsky "introduced the child into literature."[105] One of the first children he introduced was the consumptive nine-year-old Petya Gorshkov in *Poor People*. The deadening effect of this boy's demise upon his six-year-old sister renders her both a victim and a pensive child. She seems both callously matured and crassly victimized by circumstance. It is perhaps artistically fortunate that Dostoevsky was apparently content to imply the genesis of her feelings.

In a letter to Varvara Alekseevna, Makar Devushkin vividly insinuates this abrupt awakening. "A tiny little girl, the daughter," writes Devushkin,

stands leaning against the coffin, and what a miserable pensive little wretch she is! I hate to see a child grow pensive, my dear sweet Varenka; it's most unpleasant! A rag doll lies next to her on the floor — untouched; she keeps a finger on her lips and just stands there — motionless. Her mother gave her a piece of candy; she took it, but has not eaten it. Sad, Varenka, is it not?[106]

The tiny girl leans against her brother's coffin: Their fated separation is rendered more touching by the futility of their nearness. And the scene's pathos is little affected by how fully she realizes what has happened: it loses little poignancy if she believes that clinging to her brother's coffin could bring him back. But she is twice described as "pensive" and the very mechanical motionlessness of her body somehow suggests the frozen turmoil of her mind and emotions. Yet the effectiveness of this scene derives especially from the fact that the reader must himself imagine her inner reaction and thereby determine the extent of her genesis of feelings. Despite his predilection for superlatives, Dostoevsky could defer to the power of the unsaid. And here he could well afford such restraint: this little girl is soon to witness her moribund father's fixation that Petya is still alive, as well as her mother's hysterics while her father dies. Then also, the child's reaction is left judiciously unsaid: "The little girl hid herself somewhere in a corner."[107]

Notes

[1] Ernest J. Simmons, *Dostoevsky: The Making of a Novelist* (New York, 1962), p. 104.

[2] *The New York Times Book Review* (March 5, 1967), p. 32.

[3] F. M. Dostoevsky, *The Diary of a Writer:* 1873, 1876, 1877 (Paris: YMCA-Press, 1877), pp. 258–59.

[4] Dostoevsky, *The Diary* of 1876, p. 487. Compare: "Still, little girls understand faster than little boys" (*ibid.*, p. 11).

[5] *Ibid.*, p. 218. Compare: "The fantasy of these six-year-old tots is unparalled, and this is excellent; in this is their development" (*ibid.*, p. 97).

[6] *Ibid.*, p. 10.

[7] L. P. Grossman, "Dostoevsky — khudozhnik," *Tvorchestvo F. M. Dostoevskoqo*, ed. N. L. Stepanov (Moscow, 1959), p. 407.

[8] Simmons, p. 343.

[9] F. M. Dostoevsky, *Collected Works* (Moscow, 1956–1958), X, 60–61.

[10] R. A. Yantarevoy, *Detskie tipy v proizvedeniyakh Dostoevskago* (St. Petersburg, 1895), p. 64.

[11] See, for example, Vladimir Seduro's discussions of D. I. Zaslavski's admiration for Dostoevsky's depiction of Kolya — *Dostoevsky in Russian Literary Criticism* 1846–1956 (New York, 1957), pp. 256, 277, 290 — and of the book, *The Boys* (excerpts from *The Brothers Karamazov* published in 1947), which, Seduro suggests, "may well" have been a "response" to Zaslavski (*ibid.*, p. 290).

Maxim Gorky, however, was quick to find Kolya unreal, declaring that some of his utterances are not those of a boy, but of "a Tamerlain or at least a police officer" (Maxim Gorky, "Eshchyo o 'Karamazovshchine," *F. M. Dostoevsky v russkoi kritike,* ed. A. A. Belkin [Moscow, 1956], p. 395).

[12] April 12 and 13, 1880 — F. M. Dostoevsky, *Letters,* ed. A. S. Dolinin (Moscow, 1928–1959), IV, 137–38, 410.

[13] Dostoevsky, *The Diary* of 1876, p. 78.

[14] Dostoevsky, *C. W.,* X, 8.

[15] *Ibid.*, p. 36.

[16] *Ibid.*, p. 10. My italics.

[17] *Ibid.*, p. 12.

[18] *Ibid.*, p. 15.

[19] *Ibid.*, p. 22.

[20] *Ibid.*, p. 29.

[21] *Ibid.*, p. 31.

[22] *Ibid.,* p. 43.

[23] *Ibid.,* pp. 45–46.

[24] Aldous Huxley, *Vulgarity in Literature* (London, 1930), p. 57.

[25] George H. Ford, *Dickens and His Readers: Aspects of Novel-criticism Since 1836* (New York, 1965), p. 193. See also p. 62.

[26] Michael H. Futrell, "Dostoevsky and Dickens," *English Miscellany,* VII, 80.

[27] Simmons, pp. 104–05.

[28] P. S. Polzinsky, *Detski mir v proizvedeniakh Dostoevskogo* (Revel, 1891), p. 9.

[29] *Ibid.,* pp. 33–34.

[30] Dostoevsky, *C. W.,* X, 58.

[31] *Ibid.,* p. 59.

[32] *Ibid.,* p. 61. The Russian word *rebyonok* is especially effective here.

[33] At least, the concepts are also linked in the father's mind, for he is soon to say: "I don't want a good boy! I don't want another boy!" (*ibid.,* p. 68).

[34] In *F. M. Dostoevsky v russkoi kritike.*

[35] Vyacheslav Ivanov, *Freedom and the Tragic Life: A Study in Dostoevsky,* trans. Norman Cameron (New York, 1960), p. 13.

[36] Dostoevsky, *C. W.,* X, 46–47.

[37] Nikolai Trubitsyn, *Dostoevsky i deti* (Kronshtadt, 1903), p. 38.

[38] Dostoevsky, *C. W.,* II, 485–87. She is fifteen.

[39] Dostoevsky, *C. W.,* III, 408.

[40] It is tempting to infer, considering Dostoevsky's faith in a child's potential for reasoning, that he found reasoning — as it is developed in most children beyond the age of three — a not altogether positive process. This could suggest, as discussed above, that Dostoevsky may have hypothesized, in very young children, an emotional mode of reasoning which he deemed in some ways superior to the relatively rational thought later displacing it.

[41] Simmons, p. 104. See also pp. 39, 42, and 43.

[42] Polzinsky, pp. 17–20.

[43] Dostoevsky, *C. W.,* VI, 105.

[44] *Ibid.,* pp. 104, 212. Both descriptions are Dostoevsky's; he employs italics only in the first reference.

[45] *Ibid.,* p. 125.

[46] *Ibid.,* pp. 128–29.

[47] *Ibid.,* p. 134.

[48] *Ibid.,* p. 104.

[49] *Ibid.,* p. 213.

[50] *Ibid.,* p. 215.

[51] *Ibid.,* p. 216. The word "cruelly" exemplifies another descriptive device used not infrequently by the author: an adverb with an explicit connotative

function reinforced by a powerful, implicit denotative one. As has been seen, Dostoevsky often employs the word "horribly" (*uzhasno*) in this manner. Here, Kolya is perhaps somewhat masochistic and therefore "cruel" to himself, but Aglaya's conduct is cruel as well; thus, cause is subtly served up as effect.

Dostoevsky sometimes does this in reverse. Consider the following example. The protagonist of *A Gentle Creature* is wondering, immediately after the girl's suicide, whether she had "despised" him while alive:

> It's horribly interesting: Did she respect me? I do not know whether she despised me or not. I think she did not despise me. It's horribly strange: Why did it never once occur to me all winter that she despised me? (Dostoevsky, *C. W.*, X, 417).

Obviously, the two "horriblys" serve up the probable effect of his finding out that she did despise him as the partial cause of his horribly intense interest in the question. There are other, more subtle suggestions in this passage, such as the similarity of sound in the Russian between *uzhasno* (horribly) and *uvazhala* (respect), suggesting, perhaps, how horrible it was for her even to try to respect him.

[52] Dostoevsky, *C. W.*, VI, 302.

[53] Yantarevoy, p. 13.

[54] Dostoevsky, *C. W.*, IX, 70.

[55] K. Mochulsky, *Dostoevsky: zhizn i tvorchestvo* (Paris, 1947), p. 288.

[56] Dostoevsky, *C. W.*, IX, 76.

[57] *Ibid.*, p. 77.

[58] *Ibid.*, p. 202.

[59] Rakitin testifies eloquently in this regard: "You yourself are a Karamazov, you are fully a Karamazov . . . By your father, a voluptuary . . ." (*ibid.*, p. 103). See also Nicholas Berdyaev, *Dostoevsky*, trans. Donald Attwater (New York, 1957), p. 95.

[60] In the words of Ernest J. Simmons, the "Karamazov taint of carnal sensuality, which in its less vicious manifestations Dostoevsky describes as a zest for living . . . even rears its ugly head in the saint-like nature of Alyosha" (Simmons, p. 330).

[61] Dostoevsky, *C. W.*, IX, 22. My italics.

[62] Nor is the word "horribly" an isolated coincidence here; it occurs constantly when Lise and Alosha are together — four times on the very next page (*ibid.*, p. 228), and ten times on three successive pages (Dostoevsky, *C. W.*, X, 93–95) of the scene next examined below.

[63] Dostoevsky, *C. W.*, IX, 229–30.

[64] Dostoevsky was acutely sensitive to what might be termed a child cripple's adult-like suffering, as one can see from his discussion of the little girl Dunya in *The Diary* of 1876: "She was born with deformed legs, that is, without any legs at all; instead of legs she has something like a twisted braid." She is only one and a half and smiles at everyone. The doctor has commented, "We'll

give her artificial legs, crutches, teach her how to walk, and she'll never notice," and Dostoevsky remarks: "Well, God grant that she *never notice*" (p. 224, his italics).

[65] Dostoevsky, *C. W.*, IX, 231.

[66] Ivanov, p. 96.

[67] Nicholas Berdyaev writes: "Muishkin is not fully a man in the sense that Dostoievsky gives to the term; his nature is fundamentally seraphic, but deficient. Later on Dostoievsky tried to show a complete man, in Alyosha" (Berdyaev, p. 44).

[68] Dostoevsky, *C. W.*, X, 91.

[69] Note that this could be a description of Myshkin.

[70] All above, Dostoevsky, *C. W.*, X, 91–94.

[71] *Ibid.*, pp. 94–95.

[72] Raskolnikov (*Crime and Punishment*) considers yet another facet of this problem when he overhears a conversation about the women he is soon to murder. Why, he wonders, did he hear "such a conversation and such thoughts, when his own mind had just given birth to . . . *the very same thoughts?*" (Dostoevsky, *C. W.*, V, 72. The italics are Dostoevsky-Raskolnikov's.) The question common to Raskolnikov and Lise is contained both in and by the fountain image of Nabokov's *Pale Fire*.

[73] Dostoevsky, *C. W.*, X, 95–96. My italics. Maxim Gorky rather superficially considers that

> Lise has been slandered here: she did not say — could not have said, anything so vile and disgusting (Gorky, p. 395).

Gorky is seemingly unaware that such a candid declaration of "evil" is psychologically verisimilar as a masochistically perverse aspiration to avenge the bruises to which hypersensitivity and goodness are susceptible in combinaton. P. M. Bitsilli calls this feeling "horror at the awareness of human egocentricity and at being powerless to conquer it" and sees it as "pursuing a series of Dostoevsky's personages" ("K voprosu o vnutrennei forme romana Dostoevskogo," *O Dostoevskom, Stati* [Providence, Rhode Island, 1966], p. 31).

[74] Dostoevsky, *C. W.*, X, 95 and 96.

[75] Dostoevsky, *The Diary* of 1873, pp. 70–82.

[76] *Ibid.*, p. 71.

[77] *Ibid.*, p. 74.

[78] *Ibid.*, p. 74.

[79] Yantarevoy, pp. 9–35; Polzinsky, pp. 12–17.

[80] "Subsequently," writes Mochulsky, "Dostoevsky never analyzed a child's eroticism so fearlessly and closely" (Mochulsky, p. 89).

[81] Mark Spilka, *Dickens and Kafka: A Mutual Interpretation* (London, 1963), pp. 264–65.

[82] Mochulsky, p. 88.

83 *Ibid.,* p. 89.

84 Dostoevsky, *C. W.,* II, 83.

85 See *ibid.,* pp. 87 ff.

86 *Ibid.,* p. 84.

87 *Ibid.,* p. 103.

88 *Ibid.,* p. 109.

89 *Ibid.,* p. 111.

90 *Ibid.,* p. 111.

91 *Ibid.,* p. 112.

92 *Ibid.,* p. 122.

93 *Ibid.,* p. 124.

94 *Ibid.,* p. 132.

95 One is reminded of Zenkovsky's insight into Dostoevsky's "mystical ethics": "Love becomes super-reasonable, rising to a sense of inner connection with the whole world, even with the dead . . ." (V. V. Zenkovsky, "Dostoevsky's Religious and Philosophical Views," *Dostoevsky: A Collection of Critical Essays,* ed. René Wellek [New Jersey, 1962], p. 141). This concept is discussed here more fully in Chapter Five.

96 Dostoevsky, *C. W.,* II, 137.

97 *Ibid.,* p. 187.

98 *Ibid.,* p. 193.

99 A fascinating study could perhaps obtain from tracing parallels in the symbolism of awakening sexual desire in *The Little Hero* and Sologub's *The Petty Demon.* Pertinent symbols, among others, are the sun (including its rays, glowing, and shades of color), drops of water (including dew, spray, mist, etc., especially in conjunction with the sun image), and sweet fragrances (including perfume, grass, and flowers). The parallels are striking.

100 Dostoevsky, *C. W.,* II, 234.

101 *Ibid.,* p. 241.

102 An example of this "slow-start" technique is the following sentence describing Raskolnikov's feelings (*Crime and Punishment*) when he calls on the old usuress to murder her:

> He felt that he was becoming confused, that he was almost frightened, so frightened, it seemed, that if she looked at him that way, without saying a word, for another thirty seconds, he would run away from her (Dostoevsky, *C. W.,* V, 82).

For further examples of the "being wrong" device, see Lebezyatnikov's description of Sofya (*ibid.,* p. 446) and also *ibid.,* p. 441.

The Dostoevskian strange smile sometimes combines subtly with the technique of contradictory description:

> It was as if he [Raskolnikov] smiled, but it was as if it was not a smile (*ibid.,* p. 324).

Svidrigailov's face distortedly assumed a condescending smile, but he was already in no mood for smiles (*ibid.*, p. 510).

[103] One is reminded of William Empson's statement about Alice in Wonderland:

There seems to be a connection in Dodgson's mind between the death of childhood and the development of sex . . . (William Empson, "Alice in Wonderland: The Child as Swain," *The Critical Performance*, ed. S. E. Hyman [New York, 1956], p. 127).

[104] Dostoevsky, *C. W.*, II, 271.

[105] Julius Meier-Graefe, *Dostoevsky: The Man and His Work*, trans. Herbert H. Marks (London, 1928), p. 76.

[106] Dostoevsky, *C. W.*, I, 129.

[107] *Ibid.*, p. 195.

PART II

The Child as Mental Image

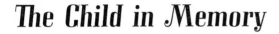

CHAPTER THREE

The Child in Memory

Father Zosima (*The Brothers Karamazov*) stresses the subsequent importance of childhood memories. "From the house where I lived as a child," he writes,

> I carried away nothing but precious memories, for a man has no memories more precious than those of his early childhood . . .[1]

It is his disciple Alyosha, however, who explains this importance. Near the novel's end, he instructs a group of children as follows:

> Know that you can have no greater and stronger force for the life ahead of you, nothing more useful and healthy than a pleasant memory, especially one preserved from childhood, from the house where you were born. They tell you a lot about your education, but such a wonderful, holy memory, cherished from childhood, is perhaps the very best education there is. A person who collects many such memories and keeps them with him is saved for his entire life.[2]

The implications of this passage are, in Dostoevsky, vast. The tenet that happy childhood memories are a force capable of mitigating life's vicissitudes [3] and its obverse, viz., that an unhappy childhood pursues one long thereafter, are continually and tendentiously propounded in Dostoevsky's works.

But was Dostoevsky in accord with his Alyosha? Evidence in *The Diary* is too plentiful to exhaust.

> Without the holy and priceless things that man preserves throughout his life as memories of his childhood, he cannot even live. [4]

And what befalls the child who is wronged? He will "take with him into life," writes Dostoevsky,

> not merely memories of dirt, but the very dirt itself, even purposely arming himself with this dirt and stuffing his pockets for the road . . . [5]

Dostoevsky neatly combines the two possibilities in an imaginary speech he attributes to the judge of the Dzhunkovsky Case (discussed above). A wronged child, he avers, will "remember to the grave."

> He will not forgive, he will hate his memories . . . You must now eradicate and re-create these memories, now, without fail, smothering them with new strong holy memories — what an enormous task! [6]

It is tempting to compare this speech with the speech of the wily Fetyukovich, who defends Mitya in *The Brothers Karamazov*. Both arguments draw deeply upon the belief that to love our children is our sacred duty — that to wrong them is a heinous sin. Fetyukovich suggests, of course, that a child whose father has not been a father to him has no father to kill. [7] In making his case, he goes so far as to cite the curious story of a young unmarried maid in Finland who was discovered to have the habit of killing her illegitimate children at birth and disposing of their bodies in an old trunk in the attic. Was this woman, asks Fetyukovich, a mother to her children? Would any of us dare to bestow upon her the sacred name of "mother"? [8]

Memories comprise a considerable portion of Dostoevsky's works, affording him ample chance to suggest in practice that childhood memories meaningfully color the remainder of man's life. Indeed, numerous passages in Dostoevsky are readily construed as rather tendentious attempts to prove this view.

A prime example is *The Peasant Marey*. Analysis of this little story reveals, besides a somewhat obvious Slavophilism, that the prisoner-protagonist, presumably Dostoevsky, draws great strength from recalling an incident of his childhood. "I suddenly felt," he asserts,

> that I could look upon these unfortunates in an entirely different manner and that suddenly, by some sort of miracle, all loathing and spite had vanished from my heart.[9]

The point is that the elixir of memory has actually altered his perceptional process; in this sense, he is a different person. But what of the Polish prisoner who also had hated the disorderly "unfortunates" around him?

> Unfortunate one! He could have no memories of any Mareys and no other outlook on the people except "Je hais ces brigands!" No, those Poles endured more than we did then!

So ends the story, its mnemonic moral unmistakable.

But let us examine this memory itself. The story's protagonist, age nine, thinks he hears the cry "Wolf!" and a peasant comforts him. Beneath the surface, one can perceive Dostoevsky working ceaselessly to effect memory's cure. He employs a favorite Dostoevskian descriptive device: the unusual smile.

Marey first looks upon the frightened boy "with a worried *smile.*" As he begins to comfort him, Marey "*smiles* some kind of maternal and long *smile.*" "I won't give you over to the wolf!" he says, "still *smiling* to him in the very same maternal way." Walking home, the reassured boy turns to look at Marey; he cannot see him clearly, but "feels that he is still *smiling* at him just as tenderly." Then, as a salutary symbol of the cure, the protagonist stops remembering for an instant, "the soft *smile* of recollection still fixed upon his face.'' Finally, as he lapses back into memory once again, he ''remembers the entire meeting with great clarity, to the last detail.

> This means that it all had settled quietly in my heart, of its own accord and without my will, and suddenly, *when it was needed,* I remembered it then, remembered this tender maternal *smile* . . .[10]

Dostoevsky thus manipulates the rough peasant's smile, first to reassure the little boy and then to illustrate how the grown man draws strength from his childhood memory. Another Dostoevskian device observed above is the painting of ''once'' with the hue of ''often.'' This too has representation here. ''Could it be, then,'' concludes the protagonist, ''that he loved little children so very much? There are such people.'' [11] One should note also the familiar theme of intensely vivid detail perceived in unusual psychic states (''with such clarity, to the very last detail''). More important, the fact that this memory appears ''when needed'' tends to render it nearly sacred.

Also worthy of note is the protagonist's discussion of how he manipulates his own memories. In his four years as a prisoner, he has relived his entire former life in constant recollections. Although these memories have almost always come of their own accord, he ''would analyze them, endow the distant past with fresh details,'' and, most important, *''direct them,* constantly correct them: this comprised my greatest delight.'' [12] This curious admission of self-indulgence in a Romantic blending of memory and embellishment is strangely similar to Vanya's encomia (*The Injured and The Insulted*) of his own vicarious involvement in the novels he has composed.[13]

The Dostoevskian doctrine that childhood memories immensely affect man's later life is perhaps still more didactically displayed in *Poor People.* Varenka frequently recalls her childhood.

> My childhood was the happiest time of my life.[14]

But it is only late in the novel that we see these memories at work. ''In my memories,'' she writes Devushkin,

there is something I cannot explain, something that attracts
so uncontrollably, so strongly, that I become numb to everything around me and forget everything in the present for
hours at a time. And there is no impression in my present
life . . . which cannot remind me of something similar in
my past, most often, of my childhood, my golden childhood! [15]

The two-page rhapsody opened on this note closes there as well: ''Oh,
how golden was my childhood!'' [16] What immediately follows, however, is the most revealing.

Now I've started sobbing like a child, carried away with
my memories. I remembered everything so vividly, my past
rose up so brightly before me, but the present is so dim, so
dark!

However evanescent, Varenka's memories of her ''golden childhood''
are nearly medicinal with respect to her painful present. Her ''sobbing like a child'' effects a direct connection with the past and facili-
tates the transmission of strength, much as the smile on the prisoner's
face above symbolized this revitalization. The intensification of detail
is typical, and within the structure of her memories, Varenka graphically conveys deep emotional appreciation of nature's beauty.

I was still a rebyonok, but even then I already felt a great
deal. . . . I would gaze at it all, listen intently — it seemed
miraculous! And yet I was still a child, a baby! [17]

Two points (both firmly in the Romantic tradition) should be noted:
the child's potential for deep experience, and the return of this experience ''when needed.''
     The life-altering potential of childhood memories in Dostoevsky
is so vital as to find representation in his literary criticism. In his
famous ''Pushkin Speech,'' he asserts that Onegin has no ''earth.''
He is ''a blade of grass, carried on the wind.'' Tatyana, however,

. . . is not like that at all: She has . . . something firm and
steadfast upon which she can lean. This is her memories of

childhood . . . Oh, these memories and former images are more precious to her now than anything else; these images are all she has left, but it is they that shall save her soul from final despair.[18]

Dostoevsky applies the healing potentials of happy childhood memories to periods of both illness and depression. In *The Landlady*, for example, childhood recollections rush to the relief of the feverish Ordynov:

Then the tender, peaceful years of his early childhood seemed to reappear for him once more, with their bright joy, inextinguishable happiness . . .[19]

This exceptionally long sentence contains "swarms of bright fragrances" that "smile at him from an endless crystal lake." As sometimes happens in Dostoevsky, these memories seem to drift into a dream; at least, after two full pages, we read that Ordynov "awakened."[20] Classification of the episode is further complicated by the fact that he continues to recall his childhood, or rather, to improvise a "wondrous fairy tale" — until we read: "Delirium passed and reality began."[21] Through all these distorted torrents of memory, dream, and delirium, however, it is to his childhood that Ordynov's mind retreats for bodily resuscitation.

Vanya (*The Injured and The Insulted*) seems to retreat to the realm of his childhood memories with Natasha after he realizes that she has irrevocably chosen Alyosha. The reader has already seen that they grew up together "like brother and sister. Oh, my dear childhood!"[22] Dostoevsky seems therefore to be showing us how memory must mitigate Vanya's grief; as with Tatyana, memories are all that remain.

Vanya's memories of himself and Natasha center around what they read together as children,[23] and late in the novel, Alyosha proposes to Natasha *in front of Vanya* that he (Alyosha) and Natasha read Tolstoy's descriptions of childhood:

Oh, Natasha! Let's read *Childhood and Youth* sometime; it's so wonderful![24]

Thus the childlike Alyosha further allies himself with children while at the same time he — the victor over Vanya in real-life romance — unwittingly invades Vanya's sanctuary of childhood memories.

Nellie is an excellent example of how Dostoevsky employs childhood memories to reveal and develop character. This young girl's memories of the past are as varied as her protean approach to the present. It is significant that Nellie's memories abruptly shed their sadness during her fatal illness near the novel's end. "Somehow especially weak and distraught,"[25] she recalls the happiness of her early childhood: "clear blue skies, high mountains with snow and ice, . . . waterfalls; then lakes and Italian valleys, flowers, trees . . ." Nellie's listeners are surprised by the fresh happiness inherent in these memories and note also their vividness of detail.

But the balance of Nellie's recollections leans grimly towards bitterness. She cannot forgive her grandfather for her mother's suffering, and she damns him, refusing to believe him dead.[26]

Dostoevsky's negative and disturbed characters are typically pursued by unpleasant childhood memories (which wax most gruesome in their dreams); and, as with Nellie, such memories often cast revealing, if embarrassing, light upon their natures and behavior. The Underground Man hated his childhood,[27] and even in school, everyone hated him.[28] Such memories trigger off, as the protagonist himself realizes,[29] a whole night-full of bad dreams (discussed here in Chapter Four). Curiously little attention has been paid to what Ruth Mortimer calls the "controlled symbolism" of dreams in Dostoevsky.[30]

Significantly, the Underground Man informs Liza:

If I had had a family in my childhood, I would not be the person I am now.[31]

It is revealing that "this person" is apparently so warped as to ignore the positive potentials of memory. In a wretched woman's happy memories of her childhood, he sees only her better loss.[32]

As mentioned above, Raskolnikov's childhood memories occur mostly in a dream. One salient instance, however, follows directly upon an enigmatic stranger's calling Raskolnikov a murderer (which he does "as if with a smile of some kind of odious triumph").[33]

Cornered by this accusation, the murderer retreats to his little room, where he collapses on his bed for about half an hour, mnemonically battered by disconnected fragments of his childhood, including the stench of cigar smoke and a

> dark staircase, slopped with garbage and littered with egg shells . . . The objects kept replacing each other and swirling like a whirlwind.[34]

Arkadi's childhood memories (*A Raw Youth*), before the birth of his "idea," reflect his painful awareness of illegitimacy and his extravagant expectations of his real father. Versilov seems to evoke in this child a strange synthesis of hope and despair.

> My every dream, from early childhood, reverberated with him, centered around him, and became him in the final analysis. I do not know whether I hated or loved him, but he filled my entire future, all my plans for life . . .[35]

The lad's ambivalence turns on the fact that although he pictures Versilov in a shimmering aura of superiority,[36] he constantly suffers from being the man's son:

> Don't you dare sit with these respectable children. You are of base birth, the same as a servant![37]

This even leads to beatings.[38]

Such ambivalence, against a backdrop of what Arkadi calls his "child-sad years,"[39] seems a prelude dangerously vulnerable to disillusionment. In Arkadi's words, ". . . it's turning out that this person is — merely my dream, my childhood hope."[40]

Arkadi's memory of his mother is succinct and Dostoevskian. "I know and remember nothing," he tells her,

> but something of your face remained in my heart for life; and there also remained the knowledge that you are my mother.[41]

This passage somehow evokes the sacred radiance of a mother's face, symbolic of a bond that is felt deeply and for life. Its words are strikingly similar [42] to those chosen for Alyosha (*The Brothers Karamazov*) : ". . . although he lost his mother at age three, he remembered her later for his whole life, her face . . ." [43] And Alyosha especially remembered, as his dying mother held him up to an image of the Mother of God, praying, "his mother's face . . . frantic but magnificent . . ." [44]

In *The Diary* of 1873, there is an interesting assertion that childhood memories, especially an early "impression of God," greatly influence seemingly unrelated actions and attitudes later in life — even twenty years later. "You laugh?" asks Dostoevsky, typically anticipating the reader's disbelief in order to weaken it. "Truly," he concedes, "all this resembles delirium . . ." [45] Also typically, he continues by effecting the deception, based upon false alternatives, that he is right if only the reader's objections *might* prove unwarranted.

The details of Arkadi's memories are instrumental in his characterization. As he tells of his childhood, a nearly electrical embarrassment seems to fill the air.

"Your recounting was excellent and brought everything back to me most vividly," declared Versilov, "but what strikes me most in your story is its richness of peculiar details . . . Not to mention the impropriety of such details, I fail to see how you could have assembled them."

"Details? Could have assembled them? But that's all I did these nine years, I tell you — collect details about you." [46]

Such collected and hoarded memories of the past seem an appropriate background for Arkadi's somewhat distorted apprehension of the present.

The most obvious correlation between the Raw Youth's childhood memories and his unstable outlook on life, however, is reflected in his unhealthy, pseudo-disillusioned attitude towards women. Arkadi does not like women because "they are coarse." [47] "Coarse," he declares, because they are "vulgarly dressed," adding, with delightful irony, "only someone morally depraved would not notice." [48]

> They openly attach a fru-fru to their posteriors in order to show they are belles femmes, openly! I can hardly help but notice and a boy will also notice, and a rebyonok, a very young boy, will also notice; it is vile.[49]

All this appears somewhat foolish and droll, albeit bizarre, until one reads of Arkadi's painful experience, at age thirteen, with Lambert's naked whore.[50] As the reader will recall, Lambert brutally lashed the naked woman with a whip; Arkadi, who attempted to intercede, he stabbed in the thigh with a fork. Ever since then, Arkadi has found nudity "despicable." "And believe me," he adds, "she was a beauty."[51]

This episode combines with another childhood memory to intensify Arkadi's uneasy aversion to the opposite sex. The youth announces later in the novel that he "horribly" hates to see women work. The main thing, it develops, is needlework.

> . . . it is, I feel, one of the sick, or rather the wrong impressions of my childhood. In my vague recollections of when I was five or six I most often recall — with disgust, of course — [52]

What follows is a lengthy description of a sewing circle, wherein the women seem to wax formidably strict and solemn.

> All these tender faces . . . suddenly became unapproachable; if I was the least bit bad, I was carried away immediately.[53]

Arkadi's last reaction seems normal enough, the implication being that he misbehaved to regain lost attention. Nevertheless, this memory serves in context to alienate him further from the female sex and perhaps even to muddy his puppy love for Katerina.

Further interesting examples of character development through childhood memories include speculations by other personages and even the deliberate defilement of such recollections.

The protagonist of *The Village of Stepanchikovo and Its Inhabi-*

tants propounds as the seed of Foma's ugly expanding pride "the first false perverted awareness of his own insulted dignity, abused, perhaps, initially in childhood by poverty, oppression, and dirt."[54] And when Foma himself, in a fit of flagrant hypocrisy, feigns shock at "the surrounding corruption," vainly apostrophizing his "golden childhood" and lost "innocence," Bakhcheev contemptuously suggests, and even offers to testify, that Foma, "as a little urchin, was already the very same brigand he is now."[55]

The perverse protagonist of *A Gentle Creature* "immediately douses with cold water" his wife's blissful recollections of her childhood. "This," he adds, was his "whole idea."[56] Her eventual suicide can be construed as eloquent proof of the consequences redounding from his deliberate desecration of pleasant memories' curative potential. His idea, as he proceeds to explain, had been to seem "an enigma" to her. His insecurity is thus developed into a savage need for self-assertion that preys upon her defences in attempting to strengthen his own.

Typically Dostoevskian is Netochka Nezvanova's statement that the "catastrophe" of her mother's death

. . . is intimately connected not only with the first impressions of my childhood, but even with my entire life.[57]

Having recounted her "affair" with Katya in exceedingly vivid detail, Netochka offers the reader a somewhat specious apology: she had been "unable to refuse herself the pleasure of being carried away to her childhood once more by means of memory."[58]

What is perhaps the most unusual incident involving Dostoevskian childhood memory also occurs in *Netochka*. By blending a recollection and its stimulus into a strangely pervasive reality, Dostoevsky nearly succeeds in erasing the edges of time itself.

Netochka tells the reader that a "present" experience instantly "resurrects" in her memory "a dark, distant childhood recollection."[59] She proceeds to relate the past incident, and the reader thus experiences it along with Netochka in her (also recollected) present, as a blend of both. The incidents occur in the same room and under nearly identical circumstances. They center around Pyotr Aleksandrovich's "changing his face" before a mirror on his way to see

Aleksandra Mikhailovna. Netochka "shudders from some kind of un-determined, unchildlike feeling." The smile on his face "disappears as if by a command," and she, "a rebyonok," shivers from fright because "he never laughed in Aleksandra Mikhailovna's presence." [60] The eerie insight into Pytor Aleksandrovich effected by this dual reality is the more striking in context, as Netochka's narration seems suddenly to acquire a new dimension.

Numerous instances in Dostoevsky's works seem intended at least partially to demonstrate his *Diary's* dictum that "the strongest and most influential memories are almost always those left by child-hood." [61] Polenka, sent by Sonya to thank Raskolnikov, "declares fervently" that she will pray for him "for all the rest of her life." [62] The Little Hero, while speaking of his wild ride on horse-back, avows that he will never forget that "mad minute" of his "childhood life." [63] The application extends even to Dostoevsky's adult narrator of *The Brothers Karamazov;* he vividly recalls from his childhood the "hysterical women" who used to "whine or bark like dogs at the whole church." [64]

There are, however, two incidents of recollected childhood in *The Brothers* that are integral to both character and plot development. The first concerns Grushenka and the fable she recalls from early childhood about "bestowing an onion." With somewhat strained logic, Grushenka informs Alyosha that she remembers the story ver-batim because she herself is the "wicked woman" therein.[65] (The reader will remember that the wicked woman's guardian angel, hard pressed to find a good deed in the woman's life, finally tells God of the time she had stolen an onion and bestowed it upon a beggar. God decrees that if the angel can pull this woman from a firey lake — her place of punishment — by an onion without breaking it, she may go to heaven. All goes carefully and well, until other sinners grab too: the wicked woman then clutches selfishly at the onion, whereupon it breaks. To this day, she burns in the firey lake).

The primary application of this story to the novel is that Gru-shenka has "bestowed an onion" by not abusing Alyosha's inno-cence. The secondary yet perhaps more important one is that Alyosha has imbued Grushenka with a thirst for confession. Most important, a pleasant childhood memory begets her sudden goodness.

The second instance is the "pound of nuts" story submitted at Mitya's trial by the old German doctor. The effectiveness of this evidence is partially prefigured by the sympathy evoked by Grigori's testimony that "had it not been for his care, the little boy Mitya would have been devoured by lice." [66] In the wake of this statement, the doctor's story of Mitya's childhood is especially effective in vouching for the defendant's character. The story itself is a simple one: the "abandoned child" Mitya was so grateful for a pound of nuts the doctor gave him in his childhood that he went out of his way to thank the man twenty years later.[67] It should be noted that underlying the "abandoned but still grateful" motif is Dostoevsky's tenet that one's childhood memories have the strongest influence in later life.

Interesting also in Dostoevsky are the childhood memories of those persons for whom much of present reality seems almost equally far removed. Indeed, one wonders if, for example, it is possible to distinguish between the dreamy fantasies of Tatyana Ivanovna's childhood and those in which she later lives [68] (*The Village of Stepanchikovo and Its Inhabitants*). Perhaps the most fascinating example is the General's (*The Idiot*) eight-page fantasy of his boyhood adventures with Napoleon.[69] Immediately following this monolithic fib, Dostoevsky characterizes the General through Prince Myshkin's eyes as:

. . . one of those special liars who, though they lie to the point of voluptuous oblivion, still, at the very climax of their rapture, secretly suspect that others do not believe them, and that they could not possibly do so.[70]

Thus, Dostoevsky typically inflicts the pain of realization while bestowing the bliss of oblivion. The emotional conflict attending the questioned veracity of the General's childhood "memory" is surely revealingly akin to his life in the present.

Perhaps the most symbolically interesting memory of childhood in Dostoevsky involves Ikhmenev's disappearing medallion (*The Injured and The Insulted*). This medallion contained, in his words, "a portrait of dear little Natasha in her childhood; she was about eight years old then, my little angel." [71] Ikhmenev's dissembled loss of the medallion is symbolic of the fact that a secret part of his heart forgives his daughter and aches for her return. When the deception is

discovered, Vanya lapses into a sentimental soliloquy about Ikhmenev's love for his daughter that is saved only in part by the vivid
reality of the fantasy world it evokes.

> . . . he would gaze with boundless love at the dear little face
> of his little loved one . . . shut himself off from everyone to
> converse with his priceless Natasha, compose her answers,
> answer the answers himself . . .[72]

Exposed, Ikhmenev hurls the medallion to the floor and tramples it
viciously. But the psychological pendulum swings abruptly back: his
wife's cry drives home to him the horror of what he has done.

> He sobbed like a child . . . In one instant the menacing old
> man had become weaker than a rebyonok.[73]

This extreme transformation ironically allies the father with the child
he would renounce, and the irony is soon extended by Natasha's long
pronouncement to the effect that her father is like a child in wrongly
deeming her to be still a child. "One cannot return the happy days of
childhood," she (also not unironically) tells Vanya. Her father
would not even recognize her now, she says.

> He loved what was still a little girl, a large rebyonok. He
> loved my childlike simplicity . . . caressed me . . . just as
> he did when I was still a seven-year-old girl . . . singing
> him children's songs. . . . I repeat, he knew and loved a
> little girl and chose not to think I would ever become a
> woman . . .[74]

Within these insights, she recounts that a month before their separation, her father had secretly bought her some earrings and was "joyful as a child, imagining how she would love the gift." But when he
discovered that she knew of the surprise beforehand, he "got horribly
angry at everyone and at her most of all." Ikhmenev's trampling of
the medallion (when his secret is revealed) thus becomes doubly symbolic: The gift of his forgiveness was also to be a surprise. His childish
anger, when this gift is discovered, thus echoes, as well as rings,
true.

Notes

[1] F. M. Dostoevsky, *Collected Works* (Moscow, 1956–1958), IX, 363–64.

[2] Dostoevsky, *C. W.*, X, 335–36.

[3] Discussing the conclusion of *The Brothers Karamazov*, Vyacheslav Ivanov asserts:

> . . . so long as the memory of Ilyusha remains alive in each of these children whom it has brought into a covenant together, it will preserve each of them from despair and collapse, from the final surrender to the spirit of not-being (Vyacheslav Ivanov, *Freedom and the Tragic Life: A study in Dostoevsky*, trans. Norman Cameron [New York, 1960], pp. 151–52).

[4] F. M. Dostoevsky, *The Diary of a Writer:* 1873, 1876, 1877 (Paris: YMCA-Press, 1877), p. 238. See also 1873, pp. 57–58, 363–64; and 1876, pp. 11, 214–15.

[5] Dostoevsky, *The Diary* of 1877, p. 249. See also pp. 262, 264, 265.

[6] Dostoevsky, *The Diary* of 1877, p. 267.

[7] Dostoevsky, *C. W.*, X, 303.

[8] *Ibid.*, p. 300.

[9] *Ibid.*, p. 370.

[10] *Ibid.*, pp. 368–69. My italics. All these smiles occur in less than one and one half pages.

[11] *Ibid.*, p. 370.

[12] *Ibid.*, p. 367.

[13] Dostoevsky, *C. W.*, III, 7 and especially 31.

[14] Dostoevsky, *C. W.*, I, 96.

[15] *Ibid.*, p. 173.

[16] *Ibid.*, p. 175.

[17] *Ibid.*, pp. 173–74.

[18] Dostoevsky, *C. W.*, X, 451.

[19] Dostoevsky, *C. W.*, I, 443.

[20] *Ibid.*, p. 445.

[21] *Ibid.*, p. 445.

[22] Dostoevsky, *C. W.*, III, 19.

[23] *Ibid.*, pp. 19–20.

[24] *Ibid.*, p. 226.

[25] *Ibid.*, p. 371.

[26] *Ibid.*, pp. 372–73, 384.

[27] Dostoevsky, *C. W.*, IV, 182.

[28] *Ibid.*, p. 183.

[29] *Ibid.*, p. 188.

[30] Ruth Mortimer, "Dostoevsky and The Dream," *Modern Philology* (November, 1956), 53, 107. Even she, in a rather incisive analysis of what touches off Raskolnikov's first dream, fails to mention this and other parallel instances.

[31] Dostoevsky, *C. W.*, IV, 212.

[32] *Ibid.*, pp. 218–19.

[33] Dostoevsky, *C. W.*, V, 283. Here Dostoevsky employs the device discussed above in *Peasant Marey*. The stranger walks off about fifty paces and turns to look at Raskolnikov once more; "it seemed" to the latter that the man again "smiled his coldly odious and triumphant smile."

[34] *Ibid.*, pp. 283–84.

[35] Dostoevsky, *C. W.*, VIII, 20.

[36] *Ibid.*, p. 21.

[37] *Ibid.*, p. 130.

[38] *Ibid.*, p. 130. See also p. 96.

[39] *Ibid.*, p. 95.

[40] *Ibid.*, p. 81.

[41] *Ibid.*, p. 122.

[42] As L. A. Zander has shown: L. A. Zander, *Taina dobra* (Frankfurt, 1960), p. 94.

[43] Dostoevsky, *C. W.*, IX, 26.

[44] *Ibid.*, pp. 26–27.

[45] Dostoevsky, *The Diary* of 1873, p. 58.

[46] Dostoevsky, *C. W.*, VIII, 127–28.

[47] *Ibid.*, p. 32.

[48] *Ibid.*, p. 33.

[49] *Ibid.*, pp. 33–34.

[50] *Ibid.*, pp. 35–37.

[51] *Ibid.*, p. 37.

[52] *Ibid.*, p. 114.

[53] *Ibid.*, p. 115.

[54] Dostoevsky, *C. W.*, II, 424.

[55] *Ibid.*, pp. 606–07.

[56] Dostoevsky, *C. W.*, X, 390.

[57] Dostoevsky, *C. W.*, II, 82.

[58] *Ibid.*, p. 172.

[59] *Ibid.*, p. 210.

[60] *Ibid.*, pp. 210–11.

[61] Dostoevsky, *The Diary* of 1877, p. 238.

[62] Dostoevsky, *C. W.*, V, 197.

[63] Dostoevsky, *C. W.*, II, 257.

[64] Dostoevsky, *C. W.*, IX, 62.

[65] *Ibid.*, p. 440.

[66] Dostoevsky, *C. W.*, X, 197.

[67] *Ibid.*, pp. 210–12.

[68] Dostoevsky, *C. W.*, II, 572–73.

[69] Dostoevsky, *C. W.*, VI, 561–69. He was supposedly ten or eleven.

[70] *Ibid.*, p. 569.

[71] Dostoevsky, *C. W.*, III, 75.

[72] *Ibid.*, p. 81.

[73] *Ibid.*, p. 83.

[74] *Ibid.*, p. 89.

CHAPTER FOUR

The Child in Dreams, Visions, Hallucinations, and Illusions

Illusion and reality may appear unwonted bedfellows, but Dostoevsky surprises them together constantly. And successfully. As Dmitri Chizhevsky asserts, "Dostoevsky's power as an artist lies precisely in his ability" to "fuse into an organic unity" the "naturalistic" and the "unrealistic."[1] In Mortimer's words, "Dostoevsky's mode of expression is the imaginative juxtaposition of the actual and the fantastic, of reality and the dream."[2] A. L. Bem employs the phrase "works-dreams" to characterize Dostoevsky's literary output.[3] All this is quite justified: the majority of his works are laced with strange relationships between what is and what seems, and each of the five major novels ends with someone presenting vivid evidence to this effect.

Crime and Punishment: Everything, even his crime, even the sentence and exile appeared to him now, in their initial impact, some sort of strange external fact which even seemed not to have happened to him.[4]

The Idiot: "And all that, and everything here abroad, and all this Europe of yours, it is all just a fantasy, and all of us abroad are just a fantasy . . . mark my words, you'll see for yourself!" she concluded almost angrily, parting with Evgeni Pavlovich.[5] [These are the very last words of the novel. Just before, as Ben points out, "one can distinctly catch the delirious whispers of Prince Myshkin and Rogozhin beside Nastasya Filippovna's body, and one is involuntarily ready to exclaim 'Just like a dream.'"[6]]

The Possessed: . . . but I am afraid of suicide, since I am afraid to show greatness of soul. I know it will be still another illusion — the last illusion in an infinite series of illusions.[7]

A Raw Youth: I have finished. Perhaps the reader is wondering: where then, did my "idea" disappear, and what is this new life that is beginning for me, about which I am so mysteriously proclaiming? But this new life, this new way just opened to me, is precisely my "idea," the very same one as before, only in a completely different form, so that it is impossible even to recognize it.[8]

The Brothers Karamazov: "Karamazov!" cried Kolya, "is it really true what religion says, that we will all rise from the dead and live on to see each other again, and everyone, and little Ilyusha?"

"Certainly we shall rise up, certainly we shall see each other, and joyfully tell each other everything that was," answered Alyosha, half laughing, half ecstatic.[9] [This passage is discussed here in Chapter Five.]

The Injured and the Insulted culminates, typically, in the following colloquy:

"Vanya," she said, "Vanya, it was just a dream!"
"What was a dream?" I asked.
"Everything, everything," she answered, "everything this whole year."[10]

Further, a disturbing intimacy between illusion and reality is predicated by the plots of works such as *Uncle's Dream*[11] and *The Dream* of a *Ridiculous Man,* as by the atmospheres of *White Nights* [12] and *The Landlady.* Still, it is this theme's mode of treatment that renders it both credible and chilling, in which endeavor Dostoevsky draws heavily upon the child.

Bem writes that Dostoevsky "had dreams of another life, and these dreams, almost hallucinations, became the flesh and blood of his works." [13] George Steiner remarks that Dostoevsky's heroes burn ideas like oxygen.

> This is why hallucinations play so large a role in Dostoevsky's narratives: hallucinations are the state in which the rush of thought through the human organism and the dialogues between self and soul are exteriorized. [14]

Mortimer calls attention to the "extraordinary number of page references to dreams" in Dostoevsky's works; [15] there are children on an extraordinary number of these pages.

The Dream of a Ridiculous Man, for example — virtually all dream — is replete with children and references thereto. On the surface, the story is not complex: an eccentric man dreams that he is wafted away, House-of-Fame style, to a blissful world where everyone is exceedingly childlike. He corrupts them and awakens.

A closer look reveals that this man, while intending to commit suicide, had met a shabby little girl of about eight on the street, gruffly refused her plea for aid, entered the building where he lived (where the children "faint from fear" [16] and the "smallest rebyonok" was having "some kind of fright-induced fit" [17]), and went to bed, diverted from suicide by the tiny girl. [18]

The dream, which brings Truth and Hope to the Ridiculous Man, is symbolically logical: touched off by a child, it is sustained by children. One even reads that these "children's" children are "the children of all," [19] which seems to suggest a paradisiacal resolution to the well-known Dostoevskian dilemma on earth: that all are guilty for all.

The dreamer stresses a favorite Dostoevskian theme. "Dreams," he avers, ". . . occur with horrifying clarity, with a jeweler's meticulous mastery of detail . . ." [20] Later, one can discern Dostoevskian prolepsis in dreamer anticipation of reader objection: "It is impos-

sible to see such details in a dream; you concocted them, upon awakening, from previous delirious feelings.''[21] This possibility is *repeatedly* parried by the unsettling Dostoevskian query: ''What difference
does it make, whether it was a dream or not, if this dream proclaimed
to me the Truth?''[22]

The Ridiculous Man employs a mode of pendulum-like description that is most typical of Dostoevsky:

> Dreams, it appears, are governed not by reason but by desire,
> not the head, but the heart; and yet what complex, crafty
> things are sometimes fashioned in dreams by my reason!
> Still, my reason encounters things in dreams that are com-
> pletely inconceivable.[23]

To summarize: (1) dreams are irrational; (2) dreams are hyper-
rational, and (3) dreams are hyper-rationally irrational. This seems
to be Dostoevsky's secret formula for creating an uneasily reconciled
whole out of extremely unharmonious halves: present one half, then
the other, and finally, work the second back into the first, such that the
resulting blend is tolerably credible. The above-mentioned ''Dostoevskian query'' now breaks down as follows: (1) maybe it was not a
dream; (2) of course it was; and (3) whether it was or not, the result
is (disturbingly) the same.

The dream's symbolism is consistent: Evoked by the child who
saved the dreamer from suicide, its childlike adults are anxious ''to
chase suffering'' from the dreamer's face.[24] Whether or not one
wishes to construe this expression of sympathy as a form of self-pity
conceived of the dreamer's inner defences against life's unpleasant-
ness, the numerous references, in so short a space, to the dream
world's denizens either as (2) or like (5) children seem almost tendentiously to ally them with the real little girl — the more so since the
dreamer corrupts their lives much as the world is corrupting hers,
abetted by his recent refusal to help her.

But, in reality, does the little girl exist? Or course: the story
ends, after a short break in the text, as follows:

> . . . I found out where that tiny girl lives . . . And I'll go
> there! I'll go there!

Yes. Yet this man's assertions sometimes bespeak the too alert confidence of madness: he is, he tells us, "accustomed to accept reality without an argument."[25] Furthermore, the borders of his dream, despite their alleged delineation, are strangely blurred. *During* the dream, the dreamer has a vision of the tiny girl he had offended,[26] and *after* the dream, he suffers for those who were in it.[27] Perhaps still more suspicious is his own view of the dream's "reality."

Even if it was a dream, all this could not have not occurred.[28]

"I'll tell you a little secret," he continues with the candor of one who furtively confides his most sacred fabrications,

Perhaps all that was not a dream at all!

The most alarming aspect of this statement is the second of its two implicit alternatives; either the story really does happen, or, *if he merely imagines that it does,* its entire "reality" rests on rent foundations. There is, after all, the subtitle, "A Fantastic Tale," and just prior to the story's end, the protagonist remarks: A dream? What is a dream, anyway? Is our whole life not a dream?[29] Can the tale's *title,* then, take on a new dimension — be construed to apply to the *whole* story? Just "before" his dream, the man says it "seemed clear" to him that both life and the world were somehow "dependent" upon him. Does the entire tale, then, transpire *in the mind* of the protagonist, and do the few words at its end, separated by a break in the text, ring out alone in some sort of insane "present reality"? Probably not, but such doubts are, in Dostoevsky, constantly disturbingly possible.

Indeed, little children, and especially little girls, constantly appear as if from nowhere in Dostoevsky's works; and exceedingly often,[30] it is difficult to be absolutely certain of their "reality." In *The Idiot,* for example, Prince Myshkin encounters a child on the street immediately prior to his epileptic fit and ensuing illness. The incident presumes to be straight narration, but one must remember that Myshkin is roaming the strange twilight land that is a prelude to epilepsy: the two preceding pages[31] could well have come from *Kotik Letaev* or *The Doors of Perception.* Moreover, the Prince has recently confided to Rogozhin that he "is beginning to think he sees things."[32] The meeting is indeed so brief as to suggest a vivid flash of expanded consciousness: "He started to speak to a small oncoming child."[33] As if in reply to an imagined reader's (or Prince Myshkin's!) question (Was the child real?), Dostoevsky immediately adds: "Perhaps his epileptic condition was growing more and more intense."

Still, the question of this evanescent child's actual existence must remain unanswered. Nor is it overly important here, except as evidence of another child who *might be* imaginary, which evidence, in especial measure of its cogency, serves further to ally the childlike Myshkin with children. One could well wonder why the adjective "small" is applied to the word "rebyonok" in so short a description: What was such a tiny tot doing on the street by itself? The word *"i"* (which follows "perhaps" in the Russian) is exceedingly difficult to translate, bearing just the slightest suggestion of "it was," i.e., "Perhaps it was his epileptic condition growing more and more intense."

The point remains moot. It should be noted, however, that *if* this child is, in fact, a shadow figure perceived only in the Prince's expanding delirium, the symbolism of illusional imagery in Dostoevsky is here as consistent as in *The Dream of a Ridiculous Man.* The source or stimulus of this "illusional" child can be found in Lebedev's daughter's baby, whom the Prince has just seen. In the stream-of-consciousness-like half-delirium that immediately follows the above "encounter," we find:

> I seem to be mixing things . . . how strange! My head seems to spin . . . And what a sweet, pleasant face Lebedev's eldest daughter has, the one who was standing with her baby, what an innocent, almost childlike expression and what almost childlike laughter![34]

"Strange," adds Dostoevsky-Myshkin, "that he had nearly forgotten this face and only now remembered it." Even so, the reader is left with the feeling that Myshkin's perception of this recollection closely approaches a vision, and that the child symbolism in the Prince's perceptions during his long, pre-epileptic wandering consistently echoes his earlier, normal conscious experience.

The question discussed above (that playfully but somewhat disturbingly asks "What difference it makes" whether something actually happened or not, if the results are the same as if it did) arises continuously in potentially unreal (not normally conscious) perceptions of children in Dostoevsky.

Marya Timofeevna (*The Possessed*), when asked by Shatov whether she really did have the baby [35] she describes, rather disarmingly replies:

> This reasoning of yours seems funny to me, Shatushka. Maybe I really did have a child, but what does it matter, whether I did or not, if it's all the same now as if there never was one? [36]

Is the memory of that which was not, she appears to be asking, any less real than a memory of that which was? [37]

"Where did you put it?" continues Shatov. "In the pond," she sighs. But Shatov, with somewhat pyrrhic strategy, asks pointblank: "And what if you never had a child at all, and this is nothing but delirium, eh?"

> "You're asking me a hard question, Shatushka," she answered pensively and with no astonishment whatsoever at such a question. "On that account I can tell you nothing — perhaps there was none; this, it seems to me, is just your curiosity; shall I not still cry for the child the rest of my life, do I not see it in my dreams?" [38]

She then shows sincere sympathy for Shatov, whose wife has left him for Stavrogin, adding that the latter (Marya's husband) came to her in a dream. "Maybe he'll come to you in reality," murmurs Shatov.

> No, Shatushka, it was a dream . . . he is not to come in reality.

Whether or not such an answer allows the construction that Marya actually views her dream world as her escape and refuge, it must be admitted that she respects this other reality with devastating insight and detachment. Indeed, the "mad" Marya, with her pensiveness, quiet flashes of wit disclosing wisdom, and alarmingly clear self-analysis, seems somehow mentally superior to those who surround her. The question of Marya's child's reality is dwarfed in importance by *the reality of the question* of its reality. (There seems little reason to disbelieve Stavrogin, who emphatically declares her a virgin.[39])

There is a Dostoevskian application of this problem to children in Leskov's story, *The Improvisers*. A "little old man tells" of how his "little children" died. He then tucks a piece of bread (given him by the narrator) up his sleeve.

> "Don't you want to eat?"
> "Not hardly. I'll take it to the children."
> "But the children all died!"
> "Well, then, up there . . . they'll each get a little apple in paradise."
> "Well, yes; and you eat the bread yourself."
> The peasant again took the bread in his hands . . . then sighed and said quietly:
> "No; still a darned sight better for the children."[40]

This refusal to believe that the little children have died, despite definite knowledge to the contrary, makes for an approach to reality, or, rather, *for another reality*, in which vividness of perception and all attending experience lay cogent claims to undeniable authenticity. (The main impact of Wordsworth's poem, "We are Seven," derives from five little children's refusal to believe that the other two have died.)

Dostoevsky's application of such "effective reality" is both multiform and broad. Petya Gorshkov's moribund father's fixation that the dead boy is still alive affords a compelling example. Stroking his little daughter's head, the man turns to his wife and asks repeatedly about their dear little Petya.[41]

A striking parallel can be seen in the bizarre conduct of Ilyusha's father at his son's funeral. After a fit of howling and writhing on the ground, the dazed man returns home and "greedily kisses" Ilyusha's shoes, wailing: "Ilyusha, dear Ilyusha, where are your little feet?"[42]

Nellie, in her fatal sickness (discussed above), also believes that her grandfather is still alive and offers eloquent proof to this effect. The treatment is strikingly similar to that in Leskov, the fixation being repeated despite all possible evidence to belie it.

> "I want to stay here and look after my grandfather, Vanya."
> "But your grandfather died, Nellie!"

Nellie grows pensive, asks Vanya to tell once again how her grandfather died, listens carefully as he does so, and then:

> "No, Vanya, he did not die!" she said decisively . . .[43]

Nellie proceeds to explain that "yesterday" her mother (also no longer living) told her that she had purposely misled Nellie, and that actually, her grandfather was still walking the streets, begging alms.

> "That was a dream, Nellie, a sick dream . . ."
> "I too thought it was only a dream," said Nellie
> . . . "But today . . . I dreamed of grandfather himself
> . . . he reproached me. He also told me that he has no
> sniffing tobacco at all, and that without this tobacco he can-
> not live."

Once again Vanya tries to dissuade Nellie. Finally, he feels he has succeeded, whereupon she admits fear of sleep, lest she see her grandfather. "I cannot leave you, Vanya," she exclaims, embracing him. "Even if my grandfather dies, I won't leave you." [44]

Netochka (who dreams repeatedly of Katya, and vice versa,[45] during their love affair) similarly refuses to believe that her mother has died:

> "No, no, not orphan, no!" . . .
> "Where's my mommy? Where's my mommy?" [46]

(These exclamations are touched off by the word "orphan," even though Netochka is already only too aware that her mother has died.)

There are relatively few Dostoevskian references to Makar Ivano-vich (*A Raw Youth*) as a child (only two [47]), yet the man is closely allied with children by what he says in the novel.[48] One of his stories, inserted "desultorily" by Arkadi, fills ten of the novel's pages and contains many significant references to children.

The tale centers around a certain Maksim Ivanovich, a rich and callous merchant. Another merchant, deeply in debt to Maksim Ivano-vich, dies, leaving his widow and five children — a boy of eight and four tiny girls — to Maksim's mercy. He is unmoved by their pleas, and the poor mother soon buries her daughters "one by one."

> Only her eldest little son remained alive, and she doted on him, trembling. He was puny and delicate, with a face pretty as a little girl's.[49]

It is the boy's misfortune, one day, to jostle Maksim Ivanovich, who instantly has him whipped. Since the lad's crying irritates Maksim, he orders that the beating outlast the screams. The boy is left barely alive.

Later, Maksim decides to become the boy's benefactor and adopts his terrified victim. When the boy, playing ball, breaks a porcelain lamp, Maksim bellows manacingly, and the child runs out to where a lovely little girl is standing by a rapid river. They are fast becoming friends when Maksim hies into view, screaming "Seize him!" The boy promptly throws himself into the river and drowns.

The incident so affects Maksim that he confesses to a priest and points with fright to *The Bible:*

> And if anyone hurts the conscience of one of these little ones, that believe in me, he had better have been drowned in the depths of the sea, with a mill-stone hung around his neck (Matthew, 18:6).

Why, asks the priest, are you so troubled about this boy when you were more directly the cause of the four girls' deaths?

> "I dream of him," answers Maksim.[50]

The priest leaves, and Maksim undertakes his own expiation, ordering an artist to paint a wall-sized picture of the suicide scene. Fanatically demanding reproduction of every detail, he insists that "all the angels of heaven" be pictured in the sky, "flying to meet" the dying boy.

The artist accepts the job but soon comes to Maksim, complaining that it is "impossible" to paint the picture as requested. Suicide, he explains, is the greatest of all sins; how then can the angels be flying to meet him?

> "But he's — a babe, he's not accountable."
> "No, not a babe, a youth: he was eight years old already, when this occurred. So he must answer for it to some degree." [51]

Maksim is minimally mollified by the adamant artist's compromise: to greet the boy with a ray of light, shining down from above.

Next, Maksim visits the widow, the boy's mother, and proposes marriage. "I want a boy born to us," he says,

> and if we have one, it means your boy has forgiven us both, you and me. The lad *commanded me* thus.[52]

She refuses, seeing that he is "not in his right mind — in some kind of frenzy." After numerous persuasions and pressures, however, including his promise to build a temple, she consents. Married, Maksim becomes a good man and does many good deeds, buying for twice its value a horse that a peasant is beating on the head; he even receives the gift of tears.

At last "the Lord answers their prayers and sends them a son," whereupon Maksim's wife concludes that the boy has "forgiven them." But a year passes, and suddenly, Maksim again dreams of the boy suicide.

> And not in vain did he dream of the youth.

The baby immediately grows ill and dies. Maksim, giving his wife everything he owns, leaves to "save his soul" and never returns.[53]

It should be noted that in addition to its prophetic function the dream medium in Makar's story serves as a channel for communication between the dead and the living. (The latter theme in Dostoevsky is explored at length in Chapter Five of the present study.)

Not only are unhealthy, warped, and undesirable characters in Dostoevsky haunted by memories of their unpleasant and sometimes unsavory pasts; in such personages, dreams join forces with recollections, and the attending symbolism is uncannily consistent and convincing.

> Throughout Dostoevsky's work there is scattered evidence that he had an uncanny insight into the nature of dream life.[54]

After visiting a "colony of tender-aged criminals," Dostoevsky wrote in *The Diary* of 1876:

> Yes, these children's souls have seen sombre pictures; they are accustomed to strong impressions which, of course, will remain with them evermore, appearing for the rest of their lives in terrifying dreams.[55]

As has been seen, the Underground Man hated his childhood; its mere memory triggers a series of nightmares.

> That night I had exceedingly ugly dreams. And little wonder: all evening I was oppressed by recollections of the penal years of my life in school, and I could not escape them.[56]

It is difficult to believe that these dreams are not further described because the next two pages are a series of nightmarish episodes from the man's childhood seen in dream-like distortion through the strange prism of his present consciousness. Indeed, these incidents, thus introduced, seem dreams first, and past second, and in this sense, the dream symbolism actually becomes one with its stimulae.

Several subtle techniques present these disturbing childhood memories as bad dreams. Not only are they introduced as dreams; the descriptions culminate in two sets of suspension points, and a fresh paragraph abruptly begins: "In the morning . . ."[57] The episodes are narrated mainly through emotions and emotional (rather than rational) reactions thereto; any sense of time in the passage is vague and uneven. Most important is the accumulation of nightmarish unbearableness effected by a series of grotesque and irrational reactions.

> My companions treated me with relentless, malicious derision because I was unlike any of them. And I was unable to bear the derision . . . the expressions on their faces somehow grew especially stupid and degenerated . . . they perceived the most obvious, eye-striking reality with a fantastic stupidity . . . I understood things . . . they had never heard of. They looked at this wildly and with derision . . . The derision ceased, but unpleasantness remained, and a cold, strained relationship began.[58]

This grotesque, illogical background of unpleasant emotions somehow reflects the narrator's inner feelings with a drugged brightness that is more dream-like than real. His companions seem irrational phantoms wearing nightmare grins. In the story's context, this passage shows translucently through a sequence of blown-up petty details caught in painfully sharp, brooding focus.

As Ruth Mortimer has noted,[59] Raskolnikov's first dream is touched off by the last lines of his mother's letter.

> The letter closed with the words, "Remember . . . when your father was living . . . how happy we all were in those days."[60]

Despite the salutary potential of Dostoevskian pleasant childhood memories, they are not immune to misuse (as by the protagonist of *A Gentle Creature*). "This last sentence had taken hold of Raskolnikov," Mortimer continues,

> but the unconscious attempt to relive a moment of that innocent happiness fails, and the childhood experience in the

dream evolves as one of intense fear and suffering, from which even his father cannot shield him.

Ruth Mortimer proceeds to espy in the dream's struggling mare "a whole class of 'sacrificial' women . . .''

Identified in the dream with the mare, helpless under the primitive passion of her tormentor, these women are translated by Raskolnikov into animals for hire.[61]

It seems a pity that Mortimer does not allude to *The Diary* of 1876, which reveals the dream to be strikingly autobiographical. "Our children,'' writes Dostoevsky, "are brought up and grow up meeting repulsive pictures.''

They see a peasant who has overloaded his wagon whip his mare, his benefactress, who is stuck in the mud, whip her across the eyes.[62]

Dostoevsky then describes a peasant he observed using a calf in a cart for a cushion, which calf perhaps died, tongue out and eyes bulging, on the way to the slaughterhouse. He is sure that no one was the least bothered by this picture, because the animal was to be slaughtered anyway . . .

but such pictures undoubtedly bestialize people and have a corrupting influence, especially on children.

All this serves as a prelude to the description of an episode from Dostoevsky's past. When he was "about fifteen years old,'' he observed the following drama of infectious brutality. A tipsy State messenger, a "strong, sturdy lad with a purple face,'' keeps striking his coachman on the back of the head with his fist. Each time, the driver whips the horses "with all his might.'' Although the animals respond vigorously, the messenger remains unappeased: His blows are not angry, but methodical. Barely able to keep his balance, the pummeled coachman "lashes the horses every second." Perhaps the fellow will beat his wife that same day, hazards Dostoevsky: "At least, *she* will pay for this" or perhaps because "She had looked and seen . . ." [63] Dostoevsky's concluding comment is highly typical:

> This repulsive picture remained in my recollections for the rest of my life. [64]

While exploring Raskolnikov's dream, one should be aware of two further parallels. The first is in Makar's story (just discussed), when Maksim saves a horse that is being beaten on the head. The second is presented by Ivan (*The Brothers Karamazov*). Prior to describing his second child victim, he asserts that Russians historically feel

> . . . a spontaneous and intimate satisfaction from inflicting pain. Nekrasov wrote a poem about how a peasant lashes his horse on the eyes, "on its gentle eyes." Who has not seen this? It's particularly Russian. [65]

In Ivan's picture, just as in Dostoevsky's *Diary*, the horse is overloaded and stuck in the mud; both animals are whipped across the eyes.

All of these details appear in Raskolnikov's nightmare. Its preface is typically Dostoevskian: "Dreams in sickness are often marked by an extraordinary vividness, brightness . . ." [66] Also typically, the artistic details of such dreams are emphasized, as is their influence upon the dreamer, after the dream. The dream begins when Raskolnikov was "about seven," and Dostoevsky tells us that its locale was even more complete with real details than was Raskolnikov's memory. The obvious inference is that dreams, especially dreams in sickness, can re-evoke details more complete and precise than those recalled by normal conscious memory. The application undoubtedly extends to perception prior to epilepsy and even to feverish hallucinations such as Svidrigailov's, discussed below, of the fourteen-year-old girl he had molested.

In Raskolnikov's dream of his childhood, he is walking with his

father towards the cemetery where his little brother is buried. Here
Dostoevsky achieves what is even for him a rare emotional intensification. Raskolnikov sees a huge cart, drawn by a small, emaciated
mare . . .

> . . . one of those who — he had seen it often — are sometimes
> strained to the utmost pulling some gigantic load of lumber
> or hay, especially if the cart gets stuck in the mud or in a
> rut, whereupon peasants always whip them so painfully, so
> painfully, sometimes even on their faces and on the eyes, and
> he feels so sorry for them, so sorry that he almost cries, and
> his mommy always used to lead him away from the win-
> dow.[67]

One should note especially that the last word, window, almost takes
the reader unawares: in his dream, the boy is *on the street*. Subtly but
relentlessly, Dostoevsky employs an undulating temporal sequence
(often . . . sometimes . . . always . . . sometimes . . . always)   to
render the occurrence nearly universal: the reader's only choice is
between the frequent and the typical. This is not accomplished, however, at the expense of the particular; vivid details abound. What is
most deceptive, however, is that all these details are merely prelimin-
ary background material. In the actual dream, Raskolnikov has only
just caught sight of a cart and horse.

When the dream is at last described, its details are at once hauntingly familiar. Their impact is intensified, and their significance seems
magnified. As Viktor Shklovsky has noted,

> It is a dream about cruelty, about the world's evil. This
> cruelty in the dream seems inherent in the entire world.[68]

Dostoevsky often promotes eloquent collaboration between the vivid
and the apparently typical.

The main part of the dream, in which the mare is brutally beaten
to death with an iron crowbar before the boy's terrified eyes, undoubtedly foreshadows Raskolnikov's killings, as Mortimer suggests.[69] Dostoevsky effectively embodies in this description the ''par-
ticularly Russian brand of sadism'' mentioned by Ivan. The peasant

Mikolka twice insists that the mare be lashed across the eyes,[70] and the gruesome details of the mare's murder greatly surpass Raskolnikov's killings as to bloody abandon. Perhaps most horrible of all is the description of Mikolka with bloodshot eyes (which seem luridly to reflect the horse's corpse) "standing as if he regretted that there was no one else to beat."

But it is the boy's trauma that interests us most. He vacillates precariously between numbness and excruciating pity, and his is the painful helplessness of trapped spectatorship.

> . . . the boy was already beside himself. With a cry he plunged through the crowd to the mare, hugged her head, bloody head, and kissed her, kissed her on the eyes, the lips . . . Then he suddenly sprang up and rushed at Mikolka, his tiny fists flailing.[71]

Just as the child's physical condition is half pain, half shock, his emotions are torn between pity and a furious need to avenge the mare's murder.

It is most important that this dream of Raskolnikov's childhood has a double projection into his present. First, Dostoevsky makes it clear that the dream's mood and atmosphere cast shadows across Raskolnikov's consciousness. "Thank God, it was only a dream!" he gasps, sitting up in horror. "But what is this? I must be getting feverish: What a revolting dream!"[72] Second, he himself projects the dream upon his present in sharp symbolic focus:

> "God!" he exclaimed. "Will I really, will I really take the axe and start to beat her head, crush her skull . . ."[73]

It is well known that Dostoevsky accorded considerable credence to his dreams,[74] and, if the episode of Peasant Marey may be presumed biographical, he was subject to hallucinations in his childhood.[75] Children such as Marya Timofeevna's, who appear both in dreams and in hallucinations, may therefore be seen to have a special significance for Dostoevsky himself. Other such combinations are two of his most pathetic girl victims: Nellie (*The Injured and The Insulted*) and Liza (*The Eternal Husband*). The only other instance approaching these two combinations concerns Svidrigailov (discussed below), who sees, just prior to his suicide, two girl victims in rapid succession — first in delirium and then in a dream.

Nellie appears both in hallucinations and dreams to herself; she does also to Vanya. During his sickness:

> Several times I awoke and each time I would see Nellie's sympathetic, anxious little face bent over me. But I remember all this as if through a dream, as if in a fog, and the dear image of the poor little girl would flash before me in the midst of delirium like a vision, like a picture . . .[76]

Later, soon after Nellie tells Ikhmenev how "evil" he is: Walking down the stairs, it was as if I could still see Nellie's face in front of me, terribly pale from my reproaches.[77]

Velchaninov is fairly haunted by various visions of Liza:

> And forever afterwards the oppressed gaze of the tortured rebyonok, looking at him in senseless fright and as a last hope, remained memorable to him and appeared to him both in conscious reality and in his dreams.[78]

And again: The dear image of the poor child rebyonok flashed sadly in front of him.[79] There is also a long passage, wherein he recalls Liza with a vividness that subtly suggests reality, beginning as follows:

> All these *conscious* thoughts always appeared to him inseparably from his memory — always bright, near, and deeply moving — of the dead rebyonok. He would re-create for himself her pale little face, recalling its every expression . . .[80]

"Debauching young girls, which runs so strangely through Dostoevsky's fiction," writes Ernest J. Simmons, "is a particular feature of Svidrigailov's immoral nature." [81] Indeed, he seems not only to dream of this, but also to live for its realization. Rakitin, in *The Brothers Karamazov*, declares that just one part of a beautiful woman's body can cause a man who falls in love with her to betray his own children.[82] Svidrigailov's passion is at once more and less specialized: he prefers young, innocent girls, but his tastes are eclectic within this category.

Such attraction to innocence is widespread in Dostoevsky. Trusotsky (*The Eternal Husband*) values innocence above all: innocence has the pungency of a ripe apple.[83] Twice Trusotsky mentally savors young girls — once, with a sweet and somehow sly smile,[84] and later, with a high-pitched snicker.[85] Fyodor Pavlovich Karamazov is "mainly" attracted to his sixteen-year-old second wife "by the innocent look of the innocent little girl." "Her innocent little eyes slashed my soul like a razor," he later declares, "sniggering vilely." [86] Similar sentiments are evinced by a "newcomer General" (*The Possessed*),[87] and by Prince Volkonsky (*The Injured and The Insulted*),[88] and such inner indecency literally overflows (*Uncle's Dream*) when the fourteen-year-old rebyonok Sonechka dances. The old Prince keeps repeating how "formed" the girl is, voluptuously drawing out his words and even drooling.[89] Razumikhin (*Crime and Punishment*) becomes enraged at Zosimov when the latter remarks, "almost licking his lips," that Dunya is a "charming little girl." [90] Afanasi Ivanovich (*The Idiot*) has a predilection for innocence; in the words of the darkly enlightened Nastasya Filippovna, he "loves babes." [91] Stavrogin (*The Possessed*) is strangely concerned, even in the published version of the novel, about dishonoring and raping little girls,[92] and he is asked by Shatov if he really enticed children and corrupted them.[93] In *Babok*, we read of a fourteen-year-old boy's corruption [94] and of lascivious dreams about a fifteen-year-old blonde.[95] The merchant in *A Raw Youth* who attempts to buy Olya offers her fifteen roubles, and forty if he finds "full honesty." [96]

Such ambitions belong occasionally to the opposite sex. There is little doubt that Grushenka (*The Brothers Karamazov*) was especially enticed by Alyosha's innocence when planning to seduce him, and The Little Hero holds a similar attraction for adult women.

Svidrigailov, however, can be considered the epitome of desiring young innocence and laughing about it repulsively. He finds the age of sixteen, with its "still childlike eyes, shyness, and little tears of shame — better than beauty." [97] This accomplished voluptuary seems especially to revel in the confusion and embarrassment of his victims, and he sees in their first blushes the splendor of a sunrise.[98]

"I especially love children — I love children in general," he tells
Raskolnikov, laughing loudly.[99]

Svidrigailov's hallucination, dream, and suicide comprise one of
Crime and Punishment's most powerful sequences. First, he sees an
image of the fourteen-year-old girl who had drowned herself after
being raped by him. The body's strange smile is somehow frightening:

> . . . the smile on her pale lips was full of some kind of
> unchildlike, boundless sorrow and supreme grievance.[100]

The victim's expression seems to combine wisdom, superiority, masochism, and even a touch of perverse pleasure. Despite the crime's
enormity, Dostoevsky waxes somewhat maudlin as he alludes to the
"offense that had steeped in shame her angelically pure soul." But
the girl's smile, faintly echoing in its own disturbing incongruity the
crime's hideous impropriety, does much to save the scene.

Still more chilling is Svidrigailov's dream of the five-year-old
prostitute. He peeks under the child's blanket and sees that

> . . . color had already filled her pale cheeks. But strangely,
> this color seemed to stand out brighter and stronger than the
> flush of a normal child's face. "It's a feverish flush,"
> thought Svidrigailov, "it's — like a flush from wine, as if
> she's drunk a whole glass. Her crimson lips are burning,
> flaming . . ."[101]

This redness is, of course, his nightmare's distortion of the sunrise-
like blush he so enjoys in his victims' burning innocence. The five-
year-old girl seems to be winking at him, and her lips "widen in a
smile." Arrant laughter fills her now "unchildlike face," the impu-
dent face, he concludes in utter horror, of a common slut.

It seems psychologically sound that Svidrigailov's conscience
should seek to see in this child a little harlot (she even holds out her
arms to him just before he awakens).[102] What renders the nightmare
most effective, however, is that the dreamer's former delight (the
blush) now horrifies him; and that the tiny girl's smile is hauntingly
suggestive of the one on his drowned victim's face.

Just as Svidrigailov is pursued by his former crimes against children in the media of hallucinations and dreams, Stavrogin is plagued by his victim in visions. In the "unpublished" *Stavrogin's Confession*, he tells of having "raped" a young girl whom he "calmly" then allowed to hang herself in an adjacent room.[103] (Actually, her shocking, almost aggressive passion [104] recalls the five-year-old slut's ostensible lust in Svidrigailov's dream, and Stavrogin's calmness is more nearly the frozen frenzy of desperate self-hypnosis.[105]

Later, Stavrogin is horrified by a vision of the girl, threatening him with her tiny fist and shaking her head.[106] "This vision," he says,

I cannot endure, because since then it has come to me almost every day. It comes not of itself, but I bring it before myself and cannot help bringing it. I cannot live without it. Oh, if I could ever see her in the flesh, even though it were an hallucination! [107]

The first contradiction in this passage raises a typical Dostoevskian question: What difference does it make, whether or not it comes by itself, if he cannot stop its coming? The second contradiction, between flesh and hallucination, is also typical and lends an eeriness to the vision itself. It is interesting that Stavrogin decides to kill the girl because his "chief hatred was at the recollection of her smile." [108] Finally, when Father Tikhon has finished reading the confession, he makes the typically Dostoevskian remark that the world is full of such occurrences.[109]

Notes

[1] Dmitri Chizhevsky, "The Theme of The Double in Dostoevsky," *Dostoevsky: A Collection of Critical Essays,* ed. René Wellek (Englewood Cliffs, N.J., 1962), p. 114.
See also A. B. Chicherin, "Poeticheski stroi yazyka v romanakh Dostoevskogo," *Tvorchestvo F. M. Dostoevskogo,* ed. N. L. Stepanov (Moscow, 1959), p. 431.

[2] Ruth Mortimer, "Dostoevsky and The Dream," *Modern Philology,* 53 (November, 1956), 107.

[3] A. L. Bem, "Taina lichnosti Dostoevskogo," *Pravoslavie i kultura* (Berlin, 1923), p. 186.

[4] F. M. Dostoevsky, *Collected Works,* V (Moscow, 1956–1958), 573.

[5] Dostoevsky, *C. W.,* VI, 696.

[6] Bem, p. 193.

[7] Dostoevsky, *C. W.,* VII, 702.

[8] Dostoevsky, *C. W.,* VIII, 619.

[9] Dostoevsky, *C. W.,* X, 338.

[10] Dostoevsky, *C. W.,* III, 386.

[11] As Bem has noted, p. 186.

[12] See *ibid.,* p. 189.

[13] *Ibid.,* p. 185.

[14] George Steiner, *Tolstoy or Dostoevsky: An Essay in the Old Criticism* (New York, 1961), p. 289.

[15] Mortimer, p. 114.

[16] Dostoevsky, *C. W.,* X, 424.

[17] *Ibid.,* p. 424.

[18] *Ibid.,* pp. 424, 426.

[19] *Ibid.,* p. 434.

[20] *Ibid.,* p. 426.

[21] *Ibid.,* p. 435.

[22] *Ibid.,* p. 427. See also pp. 421, 426, 428, and especially 432, 436, 439, 440.

[23] *Ibid.,* p. 427. Probably the most "complex, crafty" dream in all of Dostoevsky is Ivan's dream (or hallucination) of the devil in *The Brothers Karamazov.* The devil (or Ivan!) speaks of "artistic dreams"—

> such a complex and convincing reality, such events, and even a whole world of events, tied together by such an intrigue of such unexpected details . . .

There follows a fascinating discussion of whether or not the devil, who seems to be saying things that have "never before entered Ivan's head," is his hallucination or his dream (*ibid.*, p. 166).

[24] *Ibid.*, p. 432.

[25] *Ibid.*, p. 428.

[26] *Ibid.*, pp. 430–31.

[27] *Ibid.*, p. 432.

[28] *Ibid.*, p. 436.

[29] *Ibid.*, p. 441. This is strikingly similar to the Raw Youth's statement that perhaps everything is someone else's dream (VIII, 151).

[30] The reader is referred to several more such occurrences treated in Chapter Six of the present study.

[31] Dostoevsky, *C. W.*, VI, 256–57.

[32] *Ibid.*, p. 233.

[33] *Ibid.*, p. 258.

[34] *Ibid.*, p. 259.

[35] Vyacheslav ascribes some importance to this child:

> The little child for whom she weeps is only a fancy; yet, without this imaginary mourning for a child, the picture of this soul racked by the expectation of the distant Bridegroom, the beloved Redeemer, would be incomplete. (Vyacheslav Ivanov, *Freedom and the Tragic Life: A study in Dostoevsky*, trans. Norman Cameron [New York, 1960], p. 44.)

Having termed Stavrogin "the Russian Faust," Ivanov likens Marya Timofeevna to Gretchen:

> Maria's imaginary mourning for a child is almost the same emotion as that which finds expression in Gretchen's hallucinated memories (*ibid.*, p. 61).

[36] Dostoevsky, *C. W.*, VII, 155–56.

[37] Such questions are among Dostoevsky's favorites — the icing on his cake of unreality. His serving up of real results that accrue from potentially unreal causes is decidedly tantalizing.

Zander finds Marya Timofeevna's child "spiritually real, more real than everything we consider real in the usual sense of this word" (L. A. Zander, *Taina dobra* [Frankfurt, 1960], p. 92).

[38] Dostoevsky, *C. W.*, VII, 156.

[39] *Ibid.*, p. 260.

[40] N. S. Leskov, *Collected Works* (Moscow, 1958), IX, 336.

[41] Dostoevsky, *C. W.*, I, 194.

[42] Dostoevsky, *C. W.*, X, 333.

[43] Dostoevsky, *C. W.*, III, 372. It should be observed that this entire scene echoes Vanya's indiscreet answer to Nellie early in the novel: "Your grandfather? He's dead" (*ibid.*, p. 61).

[44] *Ibid.*, pp. 373–74.

[45] Dostoevsky, *C. W.*, II, 137, 165, 171.

[46] *Ibid.*, p. 132.

[47] He once speaks with a "childlike, pleading expression" (VIII, 410), and Arkadi refers to him as a "babe" (VIII, 416).

[48] Beyond what follows here, see also Chapter Five of the present study.

[49] Dostoevsky, *C. W.*, VIII, 431.

[50] *Ibid.*, p. 436.

[51] *Ibid.*, p. 437.

[52] *Ibid.*, p. 438. My italics.

[53] *Ibid.*, pp. 439–40.

[54] Avrahm Yarmolinsky, *Dostoevsky: His Life and Art* (New York, 1960), p. 326.

[55] F. M. Dostoevsky, *The Diary of a Writer:* 1873, 1876, 1877 (Paris: YMCA-Press, 1876), 25.

[56] Dostoevsky, *C. W.*, IV, 188.

[57] *Ibid.*, p. 190.

[58] *Ibid.*, pp. 188–90.

[59] Mortimer, p. 109.

[60] *Ibid.*, p. 109.

[61] *Ibid.*, p. 109.

[62] Dostoevsky, *The Diary of* 1876, pp. 35–36.

[63] *Ibid.*, pp. 37–39.

[64] *Ibid.*, p. 39.

[65] Dostoevsky, *C. W.*, IX, 302.

[66] Dostoevsky, *C. W.*, V, 59.

[67] *Ibid.*, p. 61.

[68] Viktor Shklovsky, *Za i protiv: zametki o Dostoevskom* (Moscow, 1957), p. 212.

[69] Mortimer, p. 110.

[70] Dostoevsky, *C. W.*, V, 63.

[71] *Ibid.*, p. 64.

[72] *Ibid.*, p. 65.

[73] *Ibid.*, p. 65.

[74] Yarmolinsky, p. 275.

[75] Dostoevsky, *C. W.*, X, 369.

[76] Dostoevsky, *C. W.*, III, 177.

[77] *Ibid.*, p. 304.

[78] Dostoevsky, *C. W.*, IV, 483.

[79] *Ibid.*, p. 494.

[80] *Ibid.*, p. 512. It is tempting to compare these passages with what Dostoevsky writes of his own daughter Sonya soon after her death at the age of three months. In two letters (to A. N. Maikov and S. A. Ivanova), he emphasizes that the passage of time (one month) has intensified and brightened the child's image painfully remaining in his mind (F. M. Dostoevsky, *Letters,* ed. A. S. Dolinin, II [Moscow, 1928–1959], 122, 126).

[81] Ernest J. Simmons, *Dostoevsky: The Making of a Novelist* (New York, 1962), p. 165.

[82] Dostoevsky, *C. W.,* IX, 103.

[83] Dostoevsky, *C. W.,* IV, 522.

[84] *Ibid.*, p. 544.

[85] *Ibid.*, p. 556.

[86] Dostoevsky, *C. W.,* IX, 19.

[87] Dostoevsky, *C. W.,* VII, 528–29.

[88] Dostoevsky, *C. W.,* III, 270–71.

[89] Dostoevsky, *C. W.,* II, 335–36.

[90] Dostoevsky, *C. W.,* V, 215.

[91] Dostoevsky, *C. W.,* VI, 195. See also 47, 51, 53.

[92] Dostoevsky, *C. W.,* VII, 252.

[93] *Ibid.*, p. 269.

[94] Dostoevsky, *C. W.,* X, 352.

[95] *Ibid.*, p. 353.

[96] Dostoevsky, *C. W.,* VIII, 193.

[97] Dostoevsky, *C. W.,* V, 501.

[98] *Ibid.*, p. 501. See also p. 503.

[99] *Ibid.*, p. 503.

[100] *Ibid.*, p. 531.

[101] *Ibid.*, p. 533.

[102] *Ibid.*, p. 534.

[103] His initial amorous advances cause her to "laugh like a baby." (F. M. Dostoevsky, *Stavrogin's Confession,* trans. Virginia Woolf and S. S. Koteliansky [New York, 1947], p. 49.)

[104] *Ibid.*, pp. 49–50.

[105] *Ibid.*, pp. 56–58.

[106] *Ibid.*, p. 66.

[107] *Ibid.*, pp. 66–67.

[108] *Ibid.*, p. 52. See also p. 50.

[109] *Ibid.*, p. 73.

CHAPTER FIVE

The Child as Religious Ideal

". . . I am a child of this age," wrote Dostoevsky in a letter to Mme. N. D. Fonvisin in 1854, "a child of disbelief and doubt . . ." A few lines later, however, he avowed:

> If anyone were to prove to me that Christ is outside of Truth, and if Truth *really did* exclude Christ, I should prefer to remain with Christ rather than with Truth.[1]

Joseph Frank notes that Mme. Fonvisin had given Dostoevsky a copy of the *New Testament* when he was exiled to Siberia.[2] Professor Frank asserts that what the above passage "meant for Dostoevsky cannot be truly understood unless we glimpse through its lines both the horror and glory that he had found in the house of the dead."[3]

"Both the horror and glory" is the key phrase here. Paradoxically, the horror and glory appear to be consubstantial, but perhaps this should not overly surprise us. As V. V. Zenkovsky has explained,

> . . . Dostoevsky's antinomism was rooted in his religious consciousness, and apart from this consciousness it cannot be properly evaluated.[4]

119

Bearing this in mind, one can infer that despite the strength Dostoevsky derived from religion in the house of the dead, the glory of his faith, even at its zenith, admitted of a nadir of doubt. Resolution, it appears, must rest in regeneration. Gide deems "renunciation of self" essential, in Dostoevsky, for "entering into the Kingdom of God."

The first consequence of such regeneration is that man becomes as a little child. *"Except ye be converted, and become as little children, ye shall not enter into the Kingdom of Heaven."* [5]

In Dostoevsky's world, Christ is essential, not only for eternal salvation, but for a harmonious existence on earth as well. Berdyaev writes that "outside of the Christian conception love is," for Dostoevsky, "an illusion and a lie." [6] God's parenthood, then, is essential for meaningful relationships between men. ". . . it is possible for two creatures to love one another only because God exists and is their common Father . . ." [7] But the denizens of Dostoevsky's world generally fail to recognize this parenthood. And when they do not, in the words of Vyacheslav Ivanov, "men, those children of God" embrace a "solipsistic nihilism" and "must inevitably destroy themselves and one another." [8] Indeed, man's hope for salvation in Dostoevsky manifests itself rather as a dream of the future than as the reality of the present. Instruction to this effect occurs in Dostoevsky's works either as actual dreams (Zenkovsky writes that *The Dream of a Ridiculous Man* marvellously conveys a sense of the sanctity in man) or as metaphorical ones:

". . . all will be as the children of God, and the true Kingdom of Christ will come." This was the dream of Alyosha's heart. [9]

It is of paramount importance that in both instances, hope for man predicates his becoming as a child.

Perhaps the greatest single accumulation of evidence that Dostoevsky placed such faith in man's salvation through becoming as a child is the theme in his works of connecting the living and the dead. Zenkovsky defines Dostoevsky's "mystical ethics" as follows:

> . . . our vital and genuine relationship to life is measured only by a love which exceeds the boundaries of both rationality and reason. Love becomes super-reasonable, rising to a sense of inner connection with the whole world, even with the dead . . .[10]

This is somehow suggestive of the emotional mode of reasoning posited early in the present study as characteristic of Dostoevskian thinking children. At least it implies that reason and even freedom can be a deadly trap for man; the child, as yet unspoiled by reason, is closer to the Kingdom of Heaven. If, then, Dostoevsky's "mystical ethics" predicates a love which rises even to a sense of inner connection with the dead, it follows that children should dominate the appearance of this theme in his works. Without question, this is so.

Children, especially wronged ones, seem quite inexorably destined for Dostoevsky's heaven.[11] The belief that they live on there, perceiving the living and perhaps even communicating with them, occurs in Dostoevsky with nearly tendentious regularity. It is especially prevalent in *The Brothers Karamazov;* one may therefore suppose the question to be one of his most mature, or at least terminal, concerns.

As mentioned in Chapter Two of the present study, Ilyusha says that after his death, he will await visitors at his grave. Later in the novel, we learn that Ilyusha had "ordered" the following:

> When they fill in my grave, dear papa, crumble up a crust of bread on it, so that the sparrows will come: I'll hear them flying, and I'll be happy that I'm not lying there alone.[12]

After the funeral, Snegiryov brings his wife flowers, saying that little Ilyusha sent them to her.[13]

The final scene of *The Brothers Karamazov* is most significant here. Alyosha is surrounded by the boys who attended Ilyusha's funeral and:

"Karamazov!" cried Kolya, "is it really true what religion says, that we will all rise up from the dead and live on
to see each other again, and everyone, and little Ilyusha?"
"Certainly we shall rise up, certainly we shall see each
other, and joyfully tell each other everything that was,"
answered Alyosha, half laughing, half ecstatic.[14]

Thus, the function of Ilyusha's death is to end the novel on a note of
hope. Indeed, Vyacheslav Ivanov goes so far as to say that

> . . . the final section of *The Brothers Karamazov* contains
> such a sublime glorification of the heroic child-martyr that
> we are entirely consoled, and bless his obscure sacrifice as a
> source of immeasurable comfort.[15]

Rimvydas Silbajoris, who likens the children at Ilyusha's funeral to
the Apostles, seems justified in his assertion that their pledge to preserve Ilyusha's memory is Dostoevsky's final answer to Ivan.[16] In
this respect, Kolya Krasotkin's pledge seems especially significant,
for his intellectual pretentions may be seen clearly to echo Ivan's
resounding doubt.

> Kolya's cocky exhibition of his "knowledge" turns imper-
> ceptibly into a declaration of love for Alyosha, and at the
> conclusion Kolya stands firmly with the other children at
> Ilyusha's grave, to seal the bond of friendship and love.[17]

Early in *The Brothers Karamazov*, a woman comes to see Father
Zosima, who is blessing the people. Her first three little children are
dead, and she has just buried her fourth and last, a boy of three. She
cannot forget him. Zosima tells her of another mother, centuries before, who had also wept for her dead child, her only one. She was told
by a saint that such children are so bold before God's throne that he
immediately makes them angels.[18]

The woman answers that her husband had tried to comfort her
with similar words: ". . . our little son is surely now singing with
the angels in heaven."[19] The following words of Zosima are thus
intensified by a dual prelude:

. . . each time you weep, remember fervently that your little son is one of God's angels and that he looks down and sees you, rejoicing at your tears and pointing at them to God . . .[20]

But that is not all; Zosima continues, establishing the child's presence in heaven, as it were, for a fourth time. Referring to the fact that this woman has left her sick husband in order to come to the monastery, the elder concludes:

Your boy will see from heaven that you have forsaken his father, and will weep for you. Why, therefore, do you destroy his bliss? For *he is alive and living*, since his soul shall live forever . . . And to whom shall he go, finding his father and mother asunder? Now you dream of him and grieve, but then *he will send you gentle dreams*.[21]

Dostoevskian dreams (as in Makar's story, *A Raw Youth*) are not infrequently the special medium whereby a dead child can communicate with the living.

Another such instance is brought on by the birth of Smerdyakov. Marfa, Grigori's wife, takes the crying of Lizaveta Smerdyashchaya's baby in the garden for that of her own dead little boy: "Surely, it was her boy calling her."[22] (Marfa's boy, her only child, had been born with six fingers, condescendingly baptized, and soon buried. Since then, Grigori had never spoken of the child; Marfa, only in reverent whispers.[23])

It seems logical enough to expect the discovery of a screaming Smerdyakov to dispel all notions that the dead child had been involved. But no, this time it is Grigori who theorizes; bringing the baby to Marfa, he tells her:

An orphan-child of God is akin to everyone, to us especially. *Our lost baby has sent us this one*, born of the devil's son and a holy woman. Nurse him and weep no more.[24]

These two incidents — the former stressed four times and the latter twice — serve as a background that richly reflects Ilyusha's

everlasting life, which is itself stressed three times, the third one
comprising the novel's optimistic culmination.

It is worthwhile to compare these passages with the description of
Velchaninov's feelings (*The Eternal Husband*) at sunset soon after
Liza's death:

> A tide of some kind of pure, peaceful faith in something
> filled his soul. "Liza was sending that to me, that was she
> speaking to me," he thought.[25]

Although Dostoevsky excluded Mitya from his two brothers'
conversation concerning the suffering of innocent children, he carefully developed Mitya's dream of the "poor babe." Enervated and
depressed, Mitya dreams in the courtroom of a tiny baby who is, it
seems, simultaneously starving and freezing to death. Mitya is pleased
when a peasant calls the child not "baby" but "babe": he finds more
pity in the word. But "why, why?" Mitya is compelled to ask,
whereupon he feels a flood of nearly medicinal commiseration — "a
holy pity he had never known before."[26]

As Mitya awakens, Dostoevsky skillfully blends the dream back
into reality: Grushenka's voice rings out as if in both; even the sense
of her words ("I'll go with you") applies both to the dream (wherein Mitya has just resolved to help the people there) and to the immi-
nent reality of his impending penal servitude.

Having awakened, Mitya tells everyone "somehow strangely"
that he has had a good dream. He does so ". . . with a face that
seemed illuminated by some sort of new and joyous radiance."[27]
Just as memories of childhood bring renewed strength to the ex-
hausted, ill, or depressed, this dream of a suffering child now brings
meaning and faith to Mitya. Grushenka later quotes him to Alyosha
thus: "I shall go to Siberia now *for the babe;* I did not kill, but I
must go to Siberia!"[28] And it is exceedingly significant that she
proceeds to describe the resuscitated Mitya *as a child.*

> And you know, Alyosha, I kept staring at him: such terror
> lies ahead, yet he sometimes laughs about such trifles, just as
> if he is himself a child.[29]

Still later in the novel, Mitya reveals to Alyosha the full meaning of his dream and stresses the courage and inspiration it has given him. "Why did I dream of the 'babe' at such a moment?" he begins, and one is reminded of Dostoevsky himself, who remembered the episode from his childhood in *Peasant Marey* "when it was needed."

> Why "poor babe?" At that moment, it was a prophecy! It is for the "babe" that I shall go. Because each is guilty for all — for all "babes." There are only little children and big children. All are "babes." [30]

The "babe's" symbolic effect is indeed nearly hypnotic. A. A. Belkin, in discussing "the suffering of innocent and helpless children, which attains in Dostoevsky an artistic force unprecedented in world literature," speaks of "this wild world, wherein 'the universal babe weeps.' " [31]

The theory of universally reciprocal guilt and responsibility is widespread in Dostoevsky; [32] if, in Berdyaev's phrase, he is "drunk with ideas," [33] this one proved especially heady stuff. Of special interest here is that the "babe" saves Mitya and that "all are 'babes.' "

As discussed above, Liza (*The Eternal Husband*) seems to communicate after her death with Velchaninov, her real father. Nellie's stubborn belief that her grandfather had not died has also been discussed.

> She was firmly convinced to her very death that her grandfather was calling for her, angry when she did not come . . . [34]

The reader is referred to Chapter Four above for further such examples, not primarily religious in nature.

One of Dostoevsky's most childlike adults is undoubtedly the Christ-like Prince Myshkin in *The Idiot*. The story he tells the Epanchins of his past is filled with children and strikingly allies the Prince with Alyosha. Myshkin is repeatedly surrounded by school children, as is Alyosha, and he seems to possess the latter's instinctual understanding of, and rather miraculous rapport with, little children.

Moreover, his many statements about children evince a Dostoevskian faith in their incredible potential which Alyosha also shares.

> One can tell a rebyonok everything — everything; I have always been astonished that grown-ups know children so little, even their own children. One should conceal nothing from children under the pretext that they are little and it is early for them to know. What a sad and hapless thought! Children notice only too well that their fathers consider them too little to understand anything, when actually, they understand everything. Grown-ups do not know that a rebyonok can give exceedingly deep council even in the most abstruse matters.[35]

When the Swiss schoolmaster envies Myshkin's success with the children and begins to deride him, Myshkin tells the man

> that we both shall teach them nothing; it is they who will teach us. And how could he envy and slander me, when he himself lived with children?! *Children heal one's soul* . . .[36]

The plot of the Prince's story — how he was hated for persuading the children to love Marie, a young girl abused by the towns-people, and how they brightened her last days — should be well known. The children's reaction to her death recalls that of the children at Ilyusha's funeral, which further allies Myshkin with Alyosha:

> . . . the children were not to be restrained: they decorated her entire coffin with flowers and placed a wreath upon her head. . . . when it was time to carry the coffin, the children rushed up all together to carry it themselves. Unable to carry it, they helped, all of them running after the coffin and weeping. Ever since then, the children make frequent visits to Marie's little grave: every year they decorate it with flowers. They planted roses around it.[37]

R. P. Blackmur, in an article entitled "A Rage of Goodness: *The Idiot* of Dostoevsky," argues at length that idiocy is "the very con-

dition of dramatic necessity for the novelist who would, like Dostoevsky, attempt to dramatize instinctive goodness and pity as the essence of Christianity."[38] He makes three rather complex points to
support his argument. Curiously, each of these three sub-arguments is
considerably more concerned with children, childhood, and childlikeness than with idiocy.

Blackmur's first point is the story we have just examined. He
emphasizes the fact that the doctor who was treating Myshkin for his
idiocy called him "a complete child . . . altogether a child." Blackmur also mentions that the Prince, by his own admission, "was always
attracted by children."

The second piece of evidence presented by Blackmur is the story
Myshkin tells Rogozhin about a tiny infant's first smile. Upon seeing
the smile, the baby's mother crosses herself; Myshkin asks why, and
she likens a mother's joyful glimpse of her baby's first smile to God's
gladness each time he observes a sinner praying to Him with all his
heart.[39] The Prince tells Rogozhin that this answer "embodies the
essence of Christianity, that is,"

> the entire conception of God as our own Father and of His
> joy for man — a father's for his own child — the funda-
> mental idea of Christ![40]

One is perhaps in the process of wondering how this can be construed
as a proof of "idiocy's dramatic necessity . . ." when Blackmur
abruptly proceeds to conclude:

> It is not for nothing that directly after this Rogozhin ex-
> changes his gold cross for Myshkin's tiny cross and takes
> him to his mother — herself an idiot, understanding nothing
> of what was said — to be blessed. Only an idiot can bless an
> idiot.[41]

It is not for nothing, one might observe, that this sequence of thought
appears somewhat uneven: Rogozhin's mother is described not as an
"idiot," but as a "little old lady . . . who had fallen into complete
and utter childhood."[42] Clearly, Myshkin and Rogozhin's mother

are allied, as she blesses the Prince, through their mutual childlikeness first, and second, through any common idiocy into the bargain.

Also clearly, Myshkin's statement — God as man's Father is the fundamental idea of Christ — strongly suggests Dostoevsky's religious beliefs as developed at the outset of this chapter.

Blackmur's third point "is Myshkin's outburst against Catholicism . . ."

> What his outburst amounts to is a plea for revolt against intellectual authority, against grown-up pride of all sorts, and an insistence on the meekness of the child, the submissiveness of the idiot.[43]

Again, the child to the idiot's rescue. Blackmur concludes:

> Christ ended in bloodshed, no less violent in that it was his own; and no Christ was more violent than the meek and childlike Christ Dostoevsky saw — in life visibly, in himself incipiently, and in the created figure of Myshkin the idiot potentially.[44]

It is difficult to understand how Blackmur, impressed with Dostoevsky's famous intention to create in Myshkin a "positively good man,"[45] fails to remark Myshkin's childlikeness. This is especially true in view of Blackmur's obviously fastidious acquaintance with *The Idiot's* eight initial plans:

> In the seventh plan he is made a Prince and associated with children: Myshkin is in sight.[46]

The almost choir-like congregations at Ilyusha's and Marie's graves seem to suggest the atmosphere of the Ridiculous Man's dream (of a paradise in which all are like children) and the hope that children, especially wronged ones, live on after death in the Kingdom of Heaven. These elements combine in the short story *A Heavenly Christmas Tree*. The technique employed by Dostoevsky to introduce this story is exceedingly complex. Its components, analyzed in detail at the outset of Chapter Six of the present study, afford considerable insight into his methods of introducing what are therein termed hypothetical children. The story itself is openly said to be "imagined" by its author, who has first enriched its reality through a typical Dostoevskian background of vividly particularized generalizations.

The tale proper develops through a series of irony-charged words that serve as emotional stepping stones leading conclusionwards. A little boy of "about six or even less" (typically, his age is purposely downgraded to intensify his ensuing victimization) wakes up shivering in a cold basement. "Very hungry," he approaches his sick mother several times; she lies on a mattress "as thin as a pancake." (The irony of such a description needs no mention, but it should be observed that the boy is apparently afraid to awaken his mother: Whether this is out of concern for her sick condition or from fear of possible consequences, the pathos of his hesitancy to ask even for food or warm clothing is thus intensified.) In one corner lies his father, "dead drunk," and in the other, an old woman, an "ex-nurse" who "growls" at the boy whenever he comes near.

Finally walking up to his mother and feeling her face in the dark, he notices she has grown "cold as the wall" and wonders at how cold the room has become, as he stands there awhile, "unconsciously forgetting his hand on the shoulder of the deceased."[47] Subtly, the room's coldness vaguely conveys to the boy the awful knowledge that his mother is dead.

Blowing on his little fingers to warm them, the child goes out onto the street. It is late evening, but a policeman — "a keeper of order" — turns away "so as not to notice the boy."[48] (The obvious irony that he *already* has noticed the boy is reinforced by the disturbing insinuation that to help the boy would be to destroy "the order.")

No sooner is the boy's intense hunger twice more mentioned, than he spies through a window a room-full of children playing beside a huge Christmas tree. They are eating vividly described delicacies, given to "anyone who comes near."

Feeling how painful his almost frozen fingers have become (also for the second and third times), the boy opens the door and slips in. Everyone shrieks, but a lady gives him a penny, which bounces and rings on the steps: the boy is "unable to bend his red little fingers to grasp it."

Fleeing, he "again wants to cry, but is too afraid, and runs, runs, blowing on his little hands.'' One should note three things: first, the Gogolian intensification device of transforming what is actually a first time, with the word ''again,'' into what is so easily accepted as repetition; second, the boy's being too afraid even to cry, which echoes his earlier reluctance even to wake his sick mother (both, even if he had done them, would have been ironically small compensation under the circumstances. The reader is reminded of the governess' son in *The Fir Tree and The Wedding*, who was afraid even to begin to cry when bullied. It is possible here to find that the boy's reluctance to wake his mother is rewarded in a ghastly manner: He is spared the glaring and final realization that she is dead). Finally, one should note the fourth blowing on his fingers, which presumably hurt so much that he tries to warm them even while fleeing in panic.

Next, the boy is momentarily comforted by the sight, in a bright store window, of some colorful puppets which he at first deems real. From this tiny pinnacle of delight, he is immediately hurled the more downwards: ''A big evil boy'' suddenly punches him, kicks him, and rips his clothes. Finally, the boy hides behind a pile of firewood.

Once there, ''he cannot even catch his breath from fear,'' and the reader feels that even Dostoevsky can expand pathos no further. For this reason, the reader's relief is welcome indeed: ''Suddenly,'' one reads,

> quite suddenly the boy began to feel good: his little hands and feet suddenly stopped hurting, and he started to feel warm, so warm . . .[49]

Somewhere in this ironic sentence, the reader realizes the full meaning of the word ''good'' — the boy is freezing to death.

In the short description that follows — a strange mixture of glorious delirium, dream, vision, and perhaps even heaven itself — the word ''good'' is employed four times more, with increasing cumulative ironic effect. Yet the story's lasting impression is one of fervent hope, hope that there is a place for all the boys and girls who die like this one. ''It is Christ's Christmas tree,'' the boy is told; and the mothers of all these child victims, watching them play ''like angels,'' recognize their own children and weep. The children kiss and comfort their mothers, ''imploring them not to cry because it is so *good* there . . .''

And below, the next morning, some policemen found the little body of the boy who had fled and frozen to death behind the firewood; they sought out his mother . . . She had died even before he did; *both had met before God in heaven.*[50]

Ernest Simmons finds that this story's "Dickensian atmosphere is relieved by a restraint and realism unusual even in Dostoevsky's sympathetic treatment of children."[51] Perhaps so. Nonetheless, the techniques effecting its pathos are employed with a relentlessness rare even in Dostoevsky. Moreover, it should be noted that the details of the final resplendent vision are taken from, or set up by, the boy's earlier brightly illuminated experiences on the street: The symbolism is sustained as in Dostoevskian dreams. Most important, however, Dostoevsky seems bent upon depicting a child's Kingdom of Heaven.

Children are occasionally related to the dark side of Dostoevsky's religious antinomy.[52] "God is merely an hypothesis," Kolya Krasotkin informs Alyosha (with a vengeance that slightly trembles), "but . . . he is necessary . . . if there were no God, man would have had to think him up . . ."[53] (By having Kolya spout Voltaire, Dostoevsky brings out the lad's proud presumptions to adult thinking as well as his presumably painful precocious doubt.) Nellie stresses the fact that she has read *The New Testament* and *still* "damns" her grandfather.[54] In *The Diary* of 1873, Dostoevsky digresses as follows:

. . . they say that a certain stupid and evil monk killed a ten-year-old boy in school with cruel beatings, before witnesses, besides.[55]

The Gentle Creature commits suicide by jumping out the window clutching an image of Mary and the Christchild to her breast.[56]

More significant than religion's occasional identification with child suffering in Dostoevsky, however, is the fact that statements combining children and religion in his works are made by both the most *and least* noble personages. This undoubtedly contributes to the latter's roundness.

Raskolnikov declares that "children are the image of Christ,"[57] and the Underground Man tells Liza that having children is "heavenly happiness."[58]

Furthermore, in the deranged letters sent to Aglaya by Nastasya Filippovna, there is a "picture" that at first appears quite uncharacteristic of the latter.

> Yesterday, having met you, I went home and thought up a picture. Painters always paint Christ in accord with the stories in *The Gospel;* I would paint Him differently: I would picture Him alone — sometimes His disciples did leave Him alone. I would leave only one little rebyonok beside Him. The child was playing near Him, perhaps told Him something in the language of children; Christ listened and has now grown pensive, His hand involuntarily forgotten on the child's radiant head. He is gazing into the distance, at the horizon; a thought, great as the entire universe, rests in His eyes; His face is sad. The child has grown silent . . . and, intently pensive, as children sometimes become, looks thoughtfully up at Him. The sun is setting . . . There is my picture! [59]

Unlike Nastasya Filippovna as this may seem, she immediately proceeds to effect a connection: "You are innocent; all your perfection is in your innocence. Oh, remember only that!" To feel the full power of this resolution, one has only to remember what had befallen the innocence of Nastasya. Her right to identify a child's innocence with Christ (and its abuse with Lucifer) is undeniable.

In what he himself terms a "tirade about laughter," Arkadi says that people "usually become repulsive to look upon when they laugh." [60] Only children does he exempt from this indictment, because "laughter is the truest test of one's soul," and the child's soul is innocent, pure, and holy:

> Behold a rebyonok: only children can laugh to a pleasing perfection — this is what makes them so irresistible. A crying child disgusts me, but one who laughs joyfully — is a ray from paradise, a revelation of the future, when man shall finally become pure in both heart and soul, like a child. [61]

As stated earlier in this study, Dostoevsky endowed the sun's brilliant rays, especially those of the setting sun, with a nearly mystical significance. It is significant that Trishatov should tell Arkadi, as if unwittingly continuing the latter's above developed thoughts, of an episode in Dickens' *Old Curiosity Shop,* wherein "a mad old man and his thirteen-year-old little granddaughter" observe the setting sun.

> And once the sun was setting, and this rebyonok was standing on a cathedral's courtyard, fully illuminated by the last rays and looking at the sunset with quiet, pensive contemplation in her child's soul, in her astonished soul, as if in awe at some sort of riddle, because both really are riddles — the sun, as God's thought, and the cathedral, as the thought of man . . . isn't that so? Oh, I am unable to express it, but God especially loves such first thoughts in a child . . .[62]

Significantly, Arkadi's two fathers also amplify and expand upon his finding a "ray from paradise" in the laughter of a child. Admonishing Arkadi to pray at night, Makar speaks of an inspiring July morning when he awoke near a monastery just before sunrise and sighed:

> ineffable beauty all around! All was quiet, the air light; little blades of grass were growing — grow, grass of God; a little bird was singing — sing, little bird of God; a tiny child whimpered in a woman's arms — the Lord be with you, little person, grow in happiness, little baby![63]

For Makar, even the infant's whimper seems endowed with religious significance. Versilov describes to Arkadi an earthly paradise strangely suggesting the Ridiculous Man's dream world and its child-like inhabitants. The description is part hope, part fantasy, and, significantly, Versilov both begins and ends it with a smile:

> "I picture to myself, my dear fellow," he began with a pensive smile, "that the battle has already ended and the struggle subsided. . . . Each rebyonok knows and feels that anyone on earth is — as his own father and mother. 'Let tomorrow be my last day,' each person thinks, watching the setting sun — 'it makes no difference: I shall die, but they

shall remain, and after them, their children' — and this
thought, that they shall remain thus, still loving and feeling
deeply for each other, replaces the idea of meeting beyond
the grave. . . . They grow tender towards each other, not
ashamed of tenderness as they are now, and caress each other
like children.'' [64]

There is an instance in Dostoevsky's works wherein Christ's special love of children saves a child's life.[65] In the Grand Inquisitor
episode of *The Brothers Karamazov*, Christ heals an old man ''blind
from childhood,'' whereupon ''children throw flowers before Him,
singing and shouting 'Hosannah!' '' At the Cathedral of Seville, He
sees a child's open white coffin'':

> In it there is a seven-year-old little girl, the only daughter of
> a famous citizen. The dead child lies shrouded in flowers.
> . . . He looks at her with compassion, and His lips once
> again softly pronounce ''Arise, maiden!'' The little girl sits
> up in her coffin and looks around, smiling, her little eyes
> wide open with astonishment.[66]

Under Rogozhin's murderous knife, Prince Myshkin is saved by
an epileptic fit immediately after pronouncing the words, ''Parfyon, I
do not believe it!'' [67] It is almost as though the Prince's faith that
Rogozhin could not kill him — that this could not be happening —
alters reality to the point where it *does* cease to happen. Lebedev, at
least, seems to have reached this conclusion; later in the novel, when
Nastasya Filippovna runs off with Rogozhin — thus saving Myshkin,
in a sense, from herself — Lebedev sighs and says:

> He has concealed the Truth from the clever and the wise,
> revealing it to babes — I said this once before about him, but
> now I'll add that this babe was guarded by God, saved from
> an abyss by Him and all His angels! [68]

Father Zosima's Life contains numerous references to children
and other aspects of childhood. Especially significant is the ''indelible
impression'' made by his brother's death upon his ''child's heart,''

an impression which stayed hidden there until its time came to arise and resound,'' [69] as well as the description of how, ''eight years from birth,'' he took into his soul the ''first seed of the meaning of God's word.'' [70] Also worthy of note is the fact that Zosima's ''mysterious visitor,'' who ''took a life and then gave life,'' was unable to caress his ''excellent children.''

> I cannot look upon their pure, innocent faces: I am unworthy to do so.[71]

Dostoevsky preferred Christ even to Truth and placed the child closest to Christ, and he has his Zosima testify to the child's holiness in an exhortation to ''love little children especially.'' They are ''innocent as angels,'' he says,

> and they live to show us tenderness, to purify our hearts, and, in their way, to teach us. Woe unto him who wrongs an infant! [72]

Notes

[1] F. M. Dostoevsky, *Letters*, ed. A. S. Dolinin (Moscow, 1928–1959), I, 142, As Nicholas Berdyaev and Ernest Simmons have pointed out, a striking parallel to this statement occurs in a conversation between Shatov and Stavrogin. (Nicholas Berdyaev, *Dostoevsky*, trans. Donald Attwater [New York, 1957], p. 209; Ernest J. Simmons, *Dostoevsky: The Making of a Novelist* [New York, 1962], p. 262.)

[2] Joseph Frank, "Dostoevsky: *The House of the Dead*," *The Sewanee Review*, LXXIV, No. 4 (Oct.–Dec., 1966), 802.

[3] *Ibid.*, p. 803.

[4] V. V. Zenkovsky, "Dostoevsky's Religious and Philosophical Views," *Dostoevsky: A Collection of Critical Essays*, ed. René Wellek (Englewood Cliffs, N.J., 1962), p. 131.

[5] André Gide, *Dostoevsky* (Norfolk, Conn., 1961), p. 150.

[6] Berdyaev, p. 131.

[7] *Ibid.*, p. 131.

[8] Vyacheslav Ivanov, *Dostoevsky*, trans. Norman Cameron (New York, 1960), p. 30.

[9] F. M. Dostoevsky, *Collected works* (Moscow, 1956–1958), IX, 42.

[10] Zenkovsky, p. 141.

[11] Only if there is immortality, writes Berdyaev, can the tears of children be justified. (Berdyaev, p. 157.)

[12] Dostoevsky, *C. W.*, X, 68.

[13] *Ibid.*, p. 331.

[14] *Ibid.*, p. 338. In a letter dated April 29, 1880, Dostoevsky wrote to N. A. Lyubimov that the sense of the entire novel is partially reflected in Ilyusha's funeral and Alyosha's speech to the boys. (*Letters*, IV, 139. See also p. 212.)

[15] Ivanov, p. 14.

[16] Rimvydas Silbajoris, "The Children in *The Brothers Karamazov*," *The Slavic and East European Journal*, VII, 1 (Spring, 1963), 37.

[17] *Ibid.*, p. 37.

[18] Dostoevsky, *C. W.*, IX, 63–64.

[19] *Ibid.*, p. 65.

[20] *Ibid.*, p. 65.

[21] *Ibid.*, p. 66. My italics.

[22] *Ibid.*, p. 124.

[23] *Ibid.*, pp. 122–23.

[24] *Ibid.*, p. 129. My italics.

[25] Dostoevsky, *C. W.*, IV, 513.

[26] Dostoevsky, *C. W.*, IX, 629.

[27] *Ibid.*, p. 630.

[28] Dostoevsky, *C. W.*, X, 77.

[29] *Ibid.*, p. 78.

[30] *Ibid.*, p. 105.

[31] A. A. Belkin, " 'Bratya Karamazovy' (sotsialno-filosofskaya problematika)," *Tvorchestvo F. M. Dostoevskogo*, ed. N. L. Stephnov (Moscow, 1959), p. 275.

[32] See, for example, Dostoevsky, *C. W.*, VII, 607.

[33] Berdyaev, p. 34.

[34] Dostoevsky, *C. W.*, III, 383.

[35] Dostoevsky, *C. W.*, VI, 78.

[36] *Ibid.*, p. 78. My italics.

[37] *Ibid.*, p. 85.

[38] R. P. Blackmur, "A Rage of Goodness: *The Idiot* of Dostoevsky," *The Critical Performance*, ed. S. E. Hyman (New York, 1956), pp. 239 ff.

[39] Dostoevsky, *C. W.*, VI, 250. The child's first smile has a similar religious significance for Dostoevsky in *The Diary* of 1876.

> . . . these little creatures shall only reach and live in our hearts when we, having given birth to them, shall watch over them from childhood, inseparably, from their first smile, continuing to grow deeply close to them every hour of our lives. That is a family, that is holiness! (F. M. Dostoevsky, *The Diary of a Writer*: 1873, 1876, 1877 [Paris: YMCA-Press, 1876], 96.)

[40] Dostoevsky, *C. W.*, VI, 250.

[41] Blackmur, p. 240.

[42] Dostoevsky, *C. W.*, VI, 252.

[43] Blackmur, p. 240.

[44] *Ibid.*, p. 241.

[45] *Ibid.*, pp. 248–49.

[46] *Ibid.*, p. 248.

[47] Dostoevsky, *C. W.*, X, 361.

[48] *Ibid.*, p. 362.

[49] *Ibid.*, p. 363.

[50] *Ibid.*, p. 364. My italics.

[51] Simmons, p. 318.

[52] Perhaps the most famous appearance of Doubt in his works is the foul stench emitted by Father Zosima's dead body. Little noted are the following words of Pyotr Verkhovensky to Stavrogin:

> . . . the teacher who laughs with his children at their God and at their cradle — is already ours (Dostoevsky, *C. W.*, VII, 439).

[53] Dostoevsky, *C. W.,* X, 57.

[54] Dostoevsky, *C. W.,* III, 384.

[55] Dostoevsky, *The Diary* of 1873, p. 290.

[56] Dostoevsky, *C. W.,* X, 416. See also p. 383.

[57] Dostoevsky, *C. W.,* V, 342.

[58] Dostoevsky, *C. W.,* IV, 215.

[59] Dostoevsky, *C. W.,* VI, 516–17.

[60] Dostoevsky, *C. W.,* VIII, 389.

[61] *Ibid.,* p. 391.

[62] *Ibid.,* p. 483.

[63] *Ibid.,* p. 396.

[64] *Ibid.,* pp. 518–19.

[65] Somewhat conversely, the deaths of two little girls are supposed to have killed a man in *A Raw Youth.* "That he died from this," says Arkadi,

> is a fact! How, then, could he have been resurrected? It would have been necessary to dig up those two little girls out of the grave and give them to him, that's all. At least, something like that. So he died (*ibid.,* p. 60).

[66] Dostoevsky, *C. W.,* IX, 312–13.

[67] Dostoevsky, *C. W.,* VI, 266.

[68] *Ibid.,* p. 675.

[69] Dostoevsky, *C. W.,* IX, 363.

[70] *Ibid.,* p. 364.

[71] *Ibid.,* p. 385.

[72] *Ibid.,* p. 399. Having discussed Mitya's dream of the "poor babe," Vyacheslav Ivanov concludes: "The world's unforgivable sin is the sin against children" (Ivanov, p. 95).

CHAPTER SIX

The Child in Hypothesis

Just as memories, dreams, hallucinations, illusions, and reality often fade subtly in and out of one another in Dostoevsky's works, so the Dostoevskian child frequently and bafflingly changes places with the typical child, the child in general, and the child who might well be or might well have been. This fact serves especially, together with occasional insistings to the same effect, to create the impression that the situation of a single given child is typical or virtually universal.

Moreover, children in Dostoevsky appear as if from nowhere. They pop up in unlikely places. They pop up in likely places. They see more than given credit for, and their large eyes hold deep pictures.

Sometimes, such a child seems almost artificially inserted into the text. Sometimes, one even feels that, perhaps, Dostoevsky's narrative eye is "seeing things," or rather — children. Indeed, almost any set of circumstances in Dostoevsky's works can, and does suggest, either to the author or to his characters, the existence, *behind the scenes,* of one or more children. In this sense, such children are an integral element of Dostoevsky's world, and, although they do not function as characters in their own right, they serve as an unseen dimension in his descriptive process. Both the author and his personages often obtain considerable emotional leverage by descrying such children. These children are examined in the current chapter.

Dostoevsky's introduction to the story *A Heavenly Christmas Tree* is a good working example of the effects enumerated above. Let us inquire into the nature of the techniques and devices behind such effects.

"Children are a strange lot," Dostoevsky begins,[1] "I dream of them and think I see them when I'm awake."[2] "Not long before Christmas," he continues, "I kept meeting" a ragged little boy "not possibly more than about seven" on the street. (For the reader who thinks to doubt the frequency of these meetings, let alone the boy's authenticity, Dostoevsky has readied a specious challenge to prove that the boy's age could have exceeded seven.)

The boy was "dressed for summer" despite the bitter cold, but some sort of old rags were wrapped around his neck — "this meant that still, someone had equipped him, while dispatching." Obviously ironic, the use of technical terminology is continued in the next sentence:

He was going out "to handsy;" this technical term means — to beg for alms. The term was invented by these boys themselves. There are a multitude like him . . .[3]

Even in descriptive narration, "these boys" appear as if from nowhere, quickly and typically melting into the background by means of the insistence that they are a legion. But their outlines remain visible: Dostoevsky continues to describe them until suddenly, they all flow together, as if by trick photography, *to become* the original boy:

. . . they weave in front of you, moaning something memorized; but this one did not moan, speaking somehow innocently and awkwardly, and he looked trustingly into my eyes — obviously, just beginning his profession.[4]

"Just beginning," one infers, for two reasons: The lad's lack of finesse and his abundance of trust. Such trust jars sharply with the word "profession," sustaining the theme of incongruous specialization.

Questioned, he replied that he had a sister, jobless and sick; perhaps it was true, but I discovered later that there are scads of these ragged little boys: They are sent out "to handsy" even in the bitter cold, and if they collect nothing, a sure beating awaits them.[5]

In this single, long sentence the camera works in reverse: the one boy's edges melt and dissolve, reshaping as a thousand facsimiles. At first, the original assertion that such boys are a "multitude" appears to render this one a contradiction in point of view or, at the least, a circumlocution. Actually, it is neither: Dostoevsky is now discussing those who are "new" at begging. Positing such numbers of both beginning *and* experienced children effects a subtle multiplication unusual even in Dostoevsky.

The next five sentences are eloquently ambiguous, referring equally well both to the real boy and to all others like him. Thus, the real boy seems to suffer repeatedly, even in the present, and the boy in the story that follows (discussed above) becomes at once typical of many, even without the author's saying so. (This boy's circumstances are markedly similar to those described here: filth, squalor, drunken parents, hungry children, and basement apartment; even the father's occupation, garment maker, is the same.)

Here, in the introduction, there is a lurid embellishment: Sent to a tavern with his "own" pennies to fetch more wine, the boy is forced to drink for everyone's amusement:

. . . with broken breath, he falls nearly senseless to the floor,

. . . and down my throat vile vodka
He mercilessly poured . . .

(Father Zosima deplores the effects of "vile language and wine, wine" upon ten-year-old children.[6])

Only then does Dostoevsky shift to the future in a fresh paragraph ("When he grows up . . .") to predict the rest of the boy's sorry life. He then generalizes:

But even before the factory these children become accomplished criminals. They roam the streets and know places in various basements into which they can crawl and pass the night unnoticed.

"One of them," he says, "spent the night near a policeman in some sort of basket, unnoticed." This, then, is a real boy in an introduction to the story of another real boy. But it is also more: In the story proper, the real boy there also spends the night "unnoticed" by a policeman but is found dead, bright and early, by observant policemen. And, as shown below, even the "real" boy in the story finally becomes a subtle generalization!

The introduction closes on a general note: a transition between real boys:

> By themselves, they become little thieves. Thievery becomes a passion even without any conscious awareness of crime. Before the end, they endure everything — cold, hunger, beatings — . . . one even hears things about them that seem entirely unlikely; nevertheless, they are all facts.[7]

So ends the story's preface, both blending the general case into the even more alarming exception (under the guise of the latter's surprising factualness) and helping to disguise the artificiality of the story's beginning:

> But I am a novelist, and, it seems, have composed a little "story" myself.

"It seems!" If the author is unsure, how then are *we* to know? The reader is compelled, at least subconsciously, to assume that *even if* Dostoevsky did "compose" the story, he based it on facts: The phrase "all facts" is still ringing in one's ears. But this author had yet another method for breaking down the barrier imposed by the notion of composing. "Why do I say 'it seems,'" he continues,

> I composed the story, of course, without a doubt, but I keep thinking that it did happen somewhere, once, and that it happened just before Christmas, in a certain big city when it was bitter cold.
> I keep seeing . . .[8]

So begins the story, which can hardly fail to develop in depth against such a polydimensional background. Nor is the reader surprised when the story's boy, frozen to death, is greeted by a great many such as he, children who had met nearly identical fates.

Even after the story has ended, Dostoevsky relentlessly applies his well-worn techniques:

> But why did I compose such a story . . . I promised stories primarily about real occurrences! But that is just the point: it keeps seeming to me, and I keep thinking, that all this could really have happened . . .[9]

The above epitomizes the style employed by Dostoevsky to display the hypothetical child as herein defined. Even in the present study, space permits exegesis of only a token number of examples.

Although all of Dostoevsky's works reveal a surprisingly constant application of the techniques discussed above, they are employed most frequently in *The Diary*. André Gide is impressed by Dostoevsky's power to reconstruct imaginatively a world of rich detail given only the barest facts. As evidence, he cites from *The Diary* Dostoevsky's astonishment at discovering, when he visited Madame Kornilova, how accurately he had hypothesized the details of her case.[10] It is perhaps this power which enabled Dostoevsky to present admitted hypothesis as convincing reality.

The case of the little girl who watched her mother hang herself, for example, is broached by Dostoevsky in *The Diary* of 1873 as follows. The case, he says, is well known,

> But I kept thinking I saw the entire episode for a long time afterwards — I even seem to see it now . . .[11]

The four-page description that follows is what Dostoevsky imagines, deftly developed from the undisputed facts. One should note Dostoevsky's conviction that the known facts presupposed many additional ones — also, his ability to blend them convincingly.

In a section of *The Diary* entitled "Little Pictures," Dostoevsky goes so far as to deduce the presence of little children from their absence! That is, he first "notices" that there are many more very little children in St. Petersburg than ones a bit older and then convincingly adduces this "fact" as evidence that the older ones existed but have "not survived and died." [12] After describing the warm friendship he once observed between a two-year-old boy and his father, Dostoevsky explains that he "loves" to observe strangers on the streets and to guess:

> Who they are, how they live, what they do in life, and what especially interests them at present. [13]

He then proceeds to fabricate an exceedingly credible episode in the lives of this father and son. ("Only a month before," the mother had died, "without question, from tuberculosis"; a guest talked roughly to the child; his father took him from the room; etc., etc.) All this leads, by way of a digression describing a child as "a flower, a little leaf," to two other "little pictures" of children he has observed. Dostoevsky then disparages these truly charming scenes as most empty and unserious trifles: He is "ashamed" to enter them in *The Diary*. [14] The reader is thus subtly invited to defend the significance of these pictures, which, to judge from the many previous *and subsequent* repetitions of such "empty trifles" in Dostoevsky, is precisely his desire.

One interesting example, contained in *The Diary* of 1877 and labeled "A Lone Incident," describes how an old man, a German Protestant, tore the shirt from his back in order to swaddle a newborn Jew. (The family was so indigent that not even old rags could be found for the purpose.) Leonid Grossman finds the incident "depicted by Dostoevsky with exceptional artistic attention to the tiny details of this picture of life." [15] As Grossman notes, Dostoevsky calls such squalor "the purest realism — realism, so to speak, that reaches the fantastical." [16] Also typical and effective, however, is the sarcastic treatment of this entire episode as an unusual occurrence. "A lone incident, they will say," [17] begins Dostoevsky, and he concludes, with a nearly audible snort of contempt: "A singular occurrence!" [18] He even imagines the German's thoughts that perhaps, some day, the Jew will grow up to rip off his shirt for a hypothetical Christian baby:

Will this come true? Most probably not, but, you see, it could come true . . .[19]

Dostoevsky constantly uses "the fantastical" to suggest the real, the typical, or even the universal.[20] This he does both in *The Diary* (for example, in his discussion of the "stupid and evil monk," alleged to have killed a ten-year-old boy "with cruel beatings"[21]) and in his purely creative works.

Versilov (*A Raw Youth*) seems to hope that somewhere, the inhabitants of his fantastical utopia in which all are as children really exist. He even implies that he cannot live without believing in their reality. In this sense, the so-called real world, with its unchildlike adults, presupposes the necessary existence of its ideal counterpart.

. . . it is all fantasy, even the most implausible fantasy; but I have far too often imagined it to myself, because all my life I could not live without it, without thinking about it.[22]

A much more obvious application of this attitude is contained in one of Makar's letters in *Poor People*. He tells how a little boy on the street gave him a note describing his family's destitution and imploring alms. (". . . three children are starving, so please help us . . ."[23]) For three pages, Makar intensifies the situation's reality through apt generalizations. Although he suspects, at one point, that the note is a deception (and therefore, that the starving children are unreal), he sustains the reader's pity by stressing that the bitter cold may seriously endanger the boy's health. His story culminates in convincing hypothesis:

Well, let's see — what is it like in such homes? . . . the children whine there and the wife is hungry . . .[24]

Set up by a real note, the hypothetical situation seen behind the boy is most convincing. Realistic detail further abets the effect, with the result that descriptive hypothesis is easily accepted by most readers as factual narration. Structurally, this long passage leads into and intensifies the reality of a three-page discussion of the Gorshkov situation (discussed above).

In *Winter Notes of Summer Impressions* there are three incidents in which Dostoevsky presumes the existence of children behind the scenes.

The narrator quotes, from a book of Catherine's time, an anecdote about bad breath that he had read in his childhood. This passage gives rise to a long series of vivid details beginning: "That is, just imagine for yourself . . ." His ensuing assumptions include the spectacles on the nose of the typical man who, "with the most childlike credulity," used to read similar anecdotes, the man's sumptuous steambaths on Sundays, and even his children: "horrid little Mitrofans."[25]

The narrator's two additional hypotheses carry us to London and to Paris. The first concerns a typical sick London worker, prostrate on the damp floor with his habitually intoxicated spouse and "surrounded by children who have grown savage from hunger and cold."[26]

The second description is of a typical commonplace Frenchman; in adjacent passages of somewhat scornful description, it is mentioned that he probably "begets children,"[27] whose lot seems by inference scarcely enviable. Clearly, these last two instances serve to intensify the reader's pity for the child personages in this work.

Two interesting and strangely symmetrical appearances of hypothetical children can be found to occur in *The Injured and The Insulted* and in *Notes from the Underground.* Ikhmenev can be considered to invent some children of his own in an imaginary plea to "his Excellency" for a bit of bread. ("I have a wife and little children, oh benefactor, oh father mine!"[28]) It should be noted, however, that the phrase *deti malenkie* ("little children") is customarily employed by Russian beggars who may well be quite childless.

The Underground Man invents a child in one of his several revenge rhapsodies. (If Zverkov refuses to duel, he will seek him out "after fifteen years"; Zverkov will be happily married "with a grown daughter," and he will again thrust the pistols in his face.[29]) In both these instances, the child is hypothesized for purposes of emotional leverage: first, a victim seeks alleviation of suffering; second, a would-be-victor seeks its intensification.

Katya hypothesizes a child in order to emphasize her affection for Netochka Nezvanova. Upon hearing that little boys used to beat

Netochka painfully on the street (established earlier in the novel [30]), Katya cries "Ach, those horrid things!" adding that she herself has seen one boy beat another on the street. "Tomorrow," she says,

> "I'll keep a whip hidden, and if I come upon any boy like that, I'll beat him, oh, how I'll beat him!" [31]

The Underground Man obtains what is perhaps the greatest emotional leverage to derive from the Dostoevskian hypothetical child; he confronts the prostitute Liza with seemingly endless hypothetical children. Demeaned by his comrades, he now degrades her, proclaiming the glories of a family life with children.

> "If I were a father and I had a daughter, I would probably love my daughter more than my sons," I began . . . [32]

(His sons are presumed by the hypothetical assumption.) After mentioning a father he knew who adored his daughter, he declares that fathers always love daughters more than mothers do and informs Liza that he would not permit his own daughter to marry. He admits he would be jealous . . .

> Well, what if she started kissing someone? Started to love someone else more than her father? It's painful even to imagine. [33]

Two subtle devices are employed here. First, the use of vivid detail renders the man's jealousy instantly convincing. Second, a false alternative is implied by the phrase "even to imagine." Admitting the daughter's fate to be hypothetical subtly presumes by implication the reality of her existence.

In his distorted glorification of connubial beatitude, the Underground Man asserts that "passion" will later be replaced by a "still better love."

> And children will come . . . Work will then become fun, and even though you deny yourself bread for the children's

sake, it will be fun. For they will love you for it later . . . The children grow up — you feel you must set an example for them; you are their ballast . . . is it a hardship to have children? Who says this? It is a heavenly happiness! Do you like little children, Liza? I love them horribly.[34]

Finally, his long speech comes to rest on the bliss of nursing a new-born baby, who sucks and plays with the breast. As the father draws near, the baby bends back to laugh ("as if God himself knows how funny it all is"), bites the breast, and squints as if to say: See, I bit you!

Is that not true happiness, when all three are together — husband, wife, and child? One can forgive much for such moments.[35]

Here, vivid detail both promotes realism and tempers mawkishness as the hypothetical baby makes his mark upon mother's breast and reader's mind.

In addition to the hypothetical children proposed for adoption by the Ikhmenevs and Snegiryovs,[36] there are in Dostoevsky a number of references to the children his personages may produce at some future date. (See, for example, the hypothetical children of Dunya in *Crime and Punishment*, Liza in *A Raw Youth*, and even of Makar Devushkin.[37]) Perhaps the most interesting of these are the children hypothesized by Stephen Verkhovensky in *The Possessed*. (He is considering marriage to Darya Pavlovna but is tormented by the thought of marrying "someone else's sins.")

Married life will corrupt me and take away my energy, manliness, and steadfastness of purpose; children will come, not mine, I suppose, that is, obviously not mine: a wise man can look into the eyes of Truth . . .[38]

Thus, Dostoevskian children can be found to lurk behind and to effect emotional leverage in diverse circumstances: an ancient anecdote, poverty in London and Paris, a plea for help, a dream of revenge, and even a deranged man's need to degrade a prostitute. Indeed, Dostoevsky's hypothetical children sometimes suggest the after-thoughts of a painter loath to leave his canvas. Consider the following episode in *A Raw Youth*.

Arkadi and a friend, as is their sordid habit, glue themselves to a young girl on the street; they converse across her in obscenities until she screams: "Oh, what vile beasts you are!"[39] Arkadi describes the victim as

> . . . a very youngish girl, perhaps only about sixteen or even less, very cleanly and modestly dressed; perhaps . . . returning to her mother, an old widow with children; but there is no need to be sentimental.[40]

Arakadi's typical distaste for his own emotional effusiveness serves as an Aesopian apology for Dostoevsky's invention of these children. But this does not entirely erase the reality of their existence; the children are now allied with their older sister, or vice versa, such that her age can be lowered still further. (She was described as "about sixteen or even less.") The next sentence opens: "The little girl listened for a while, walking faster and faster . . ." (Thus, by the time she screams in her tormentors' faces, she has been reduced from "about sixteen" to "a little girl.") Once again, Dostoevsky evinces skill at stretching tender age to dramatic advantage. Here, the girl is old enough to be vividly shocked by all the obscenities she hears, yet young enough to be a childlike, and hence, a more pathetic victim. The girl's mental age and physical appearance are thus compelled to engage in strange and subtle combat.

Tatyana Pavlovna invents hypothetical children as models of deportment for Arkadi in his childhood.

> . . . she used to compare me to some kind of fantastic little boys, her acquaintances and relatives, who always seemed to be much better than I . . .[41]

The pictures of Nellie that pursue Vanya have been discussed as near-hallucinations; late in the novel, when he has recovered from his illness, her childhood recollections evoke vivid images in Vanya's mind that seem to be part memory and part hypothesized embellishment.[42]

Possibly the most fascinating of all Dostoevsky's hypothesized children are those projected far into the future. Makar asks Arkadi if he knows how long the memory of a man can remain on this earth. The answer is a hundred years. "His children or even his grandchildren," it seems, can remember his face that long; then, memories of the man are passed along by those who have never seen him. "So be it!" he continues, focusing upon himself:

> Forget me, dear ones, but I shall still love you from the grave. I shall hear your happy voices, little children, hear your footsteps on your ancestors' graves on memorial days. Live then, in the sunshine, be joyous, and I shall pray to God for you, I shall visit you in dreams . . .[43]

In this remarkable passage, Makar apostrophizes the children of future generations. There are bold echoes here of two themes discussed above: man's life after death and his communication with the living, especially in dreams.

Vladimir Nabokov, in his study of Gogol, is impressed that the latter, in one of his inimitable disgressions, carries the reader as far as the second generation.[44] It is difficult to say how far Makar's proposal extends, but Dostoevsky explicitly overtakes, in two unusual digressions, the fifth and sixth generations.[45]

In A Vile Tale, the tipsy Ivan Ilich lapses into a lengthy aberration concerning a wedding party he is preparing to grace with his intrusion. This amazing passage rambles ahead nine months (when the bride will probably have given birth because "they are as fertile as rabbits"); lurches back to the present (his visit will honor them: He is "the father, they are his children"); and, finally, soars ahead five generations into the future:

> . . . Pseldonimov will tell his children how the General himself attended his wedding party and drank to his happiness! Yes, and these children will tell their children, and those their grandchildren, as a sacred family story, how a highest

official, a leader in the government (by that time I'll be both) favored them . . . etc., etc.[46]

Though less interestingly, The Gambler also strides hypothetically into the future for "five or six generations."[47]

There are two most unusual, even in Dostoevsky, instances of hypothetical children (for whose depiction the style employed is somewhat Gogolian) in *The Brothers Karamazov*. Both occur late in the novel.

The first concerns the man Ivan thinks he sees upon his sofa soon after being told by his doctor that hallucinations in his condition are "very possible." This amazing "visitor" passes through no less than eight stages of materialization (from "some kind of object" to "someone, who had entered, God knows how, because the room had been empty" to "some kind of gentleman" to "a well-known sort of Russian gentilhomme" etc., etc.). Finally, he crystallizes as some kind of landowner who had recently been transformed into a "high-society parasite." The passage here discussed concludes a description of "such parasites."

> . . . usually solitary men, either bachelors or widowers; perhaps they have children, but their children are being brought up — it always turns out — somewhere far away, at some aunt's, whom the gentilhomme, as if somewhat ashamed of the relationship, *almost* never mentions in good society. Little by little they become completely accustomed to the children's absence, occasionally receiving from them a Christmas card or birthday greeting which they sometimes *even* answer.[48]

This passage employs Gogolian methods to intensify the reality of hypothetical children. Generally, one should observe here the detailed elaboration of a somewhat remote possibility until it becomes the probable or even the actual. (By the time a hypothetical child's letters are occasionally answered, the child himself has subtly become more real.) Also Gogolian is the strangely spectral reality that redounds from a series of concrete details. (The children are somehow held vaguely behind the scenes even though, one feels, they are exceedingly eager to make an appearance.)

Gogolian also is the subtle interplay of apparently unrelated details and plot development. There is a synergistic intensification common to both these hypothetical children and the brothers Karamazov themselves. (The reader is referred to Fyodor Pavlovich's unconscionable neglect of his three children,[49] not to mention a probable fourth.)

Most Gogolian of all, however, is the fact that the exception returns to haunt the rule: *Even the attention* paid to the children renders them more distant — through its flagrant insufficiency alone — and the men become *more solitary than ever*. It is this descriptive ability *to draw closer while apparently moving away* (Gogol, of course, often employs the converse to advantage, but usually not without the same "haunting return") that especially marks this passage as Gogolesque. Let us examine its workings in detail.

To begin with, one should note the abrupt initial displacement of the hypothetical by the real, followed by the latter's immediate abdication: The "perhaps" children suddenly become a reality ("their children") only to be demoted, by means of qualification ("it always turns out"), back to the rank of "perhaps" once again, i.e., *if* they have any children, "it always turns out . . ." The protean role of "almost" seems obvious. This word hints furtively at a number of contemptible alternatives: either there are only a very few times when the man dares to mention the aunt, or he very occasionally slips and must cover up, or, perhaps, he manages to stop in mid-slip, but only after an incipient pronunciation of her name, which hapless syllable he is also compelled to disguise.

Far more subtle, suggestive, and complex is the Gogolian interplay of meaning within the last sentence. First, the slow, steady, even deliberate ("little by little") recognition of a lack of recognition ("accustomed to the children's absence") is rendered especially humorous by the seasoning of "completely." Second, the momentary implication that "as they receive reminders, they forget" is yet more pleasantly perplexing. Third, this implication, with all its pyrotechnical flashes of suggestion — ranging from "the cards put his conscience at ease that the children are still alive, etc., and thus actually are conducive to his forgetting" to "his diabolical lack of concern for the children is sufficiently brazen to pretend the cards do not exist" — this implication *is* momentary because the word "even" is knocking disturbingly at Meaning's back door. In the present context, this word effects a lurch in *both* directions, making it possible for the man's "answers" to be both more and less attentive to his children, depending upon whether the point of view is taken to be the narrator's or the parasite's, respectively.

Further hypothetical children dressed in Gogolian style appear at Mitya's trial. In and of itself, the description is less complex, but its preparatory introduction deserves some notice. In fact, several elements immediately preceding the passage are strikingly suggestive of Gogol's *The Overcoat*. One of the three judges, for example, has a *"hemmoroidal face"* [50] and wears a red ribbon — "of what Order I just *do not remember.*" The prosecutor *"seems somehow* awfully pale.*"* He has *"almost* a green face,*"* quite different from two days before, when he *"still had his own appearance.*"* The narrator informs us that he would give more details of what was said in the official proceedings but he cannot continue "just because, *even,* he failed to hear much of it, neglected to be attentive to some more of it, and *forgot to recall* still more, but *mainly because"* he has *"literally* neither the time nor the place.*"* [51] All this, it seems, is a most appropriate introduction to the jury's four officials, "petty people of low rank." It is during the rather Gogolian description of these petty officials that hypothetical children appear in good force:

. . . who had, surely, old wives, impossible to present anywhere, and heaps of children each, perhaps even barefooted . . . [52]

The passage is brief, but meaty. Consider, for example, the unpleasantly suggestive Gogol-like pun, "heaps," the more literal connotations of which, though somewhat rough, are at least softened by bare feet. As above, the word "even" mockingly hints at betterment and is humorously vindicated by the "bare feet" despite its almost disenchantingly pejorative function. Also as before, the real subtly usurps the hypothetical's domain: the "surely" existing wives exist even more surely as one tries, uneasily, to find *somewhere* to present them, much as one searched in "good society" for a place to allude bravely to that distant aunt.

The tiny tale *A Hundred-year-old Woman* displays several varieties of the Dostoevskian hypothetical child. Most of the story is a continuation, in the narrator's imagination, of an incident recounted to him by a female acquaintance. (This woman, while buying some shoes for her little girl, meets a tottering hundred-and-four-year-old woman, who mistakenly refers to the daughter as a granddaughter, "thinking, apparently, that everyone had granddaughters." [53]

Later, at home, the narrator suddenly recalls the old woman and hypothesizes as follows:

> Her granddaughters, and perhaps her greatgrand-daughters, though she calls them all "granddaughters" anyway, . . . live in a basement, or, perhaps . . .[54]

She visits them. Her great-grandchildren, a boy and two little girls, run up to greet her "instantly."

> Usually, it seems, such exceedingly old women are always very close to children: they themselves become very much like children in their hearts, sometimes even exactly like them.

She has brought some sweets for the children, and her rather incoherent speech suggests the little old man's in Leskov's *The Improvisers*. The old woman's smile augers of her demise, "growing cold upon her lips." (Nellie, just before dying, smiles a "dead smile." [55]) The old woman grows motionless, her left hand remaining on the shoulder of little "Misha, a boy of about six." (If one remembers Nastasya Filippovna's letter, this somehow allies the old woman with Christ.) Misha observes her "with large, astonished eyes." (The mention of a child's "large eyes" frequently introduces a genesis of feelings.)

As she grows forebodingly motionless, the children (typically) back into a corner, startled, and watch the dead woman "from afar." Dostoevsky's conviction that childhood memories alter entire lives now blends rather tendentiously with Makar's theory of how long man is remembered:

> Misha, as long as he lives, will remember the old woman and how she died, her hand forgotten on his shoulder, and

when he does die, no one on the entire earth will recall or discover that once upon a time there was an old woman who lived for a hundred and four years, why and how — no one knows.[56]

The narrator adds that there is "something somehow deeply peaceful and almost holy, something even portentious and peace-making" about hundred-year-old people as they die. (The reader is now even more strongly reminded of Nastasya Filippovna's Christ.) The narrator's conclusion [57] reminds one of Dostoevsky's claim that his "Little Pictures" are merely "empty trifles." But frequency of occurrence and mode of depiction belie both assertions.

Perhaps the most doctrinaire use of an hypothesized child in Dostoevsky's works is one alluded to by Father Zosima. The passage follows close upon his admonishment to "love children especially."

You pass by a little rebyonok — pass by spitefully, with wrathful soul, uttering obscenities; you may not have noticed this child, but he has seen you, and your unseemly, ignoble image may remain forever in his defenseless little heart. You may be unaware of it, but perhaps you have already sowed in him the seed of evil . . .[58]

Father Zosima thus employs a hypothetical child to point up several of Dostoevsky's deepest convictions: that childhood impressions, partially because of the child's unacknowledged potentials, are far stronger than we realize; that memories thereof are also the strongest, affecting attitudes and actions for the rest of our lives; and that life's most heinous horror is the suffering of innocent children.

Notes

[1] One may presume that the narrator *is* Dostoevsky: The story first appeared in *The Diary* of 1876.

[2] F. M. Dostoevsky, *Collected Works* (Moscow, 1956–1958), X, 359.

[3] *Ibid.,* p. 359.

[4] *Ibid.,* p. 359.

[5] *Ibid.,* p. 359.

[6] Dostoevsky, *C. W.,* IX, 394.

[7] Dostoevsky, *C. W.,* X, 360.

[8] *Ibid.,* pp. 360–61.

[9] *Ibid.,* p. 364.

[10] André Gide, *Dostoevsky* (Norfolk, Conn., 1961), p. 95.

[11] F. M. Dostoevsky, *The Diary of a Writer:* 1873, 1876, 1877 (Paris: YMCA-Press, 1873), 204.

[12] *Ibid.,* pp. 330–33.

[13] *Ibid.,* p. 331.

[14] *Ibid.,* p. 333.

[15] L. P. Grossman, "Problema realizma u Dostoevskogo," *Vestnik Evropy* (February, 1917), p. 80.

[16] Dostoevsky, *The Diary* of 1877, p. 122.

[17] *Ibid.,* p. 121.

[18] *Ibid.,* p. 123.

[19] *Ibid.,* p. 123.

[20] The attitude, of course, stems from his belief that "truth is far stranger than fiction." A well-known letter from Dostoevsky to N. N. Strakhov in 1879 contains the following:

> Facts from the newspapers are more fantastic than fantasy, but who will notice and use them? (F. M. Dostoevsky, *Letters,* ed. A. S. Dolinin, II [Moscow, 1928–1959], 169–70.

See also Dostoevsky, *The Diary* of 1876, pp. 127–28.

[21] Dostoevsky, *The Diary* of 1873, p. 290.

[22] Dostoevsky, *C. W.,* VIII, 519.

[23] Dostoevsky, *C. W.,* I, 179.

[24] *Ibid.,* p. 181.

[25] Dostoevsky, *C. W.,* IV, 75. The reference, of course, is to the bestial child hero of Fonvisin's play, *The Minor.* Inserting the word "horrid" here in the English perhaps overconveys the uncomplimentary ending *"-ushki"* (*Mitrofanushki*) plus the connotations evoked in those familiar with the name Mitrofan.

[26] *Ibid.,* p. 98.

[27] *Ibid.,* p. 130.

[28] Dostoevsky, *C. W.,* III, 78.

[29] Dostoevsky, *C. W.,* IV, 204.

[30] Dostoevsky, *C. W.,* II, 86.

[31] *Ibid.,* p. 169.

[32] Dostoevsky, *C. W.,* IV, 212.

[33] *Ibid.,* p. 213.

[34] *Ibid.,* pp. 214–15.

[35] *Ibid.,* p. 215.

[36] Dostoevsky, *C. W.,* III, 76 and X, 67, respectively.

[37] Dostoevsky, *C. W.,* V, 379; VIII, 336; and I, 187, in that order.

[38] Dostoevsky, *C. W.,* VII, 132.

[39] Dostoevsky, *C. W.,* VIII, 104.

[40] *Ibid.,* p. 104.

[41] *Ibid.,* p. 26.

[42] Dostoevsky, *C. W.,* III, 371.

[43] Dostoevsky, *C. W.,* VIII, 397.

[44] Vladimir Nabokov, *Nikolai Gogol* (New York, 1961), p. 79.

[45] Also the second. See Dostoevsky, *C. W.,* VIII, 519.

[46] Dostoevsky, *C. W.,* IV, 18.

[47] *Ibid.,* p. 308.

[48] Dostoevsky, *C. W.,* X, 161. My italics.

[49] Dostoevsky, *C. W.,* IX, 15, 20–21.

[50] In this connection, at least ten children (of little significance and questionable actual existence) are seen or mentioned in Mr. Prokharchin's strange mixture of fever, dream, and delirium; these children surround a "hemmoroidal face" that "flashes before" the moribund man (Dostoevsky, *C. W.,* I, 404–05).

[51] Dostoevsky, *C. W.,* X, 191–92. My italics.

[52] *Ibid.,* p. 192.

[53] *Ibid.,* p. 373.

[54] *Ibid.,* p. 373.

[55] Dostoevsky, *C. W.,* III, 385.

[56] Dostoevsky, *C. W.,* X, 376.

[57] *Ibid.,* p. 377.

[58] Dostoevsky, *C. W.,* IX, 400.

PART III
The Child As Modifier

CHAPTER SEVEN

The Adult as Child

Unquestionably, Dostoevsky had a flair for crowding people into cramped rooms and proceeding to bring out the worst in them. He was perhaps yet more accomplished, however, in the converse of this procedure: bringing out the goodness in villains, in which process he wielded childlikeness to great descriptive advantage.

In fact, the presentation of both positive and negative characters in Dostoevsky draws heavily upon the child. To bring out the child in a "positively good" personage is to enhance his goodness while doing his credentials little damage. Childlikeness seems ready-made to convey credible virtue. Even the most remote descendants of Rousseau seem imbued with the subconscious assurance that childlikeness is next to Godliness.

But why and how are Dostoevsky's negative personages believable and round? First, they are like children. Second, they like children, frequently with much more than the love, as Ivan puts it, that a sadist feels for his sacrificial victim. And human nature helps. For some reason, we are far more ready to believe a man bad than good, and the artist's only real challenge is to keep his villains human — to redeem, as it were, their evil. Dostoevsky does this largely via the child. In fact, Dostoevsky's most villainous characters are surpassed in childlikeness only by his "positively best" ones.

Let us put this premise to the strongest possible test by turning

161

first to Dostoevsky's most copious collection of "villains," *The House of the Dead.*

Besides the little ten-year-old girl, "a little angel" who gives the narrator a small coin, and the "tiny little girls" who sell bread to the prisoners,[1] there are virtually no children in *The House of The Dead.*[2] Yet the prisoners are astonishingly often described as childlike and allied with children or childhood.

The prisoners, writes Goryanchikov, would relate the most hideous, gruesome crimes "with the most irrepressible, the most childishly happy laughter."[3]

Sometimes they would tell stories and laugh like children.[4]

. . . in many ways, the prisoners were utter children.[5]

"A few kind words" from their keepers,

and the prisoners would nearly undergo a moral resurrection. They would become as joyful as children and, like children, would begin to love.[6]

(Here, one is nearly tempted to infer that *theirs* is the Kingdom of Heaven.) The prisoners put on a Christmas play:

Like children, the prisoners rejoiced at each little successful effect . . . In a word, they were children, fully children, despite the fact that some of these children were as old as forty.[7]

The curtain about to rise:

What a strange sheen of childlike joy, of pure sweet pleasure shone . . . in these eyes, which had sometimes flashed with terrifying fire![8]

They hear a rumor:

Prisoners are as gullible as children; they themselves know that the news is nonsense . . . yet they all seized upon the news, judging and loving it . . .[9]

The prisoners await the arrival of a new horse:

They were happy as children.[10]

They adopt a pet goat, Vaska:

Their adoration of the goat went so far that some of them, like children, got the idea: "Why not paint Vaska's horns gold!"[11]

We have barely scratched the surface, but it should be clear that the prisoners are constantly described as little children, and, for the most part, as happy, joyous ones. In context, these patches of radiant joy serve to relieve the more normal atmosphere of brutal gloom and to render the convicts more human and believable. Let us turn to specific instances.

The most childlike of all the prisoners is a Dagestan Tartar, Aley (the youngest of three brothers there), "no more than twenty-two and by his appearance, still younger." His smile is "so trustful, so childishly open-hearted." They seem to consider him "a boy" and to talk with him "about childish things." But these are only half of the references within a single paragraph! Goryanchikov constantly refers to Aley as "the boy" and deems him "innocent as the purest little girl."[12] Perhaps the most interesting aspect of Aley's childlikeness is the fact that Goryanchikov seems to adopt him, in prison, as his own son, even teaching "the boy" to read and write. At one point, Aley embraces and kisses him:

"You've done so much for me, so much," he said, "become my father — my mother wouldn't have done that much: you've made me into a person; God will repay you, and I'll never forget you . . ."[13]

One can infer that Dostoevsky considered memories of childlike adults similar in effect to those of children. At least such passages, however sentimental, lend dimensions of reality to the dark prison barracks.

As he watches the prisoners' theatrical production, Aley's child-like face seems to reflect the birth of what Alyosha has termed, above, a holy childhood memory:

> Aley's sweet face shone with such a childlike, excellent joy
> . . . When everyone burst out laughing, I would turn to-
> wards Aley and look into his face.[14]

This almost holy radiance lasts late into the night: falling asleep, Aley still laughs about the play with his brothers, and as he sleeps, Goryanchikov "involuntarily" looks long and deeply into his "peaceful, childlike face." [15]

The next most childlike convict is probably Sirotkin (whose very name, derived from the root of the Russian word for orphan, suggests an abandoned child) : "a young prisoner, an exceedingly good looking boy."[16] Dostoevsky typically works the man's age down: From "young" and "boy," Sirotkin goes to "not older than twenty-three" to "boy" again to age ten to age seven! (All in half a paragraph) : When spoken to, he "would look at you like a ten-year-old child," and when he had money, he would purchase some sweets — "as if he were only seven years old." All this age manipulation serves both to intensify the boy's previous genesis of feelings (when he could not endure the life of a recruit) and to engage the reader's interest in Sirotkin's story of how he had bayonetted to death his commanding officer.[17]

The prisoners in *The House of The Dead* often consider each other children, as if Dostoevsky's word, via Goryanchikov, is insufficient. Occasional juxtapositions make for somewhat unsettling ironies.

The brigand Orlov, for example, is described by Goryanchikov as "a unique villain, who had slaughtered both old men and children in cold blood . . ." [18] No sooner has the reader received this information than Orlov, questioned by Goryanchikov, appears to survey the latter in a rather disturbingly suggestive manner: "as if I had suddenly become in his eyes some sort of stupidish little boy . . ." [19]

Another convict, Petrov, repeatedly serves the purpose of promoting the prisoners' childlikeness.

> One could have compared him to a worker, a burly worker, a bear for work, who has as yet been given no work, and so he sits waiting and playing with little children.[20]

> I think he generally considered me some sort of child, almost an infant . . .[21]

> He treated me decidedly like a child . . .[22]

Yet another example is the haughty Almazov (his name, in Russian, means "of the diamonds"), who, when helped in his work by some fellow prisoners,

> started to look upon us condescendingly, as one regards very young children . . .[23]

As one could well expect from the story *Peasant Marey,* memories of childhood play an important, often panacean role in the prisoners' present lives. At Christmas, Goryanchikov Dostoevskianly declares:

> . . . who knows how many memories were destined to rise up in the hearts of these outcasts at the coming of such a day! The Christmas holidays make deep impressions upon the memories of the common people, beginning in early childhood.[24]

This apparently causes one convict, Akim Akimych, to view "with some kind of anticipatory esteem" an ordinary suckling pig:

> Perhaps he was accustomed from early childhood to seeing a suckling pig on the table on that day and had concluded that a suckling pig was essential for that day, and I am convinced that if he had not at least once tasted of suckling pig on that day, he would have experienced certain pangs of conscience from unfulfilled duty for the rest of his life.[25]

One should note that this simple man's attitude (part conditioned reaction, part deep belief) is subtly reflected by the very wording — by its nearly hypnotic repetition: "suckling pig . . . that day . . . suckling pig . . . that day . . . suckling pig . . . that day."

On Christmas Eve, Akim Akimych performs a lengthy series of rituals, the indisputable necessity of which has been his firm conviction ever since childhood. Then, having prayed to God, he falls into "the halcyon sleep of an infant." [26]

All such holidays seem to bring out the childlike best in all the convicts.[27] The Easter Service, for example, evokes a long series of pleasant, stabilizing memories in the protagonist.[28] We have observed the transfigurement of Aley's face at the prisoners' theatrical production. Two other convicts, arguing over who should play the part of a nobleman, dispute "like little children," and when a third prisoner gets the part and plays it successfully, Goryanchikov hypothesizes that "still in his childhood" and "as a bare-footed little urchin" he had chanced to see the real thing.[29] The prisoner Baklushin "suffers like a child" when considered a less talented actor than someone else.[30]

Perhaps the most unusual Dostoevskian illustration of how childhood experiences and memories are beneficial later in life is a strangely negative one. For three pages, the prisoner Aleksandr harps on his theory that had he not "grown up under the whip" from earliest childhood, he could never have "survived" a punishment of four thousand lashes inflicted upon him in *The House of the Dead*.[31] "Beaten for fifteen straight years, beginning as far back as he could remember," he "got used to it." One can easily argue that with a more placid past the man might well have avoided prison in the first place, but, given the facts, his contention is most convincing.

These adult "villains" are thus painted as part children and pictured against a background of childhood memories that further highlights their childlikeness. This surely renders them rounder and more credible, yet not un-ironically so, for many of these men are former specialists at child victimization. One brigand, for instance, tells

how he had slaughtered a five-year-old boy, how he first lured him with a toy, led him off somewhere into an empty barn, and then butchered him there.[32]

Especially lurid and typical of Dostoevsky is the following description, contained in a digression with the alleged intention of illustrating that highly diverse crimes lead to the same punishment. "One killed . . . defending his freedom, his life, often dying of hunger," while

> another slices up little children for the pleasure of slicing, to feel their warm blood on his hands, to savor their suffering and their last swan-like flutter beneath the blade.[33]

One should remark the casual atmosphere conveyed by the word "another." The narrator, it seems, could have indicated, with equal ease, any one of several who surround him. This effect is abetted both by one man's being described as a type and by the introductory word "often," which subtly promotes symmetry even as it insists upon repetition. Moreover, the more of the latter criminal type, the more (then compoundedly plural) child victims.

Most haunting, however, are the *implied* exploits of another prisoner, the Tartar Gazin: no facts are given, but the descriptive technique employed is perhaps all the more convincing. There were, we are told, "strange rumors" about this man.

> . . . that he had loved formerly to slaughter little children, purely for his own pleasure: he would lead a child off to a convenient place; at first he would frighten the child, torture it, and then, having fully enjoyed the terror and trembling of his little victim, he would slaughter the child slowly, quietly, and with delight.[34]

This lurid account tends to take the reader by surprise: such details are indeed "strange rumors." Even greater effect is obtained by a sudden shift, after the colon, from the possible to *the habitual*. The word "convenient" disturbingly hints at Gazin's diabolical detachment from his own insane pleasures.

Gazin's characterization seems to gain in persuasiveness by dint of imputation: rumors woo, perhaps, where facts offend. The next sentence boldly develops this Dostoevskian descriptive reverse psychology:

Perhaps all this had been thought up, due to the depressing effect Gazin had upon everyone, but all these inventions somehow suited him, somehow fitted his face.

So confident, now, is the protagonist of his strange rumors' convincingness, that he dares to assume them false! But only for an instant. One still feels Gazin easily could have committed such crimes and — partially because of the vivid emotions described above, partially because of the reverse psychology carried by "inventions" — even that he probably did. To sum up: the rumors become so vivid that the reader instinctively challenges the obviously false assumption (no one knew for sure) that they were in fact mere fabrications. At this point, Dostoevsky has Goryanchikov rush to the reader's aid: the rumors did *seem* very true. Typically, the description comes to rest on Gazin's smile:

. . . but there was always something proud, mocking and cruel on his face and in his smile.[35]

If the child in criminals adds depth and credibility to their depiction by pointing to their goodness, what of those who live within the law? What of those who enforce its consequences? Does the child figure negatively in the description of such persons?

In a rather lengthy digression about executioners, Goryanchikov remarks that "the characteristics of a butcher can be found, in embryonic form, in every contemporary person."[36] And about the executioner himself, he says: "Even children know that he "renounces his own father and mother."[37] This complex, nearly metaphorical relationship emphasizes that children instinctively recognize the executioner as denying the child in himself. And thus, childlike convicts are the more convincingly sympathetic when punished by unchildlike executioners.

Dostoevsky's range of metaphorical, or nearly metaphorical, child criminals is quite impressive. Of one convict, Osip, Groyanchikov makes the following statement:

It was strange even to look at this seven-year-old Hercules.[38]

Another instance seems balanced on the brink of metaphor:

> One man especially stands out in my memory — one who killed his father. He was a nobleman, had held a post, and had been, for his sixty-year-old father, something of a prodigal son.[39]

Yet another description blends hypothetical children with analogous metaphorical ones.

> "A settler's but an infant child, by all he looks upon beguiled," they say in Siberia about settlers. This adage can be enlarged upon and fully applied to vagrants.[40]

A description of vagabonds, always lured on by something new, then comes to rest on some who "even marry, beget children, live about five years in one place, and then suddenly, one fine morning, vanish somewhere, leaving behind a bewildered wife, children, and the entire county in which they are registered." Besides introducing a "little old" convict of about fifty "who, they say, has children somewhere,"[41] this strange bit of narration paints the odd picture of a childlike father who leaves his children when he is enticed away like a child.

Another case of strange child juxtaposition is one of Goryanchikov's first impressions in prison: a little old man of about sixty who had burned a church. This man, twice described as childlike ("peaceful and timid as a child" and in his laughter there was much "childish open-heartedness"[42]), often cries and wails: "Oh my dear little children, my dear little children, we shall never see each other again!"[43] The separation of a childlike adult from his children is perhaps doubly pathetic.

On a per page basis, there are more references to adults as children or childlike in *The Injured and The Insulted* than in any other of Dostoevsky's works. No little irony ensues from the fact that two exceedingly childlike adults live in sin, while another childlike young woman appears to threaten their relationship and a childlike father deplores it. (And only the insights of an adult-like child resolve the situation.)

The seventy-nine adult-as-child descriptions in this novel apply principally as follows: Alyosha — 28, Natasha — 18, Katya — 16, and Ikhmenev — 7.

Vanya, the protagonist, is quick to say of Alyosha that "despite his nineteen years, he was still a perfect child." [44] As if in echo, Natasha soon tells Vanya that Alyosha is a child, whereupon Vanya asks her somewhat rhetorically how such a person ("still a boy") can marry. [45]

Vanya's first impression of Alyosha, as the latter arrives to abscond with Natasha, is most revealing. It contains several deeply Dostoevskian ideas, though its words can be found to gird omniscience with the fabric of opinion.

> It seems to me that this child could never lie, even in jest, and that even if he were to lie, he would surely suspect nothing bad in it. . . . To offend or deceive him would be as sinful and pathetic as it is sinful to deceive and offend a child. He was very naïve for his age and understood almost nothing of real life; however, he would have known nothing of life, one felt, even at the age of forty. Such people seem destined to eternal non-adultness. It seems to me that no one could have failed to like him; he would win you over like a child. [46]

First, one should observe several Dostoevskian descriptive techniques at work: the convincing initial contradiction (that somehow seeks to undermine certain connotations of the word "lie"); the initial overstatement ("this child") subsequently modified to suit the real purpose (childlikeness) and thereby strangely corroborated; and the effective descriptive use of appealing childlike helplessness.

The moral implications of this passage, however, are yet more engaging. If the child in Alyosha is innocent and enticing, it nevertheless tends to shield him from responsibility for the chaos he causes. "He is a child," says Natasha. "He was brought up wrong. How can he understand what he is doing?" [47] And just as it tends to render his innocence invincible, the child in Alyosha casts an aura of ironic pathos about the suffering he experiences and inflicts upon others. In Natasha's words: "Oh, we are cruel children, Alyosha!" [48] But if Alyosha is playfully numb, others are not. For one thing, anguish too frequently reigns in the Ikhmenev family; for another, there is always the burning question: What sort of father might this child become? Even when Alyosha crawls to Vanya "sad and distraught," saying that he is unworthy of Natasha's love and that he is "crude and evil," his remorse is rendered both unconvincing and irrelevant.

> . . . he felt himself a child before her, and she always considered him a child, too.[49]

Natasha is only seventeen, yet she is aged down almost immediately. When Natasha is unjustly accused of seducing Alyosha, Vanya declares:

> . . . she was as happy and innocent as a twelve-year-old child.[50]

As the novel proper begins, Vanya meets Natasha once more, and he finds her "somehow little developed" during the years of their "long separation,"

> just as if she had not changed and had remained the very same little girl . . .[51]

We have seen the importance and frequency of Ikhmenev's still considering Natasha a child. Natasha has been telling Vanya "how much pain there is in life" when she slips (calling him Alyosha) and "smiles at her mistake."

> "I'm looking at your smile now, Natasha. Where did you get it? You never had one like that before."
> "And what about my smile?"
> "Still the same childish open-heartedness, true, but it also has—but when you smile—it also seems that something terribly pains your heart." [52]

The technique should be most familiar: clinging firmly to child-likeness with one narrative hand while reaching for deep adult feelings with the other. Here, Dostoevsky employs one of his favorite descriptive devices: the strange smile.[53]

This childlike affair is endangered by two other, strangely symmetrical children: the too unsympathetic Ikhmenev and the too sympathetic Katya. Alyosha, it seems, is forever on the verge of reevaluating the understanding he finds in the latter's arms.

> She was a perfect child, but some kind of strangely *convinced* child with strict rules and a passionate, innate love for goodness and fairness. If one indeed could still call her a child, she belonged to the group of *pensive* children . . . It was interesting to peer into this reasoning little head and observe how perfectly childlike feelings and ideas mixed there with deep experiences and thoughts about life . . . She loved to think her way to the truth, but was so unpedantic, so full of infantile, childish escapades . . .[54]

Typically, an initial overstatement is convincingly qualified. Also typically, a stubborn insistence upon childlikeness is then persuasively projected deep into adulthood. Vanya continues:

> This naïve duality of child and pensive woman, this childlike and exceedingly righteous thirst for truth and fairness, and an unwavering faith in what she desired — all this illuminated her face with some kind of pure, sincere brightness and endowed it with some kind of lofty, spiritual beauty . . . Katya had already told Alyosha much, with all the sincerity of childhood . . . Katya had a great advantage over Natasha: the fact that she herself was still a child and, it seems, was destined to remain a child for a long time to come. This childlikeness of hers and her bright mind, combined with a certain insufficiency of reason — all this somehow made her closer to Alyosha. He felt it, and for that reason, Katya attracted him more and more strongly all the time.[55]

One should note the use here of some convincing lexical hocus-pocus. Immediately prior to stating how closely Katya's childlikeness and partial adult-likeness ally her with Alyosha, Vanya described her by a phrase ("destined to remain a child for a long time to come") that strongly evokes an earlier description of Alyosha ("destined to eternal non-adultness"). As remarked above, Natasha's quantitative childlikeness exceeds Katya's by two references, although the latter's is perhaps qualitatively the more convincing and emphatic. The technique here may well seem somewhat contradictory. Nevertheless, to be childlike *compared with a person well established as exceedingly childlike* is surely, however unfairly, to be doubly so.

But perhaps Katya never really threatens Natasha: Vanya finally confesses to a "strange but deep conviction" concerning Katya:

> . . . she was still so completely a child that she was fully ignorant of the mystery of relations between man and woman.[56]

But then this amazing person claims that those who call her a perfect child are themselves like children! [57]

At times, this "love triangle" becomes absurdly juvenile: The three participants appear to be playing house in some sort of enormous nursery. (One by one, each of the three is called a child on a single page.[58]) But the game's moral implications are not so easily dismissed: someone, it seems, has left matches on the playroom floor.

A ready suspect is Ikhmenev. But he too is a child. As shown above, he wrongly considers Natasha still a child, "rejoycing like a child" [59] while imagining her happiness at receiving a present he plans to give her. This man, Natasha's father, whom Volkonsky dubs a "sixty-year-old infant," [60] also "sobs like a baby," becomes "weaker than a child," [61] grows "impatient as a child," [62] and even smiles like a child.[63]

One would perhaps then blame Natasha's mother — but no. At least, as Vanya says:

> I think that Aleksandra Semyonovna was, to a great extent, just as much a child as Nellie.[64]

Virtually every major character of each of Dostoevsky's five major novels is at least once described as a child or as childlike. As mentioned above, "positively good" persons are the most childlike, with "villains" an impressively close second. Let us examine the major works in chronological order.

Raskolnikov, the murderer in *Crime and Punishment*, richly exemplifies the Dostoevskian childlike adult "villain." Key episodes in his often grim story contain surprisingly much of the child. Indeed, Porfiri Petrovich's psychological pursuit of the killer is to a great extent based on the latter's being "just like a child." [65] As Raskolnikov kills Lizaveta, she becomes frightened "like a little child." [66] Accused rather playfully by the wily Porfiri of having committed the murders, Raskolnikov denies it "like a frightened little child, caught at the scene of a crime," [67] and, when the killer finally goes to confess, he says he is "becoming a child." [68] On the way, he meets a beggar woman and her child [69] and gives them money. Earlier, he had saved a young girl from being molested [70] and had expressed pity for and helped the Marmeladov children. When little Polenka comes to thank him, he asks that she pray for "the slave Rodion"; he soon recalls this and "laughs at his childish trick." [71] Moreover, Raskolnikov says to Sonya, deep in the novel:

> . . . and the children? How can Polechka not perish? Have you not seen the children on street corners here, whose mothers are asking for alms? I have found out where these mothers live, in what conditions. It is impossible for the children there to remain children. There, seven-year-olds sin and steal. And yet *children are the image of Christ: "Theirs is the Kingdom of Heaven."* He commanded us to honor and love them; they are the future of humanity . . . [72]

Finally, it is twice mentioned in the epilogue that Raskolnikov had been seriously burned while saving two tiny children in a fire.[73] Furthermore, in Raskolnikov's stream of consciousness just prior to the murders, we learn that he has long been pondering "one question." Why are criminals so easily tracked down and why do they almost always leave such revealing evidence behind them?

> . . . in his opinion, the most basic reason lies not so much in the situational difficulty of hiding the crime as in the criminal himself; the criminal himself, and almost anyone at the

moment of his crime, experiences some kind of weakness in both will and reason, which are perversely replaced by *a childlike phenomenal flippancy* precisely at the very moment when reason and carefulness are the most essential.[74]

In Chapter Four above, Raskolnikov's long dream about the butchered horse is adduced as vivid evidence that his childhood has a profound influence upon his behavior and attitudes later in life. The mere fact that such detailed attention is given to his childhood when he is an adult is of itself significant. Slides of Raskolnikov's childhood thus tend subtly to superimpose themselves upon the reader's apprehension of this murderer's present.

One can almost instantly conclude that this strange concentration of children both around and in Raskolnikov makes him a rounder character. In fact, it is perhaps a tribute to Dostoevsky's descriptive technique that Raskolnikov, despite the child in him, arouses such revulsion in the reader: half sweaty schemer, one feels, and half trapped rat.

In Sonya's shabby little room by the light of a dying candle, "prostitute and killer" are "brought strangely close together" reading the "Eternal Book."[75] The scene is famous. It is less well known, however, that this copy of *The New Testament* was brought by Lizaveta,[76] who "died like a child" under Raskolnikov's axe. Even more important is the fact that this "prostitute and killer" are *by far* the most childlike adults in *Crime and Punishment*.

Though the reader learns of Sonya's grim fate at the novel's outset, she is described in detail only much later, as she invites Raskolnikov to her father's funeral service:

> . . . a girl, still very youngish, almost resembling a little girl . . . she grew timid, like a little child . . .[77]

Twice she dares "timidly" to look at Raskolnikov, who notices "in her face and in her whole person," as he regards her intently,

> one special characteristic; in spite of her eighteen years, she still seemed almost a little girl, much younger than her years,

almost completely a child, and this was at times even humorously evident in certain of her actions.[78]

Sonya's childlikeness allies her with Dostoevsky's child victims and
somehow sustains her freshness throughout the long series of tribulations to which she is subjected. Indeed, it is difficult to believe that she
is both an innocent child and an "accomplished" prostitute as well.

It is no coincidence that the two "child criminals" are brought
together by *The Bible* brought by Lizaveta, who dies "like a child."
This complex of circumstances carefully prepares for the scene in
which Raskolnikov "confesses" to Sonya. As usual, unusual smiles
frame the picture. "Suddenly smiling somehow palely and strength-
lessly for approximately two seconds," Raskolnikov professes to
know who killed Lizaveta.[79] How could he know? "Guess," he tells
Sonya, "with his former distorted and strengthless smile."[80] "Why
must you frighten me so?" she asks, "smiling like a child." Raskolnikov hints the truth to her; and suddenly, as she begins to understand, he seems to see in her face the Lizaveta he has murdered . . .

with completely childlike fright in her face, exactly like tiny
children, when they suddenly become afraid of something,
staring uneasily at whatever is scaring them, move back-
wards and, raising up a little arm, prepare to cry. Sonya now
acted almost exactly the same way . . . her terror suddenly
communicated itself to him: the very same fear took hold of
his face, and he began to gape at her the very same way, even
with almost the very same *childlike* smile.[81]

The italics are Dostoevsky's. This childlike smile (which strangely
unites three very different victims much as *The Bible* does before),
occurring at one of the novel's most dramatic moments, can hardly
fail to convey several Dostoevskian ideas. Murderer, murdered, and living sacrifice are all children before God. This is perhaps the one hope
common to all men: realizing the adult's child's potential first on
earth and later, in heaven.

The prostitute Sonya is also significantly allied with children.
Children often come to see her.[82] She dreams of the child Polechka,[83]
and she calls her mother childlike three times on a single page.[84] And

she becomes excited and vexed "just as a canary or some other kind of tiny bird would get angry," [85] which is revealing if one recalls Prince Myshkin's description of children as little birds. All these trimmings tend further to hide what Sonya has been forced to become.

Not only does the child intensify Lizaveta's murder and Raskolnikov's strange, insinuated confession; the child plays a dramatically descriptive role in Svidrigailov's attack upon Dunya. Given her assailant's particular brand of lust, Dunya's childlikeness renders her fright doubly dramatic. "Why are you afraid, like a child?" asks Svidrigailov, and his face "twists itself" into a condescending smile, but his agitation demolishes this smile. Even before Dunya consciously notices Svidrigailov's menacing unrest, she seems to sense it:

> . . . she was overly bothered by his remark that she was afraid like a child . . .[86]

The range of adults likened to children in *Crime and Punishment* is great and extends even to such scoundrels as Luzhin and Svidrigailov. (The former becomes frightened "like a little child" [87] and the latter admits hiding from Raskolnikov "like a schoolboy." [88]) Especially emphasized is Dostoevsky's insistence that the painters Nikolai and Dmitri behave like little children — three times on a single page, the first reference followed in parentheses by: "the word for word expression of witnesses." [89] Even the presumably compulsive confessor Mikolka (who seems almost to have leapt to life from some obscure newspaper clipping) is described as a child by Porfiri Petrovich.[90]

Significantly, one of the very few *unchildlike* adults in all of Dostoevsky is Porfiri himself. The resulting inbalance between all-adult punisher and part-child criminal, notwithstanding Porfiri's apparent hopes for Raskolnikov's ultimate salvation, makes for a strange spider-and-fly relationship that abets two effects. Raskolnikov, who becomes even more a child because Porfiri is less, seems the more victimized and the less responsible for his crime. This, in turn, renders his final confession the more noble and his eventual salvation the more likely.

Whereas Dostoevsky endowed his killer and prostitute with most of the adult childlikeness in *Crime and Punishment*, there are four such principal recipients in *The Idiot*. Myshkin, the most obvious choice, is the most childlike. Aglaya is the next most childlike and the most complexly so. Her mother can perhaps be called a humorous child, and Nastasya Filippovna, a surprising one, at least, for the present. (As shown below, Dostoevsky employed childlikeness to round out his so-called infernal women much as he did his criminals.)

Myshkin is probably the adult most repeatedly and unequivocally described as a child in all of Dostoevsky's works.[91] He is even said to need a nurse,[92] to need a bib and supervision while he eats,[93] and to be fit for playing blind man's buff.[94] General Epanchin immediately describes him as "an utter child and so pathetic."[95] (Curiously enough, Epanchin himself has just been compared to a child by Dostoevsky.[96])

Most important, it is the childlike and Christlike Myshkin who most often perceives the child in others and even in himself.

> I'm in my twenty-seventh year and yet I know that I'm like a child.[97]

Myshkin's story early in the novel about the Swiss children and the girl Marie has been discussed in Chapter Five of the present study. While telling this story, the Prince repeats the opinion of his doctor

> that I myself am a perfect child, that is, entirely a child, that only in face and figure do I resemble an adult, but that in development, soul, character, and perhaps even in mind I am not a grown-up and shall remain that way, even if I live to the age of sixty.[98]

Having denied the above statement so unconvincingly as to confirm it, the Prince continues:

> . . . my friends have always been children, but not because I myself was a child, but simply because I am drawn to children.

He even concludes:

Perhaps they will consider me a child even here — let them! [99]

Immediately after his story is finished, the Prince tells Lizaveta Prokofevna:

. . . I am simply sure that you are a perfect child in all, in all, in all that is good or bad, despite your years.[100]

She instantly agrees and returns the compliment:

. . . I am a child . . . I find your character completely identical to my own: like two peas in a pod.[101]

Actually, she had already likened herself to a child,[102] and later in the novel, the Prince calls her a child once more:

Oh, what a little child you are, Lizaveta Prokofevna! [103]

This is not to say that other personages do not call each other children, merely that Myshkin does most of it. Ippolit, for example, asks Lizaveta Prokofevna to ''save'' his ''poor little innocent brother and sisters,'' exclaiming:

You — are holy, you yourself are a child . . . [104]

It is somewhat amusing that Lizaveta Prokofevna, such a child herself, becomes vexed at her daughter Aleksandra, who sees and re-counts an unusual number of dreams, innocent dreams, ''like those of a seven-year-old child.'' [105]

Myshkin also descries the child in Aglaya; late in the novel, he tells her:

I love horribly that you are such a child, such a good, kind child! Oh, how wonderful you can be, Aglaya![106]

This is strikingly similar to what the Prince has told Kolya Ivolgin shortly before:

What children we still are, Kolya! And . . . and . . . how good it is that we are children![107]

Still more significantly, the Prince surprises the child in Nastasya Filippovna (although she is earlier described by Dostoevsky as "laughing and clapping her hands like a little girl"[108]). Near the novel's end, Myshkin exclaims to Evgeni Pavlovich Radomsky:

. . .I love her with all my soul! Why, she's — a child; she's now a child, entirely a child! Oh, you know nothing![109]

In connection with Dostoevsky's treatment of "villains" and criminals, this declaration about the "fallen" Nastasya Filippovna is most revealing. Can one assume, then, that she is still largely the same child that was led astray (by Totsky) and therefore, that she yet possesses great potential for salvation but acts like a child who "does not know any better"? We have Dostoevsky's word:

He had quite rightly told Evgeni Pavlovich that he loved her sincerely and completely; in his love for her there was truly a sort of attraction to some kind of pathetic, sick child, whom it is difficult and even impossible to leave on its own.[110]

Perhaps yet more remarkable is the fact that Myshkin *physically* treats both the wayward Nastasya Filippovna and her wild paramour, Rogozhin, as infants. One should observe that this occurs immediately after the latter two have "misbehaved" at their worst. Late in the novel, Nastasya Filippovna launches a bitterly brutal emotional attack upon Aglaya that ends in a momentary faint and then continued frenzy. Myshkin sits next to Nastasya Filippovna and, looking at her fixedly, strokes her "on the head and face with both hands" as if she were "a little child." [111] She babbles incoherently, and he drinks it all in with what seems almost supernatural empathy.

> . . . he smiled quietly, and no sooner did it seem to him as if she was beginning to grow sad or cry again, reproach or complain, he would immediately begin to stroke her head once more, tenderly passing his hands across her cheeks, admonishing and consoling her like a child.[112]

Then, when Rogozhin has murdered Nastasya Filippovna, Myshkin sits beside him in the same manner, stroking his head, hair, and cheeks with a trembling hand.[113] And this is how they are found, Rogozhin, feverishly delirious, and Myshkin, apparently mad.

> . . . each time the patient cried out or babbled deliriously, he would hurriedly pass a trembling hand across his hair and cheeks, as if caressing and consoling him.[114]

A high percentage of near madness in all participants of both scenes tends somehow to salvage a mawkishness that could otherwise evoke disgust and disbelief. Far more important, however, Myshkin treats both persons as infants immediately following their sins. If they are *then* to be saved, it seems, he must find the child in them at once and at all costs — sanity, perhaps, included.

Myshkin thus can be seen to find childlikeness in Lizaveta Prokofevna, Aglaya, Kolya Ivolgin, Nastasya Filippovna, and even in the savage Rogozhin. He also finds childlikeness in the laughter of Keller and Ganya. Once again, it should be noted that the subjects of his discovery have just acted rather ignobly. Just as before, the child appears, in both meanings of the word, to redeem the "villain."

After the "son of Pavlishchev" deception, Keller feels a strange need to confess to Myshkin the errors of his previous ways. Some of his stories are so "humorously" told that both he and the Prince "finally laugh like maniacs."

> "The main thing is that you have a childlike trustfulness and exceptional truthfulness," the Prince said finally. "Do you know that this alone redeems you greatly?" [115]

Soon after Ganya has so disgusted his own sister that she spits in his face and he, having seized her in a rage, has slapped the interceding Myshkin's face, he apologizes to the Prince. As they converse, Ganya laughs good naturedly. "I'm amazed," says Myshkin,

> that you laugh so sincerely. Truly, you still have the laughter of a child. Recently you came in to make up and said "I'll kiss your hand if you like" — that's exactly how children would make up.[116]

It is most important that Myshkin finds the villain-redeeming child in the laughter of these two people. As observed above, both laughter and smiles are not infrequently employed to signify, in Dostoevsky's works, the child's holy potential — the child's right to enter the Kingdom of Heaven. (The reader is especially reminded of Arkadi's statement that a baby's laughter is a ray from paradise and Myshkin's story of a child's first smile.)

In *The Idiot*, Lizaveta Prokofevna sees a positive quality in the Prince's laughter from the first,[117] as does he in her daughters'.[118] Even the embittered Ippolit smiles "some sort of childlike smile"[119] just prior to crying "like a little child."[120] Especially suggestive is Lebedev's story of a high official who always used to "smile, smile like a little child" and finally gave up his soul to God "like a little child, like a little child."[121] Here, the man's childlikeness, brought out by his smile, seems almost tendentiously to emphasize his closeness to God.

But let us return to Aglaya. We have seen that Myshkin finds the child in her; his findings are well founded. The General states that Aglaya "laughs like a child,"[122] and she is subsequently described by Dostoevsky as "bursting out laughing, entirely like a child."[123] Childlikeness in Aglaya seems initially to serve a typically redemptory purpose: in every one of her peevish antics, Dostoevsky writes, "something childlike peeked out."[124] Later in the novel, however, when this young lady's relationship to Myshkin has grown more important and complex, it appears that her childlikeness symmetrically reflects the child in him. Whereas she, as do her mother and Nastasya Filippovna, doubts Myshkin's manliness and marvels uneasily at the idea of such a child marrying, the Prince seems to see the child in

Aglaya as, perhaps, only another child could, but seems as unequipped to act upon his knowledge as he is equipped for such insights. Almost in one breath, Aglaya speaks of running away from home and of taking up teaching together with Myshkin, "because he likes children so much."

> He could not understand how in such a stern, haughty beauty there could turn out to be such a child, a child who truly even *now* was unable to understand *some words*.[125]

Yet, only six pages later, the process works in reverse. Aglaya evinces considerable insight into the feelings behind Nastasya Filippovna's bizarre correspondence, whereupon Myshkin looks at Aglaya in amazement.

> . . . he found it strange to realize that this child had long been a woman.[126]

In both instances, Myshkin and Aglaya seem close as perhaps only two children can be, yet therefore, perhaps, only the less able to make something of their relationship in the "adult" world around them. In this sense, their dilemma is a miniature of Myshkin's essential problem: as a holy child, he is endowed with fabulous potentials but as a man, he cannot realize them in his present environment. In his own words, he is "drawn to" children, and, one feels, he is perhaps only as close to others as they are childlike. And this can be seen to include even his understanding of others, once one acknowledges Dostoevsky's penchant for pointing to the child in alleged villains.

Near the novel's end, in a burst of triumphant optimism, Myshkin expresses disbelief that man can be unhappy:

> Look at a child! Look at God's sunrise![127]

This ecstatic pronouncement seems a prelude to the Prince's epileptic fit. It is interesting to speculate that this seizure represents an escape from even the thought that the child, for whom Myshkin feels such deep, empathetic love, can grow up so unfulfilled and even so abused in the world as he finds it.

The Possessed contains relatively few childlike adults; nor does its title promise otherwise. The most childlike adult by far is Stepan Trofimovich, who, ironically enough, is the unchildlike hero's tutor. The novel's other most childlike adult personages are Marya Timofeevna and, perhaps surprisingly, the suicide Kirillov. All the other characters are described at least once or twice as childlike except for Stavrogin, who never is, unless one counts the likening of his three outrageous pranks to those of a naughty boy.[128] This is of itself greatly significant in Dostoevsky, and especially so since Stavrogin seems an immensely powerful possessor of unrealized potentials.

After two brief suggestions that Stepan Trofimovich is quite childlike,[129] we are told that Stavrogin, as an eight-year-old child, grew up entirely under his care. The tutor's "secret," we read, was his being himself a child.[130] (The secret, one can infer, perhaps not of his success, but of his failure.)

The aging tutor complains like a child [131] and even lies like a little boy; [132] finally, he refers to himself as a child considering marriage.[133] "I am a capricious child," he says, "with all a child's egoism but minus its innocence." [134] Even the most childlike of The Possessed, one can conclude, is a misguided child. In Stepan Trofimovich's words:

So it's not enough that we are old children, we're evil children besides? [135]

In the words of the novel's narrator:

. . . and now he suddenly sobbed, sobbed like a tiny naughty boy awaiting the whip his teacher has left to procure.[136]

Marya Timofeevna is exceedingly childlike when seeking acceptance by her husband and his mother. Dostoevsky, one can conclude, brought out the child in Marya to stress her helplessness and, perhaps, her superiority. Approaching Varvara Petrovna at church, the cripple says she has come only to kiss the lady's hand with an exceedingly childlike expression, like a child who grows affectionate, requesting something . . .[137]

Later, Stavrogin visits Marya and she wants to kneel before him.

"No, that's utterly impossible," he splendidly smiled to her, causing her to burst into joyous laughter. He kept tenderly admonishing her, like a child, with the same mellifluous voice . . . [138]

Stavrogin's smiles are nearly all cold, haughty, and aloof. Here, it seems that Marya's childlike helplessness elevates and softens the callous man who is guilty before her but before whom she would kneel.

The same transformation is effected when Stavrogin comes again and finds Marya asleep. Stavrogin's eyes feed viciously upon her fright as she awakens to find him coldly watching her. But as she starts to cry, "just like a frightened child,"

. . . the guest remembered himself; his face changed in a single instant, and he walked over to the table with the most warm and tender of smiles.[139]

Such attitudes are indeed rare in Stavrogin and seem directly induced by Marya's childlike helplessness. The fact that even though he is himself unchildlike, Stavrogin has at least some threshold of pity and receptivity to childlikeness is most important. The man remains just human enough to engage much of the reader's credence and understanding that he otherwise would not.

Pyotr Stepanovich is several times referred to as a little boy, but the occurrences are usually disparaging and not overly significant.[140] There is, however, one revealing instance. This is the well-known scene where Pyotr tells Stavrogin his scheme about Ivan the Tsarevitch. Pyotr first deplores the current state of affairs, describing a child of six he has seen leading his drunken mother home.[141] Typically, Stavrogin's reaction is scornful laughter. When he learns of Pyotr's plan to amend all this, Stavrogin smiles maliciously.

Why are you laughing so maliciously? Do not frighten
me. I now am like a child myself, and one smile like that can
scare me to death.[142]

Kirillov is often described as childlike and associated with children. This makes for a sharp, dramatic contrast when Stavrogin visits
Kirillov. The latter is happily playing ball with a tiny child who, at
the first sight of Stavrogin, bursts into such a "long fit of childish
crying" that he must be carried from the room.[143] Stavrogin asks
Kirillov if he likes children, and the latter answers affirmatively.[144]

Also in sharp contrast to Stavrogin, Kirillov smiles like a child.
Early in the novel, for example, Kirillov laughs "a most joyous and
pure laugh."

For an instant his face took on an extremely childlike expression, and, it seemed to me, one that suited him very
well.[145]

The fact that, in Dostoevsky, childlikeness *suits* Kirillov suggests,
perhaps, that his potential is closer to the surface than is Stavrogin's.
Nor is the difference accidental: this description is soon repeated.

. . . he suddenly smiled his recent childlike smile.[146]

Since both these men commit suicide, it is tempting to speculate
as to why one is so closely allied with children and the other almost
purposely — in Dostoevsky — estranged. An analysis of their diverse
motivations is revealing. To oversimplify: Kirillov seems motivated by
hope; Stavrogin, by despair.[147] In terms of the present study, one can
hazard that Stavrogin takes his life partially because he fails to find
the child within himself; Kirillov, because he hopes to realize, by
becoming "an angel of God," [148] the child he senses within.

Except for thirty-five references to Arkadi as or like a child, *A
Raw Youth* is quite barren of unusually childlike adults. Like
Nastasya Filippovna, however, Katerina Nikolaevna is more a child
than one would perhaps expect. Like Stavrogin, Versilov is one of the
very few unchildlike adults in all of Dostoevsky. His dream that men

will someday be as children, however, renders him even more different from Stavrogin than is Kirillov. Makar Ivanovich is discussed as a child in Chapter Five above.

Nearly half of Arkadi's childlike labels are self-imposed and most of these, in adolescent disgust. His being considered a child by Versilov and by Katerina Niklaevna is considerably more significant.

Not only does Arkadi harbor hopes for his "future father"; he feels a secret fear that Versilov will fail to esteem his "future son." The following is typical.

> . . . Versilov might think (if only he deigned to think of me) that here goes a little boy, a retired schoolboy, a teen-ager marveling at the entire world.[149]

(One is reminded of Kolya Krasotkin courting the respect of "Karamazov.") Later, Arkadi also suggests Kolya as he accuses Lambert of treating him "like some sixteen-year-old."[150] And, as "the fledgling" who wants to challenge the Prince to a duel,[151] Arkadi suggests the proud Ilyusha Snegiryov.

But Versilov's opinion of Arkadi remains the cynosure of the latter's hyper-sensitive hopes and expectations. Versilov talks to him "decidedly as to a child"[152] and even "most stupidly, as if to a little one."[153] It is hardly difficult, then, to imagine Arkadi's feelings when he reads, in a note from Versilov to Katerina Nikolaevna:

> Spare him, he is not yet an adult, almost a boy, undeveloped both mentally and physically . . .[154]

In fact, Arkadi's is a dual mortification, for he has furtive hopes for Katerina's love as well. He is thus in agony when, in a long conversation they have later, she answers him

> as one answers a little child's childish, pesky question, in order to get rid of him. I suddenly understood this, and was ashamed, but I was unable to tear myself away.[155]

Still later, when pricked by Tatyana Pavlovna (Arkadi's thorn of common sense) : "In love, puppy?" — he declares himself ready even

to seem "a petty urchin" in the eyes of Katerina if only she realizes
how high he has placed her happiness.[156] (The reference is to his
good intentions concerning the hidden letter.)

No little irony ensues from Arkadi's words to his sister:

What a beauty you are today, Liza. And yet you're still
terribly much a child.[157]

(Unbeknowns to him, she is now *with* child.) Later, when Arkadi is
told of his sister's condition, he himself cries like a child:

A little child suddenly showed itself from within the young
man. A little child, then, must have still been living in an
entire half of my heart. I fell on the sofa and whimpered.[158]

Arkadi's recognition of the child in Katerina Nikolaevna draws
deeply upon her smile. On a page where he mentions her smile no less
than ten times (for example, "You smile even in fear . . . You always smile . . . I cannot endure your smile!"[159]), Arkadi describes Katerina's face:

"The expression of your face is childlike playfulness and
infinite open-heartedness — there!"[160]

On the next page, he calls her face "the face of a country beauty"
— and a long series of adjectives describing her face culminates in:
"modest and virgin, I swear it."

More than virgin — childlike! — That's your face![161]

Grushenka (*The Brothers Karamazov*) is even more childlike
than either Nastasya Filippovna or Katerina Nikolaevna. Just as the
children in the latter two are "discovered" by the childlike Myshkin
and Arkadi, so now the reader sees the child in Grushenka through
the eyes of the childlike Alyosha.

Alyosha was struck most of all by this face's childlike, open-hearted expression. Her gaze was that of a child; her joy was a child's, and even now she walked over to the table "joyously" as if expecting something with the most childlike, impatient, and trustful curiosity. . . . her manner of speaking and intonation seemed to Alyosha some kind of nearly impossible contradiction compared to the childishly open-hearted and joyful expression of her face and her quiet, happily shining infant's eyes! [162]

The narrator of *The Brothers Karamazov* uses the phrase "still a little girl"[163] in conveying the rumor of Grushenka's having been "deceived" and "abandoned" at the age of seventeen by an amorous officer. Besides stressing the genesis of her feelings, this phrase subtly prepares the reader for her behavior during Alyosha's visit. Alluding bitterly to the man who wronged her five years before when she was a "stupid little girl," she implies that the incident may yet cause her to commit suicide and starts sobbing "like a tiny child."[164] She echoes this description much later, at Mitya's mad celebration, by referring to the incident of five years before, when she was a "stupid little girl."[165] And here, her childlikeness carries over, by implication, into the present: she admits of loving the officer "all these five years."

All three brothers Karamazov are repeatedly described as child-like, and several of the twenty-eight instances (Alyosha — 13, Mitya — 8, and Ivan — 7) have been discussed above. Significantly, the suffering of innocent children brings out, at different times, the child in each of them.

Alyosha, as discussed in Chapter One above, is called by Lise "the smallest boy possible" because he has been "associating" with little boys, including the suffering Ilyusha.[166] Silbajoris calls Alyosha "the child of God";[167] Mikhailovsky calls him "a babe";[168] Wasiolek, "a child in the mildness and quickness of his heart";[169] and M. A. Antonovich, "the author's most favorite baby."[170] When Father Zosima dies, Alyosha's weeping causes his face to swell up like a little child's.[171] Actually, Alyosha is so constantly referred to and described as childlike that the narrator seems to feel it his duty to inform the reader that this child is part man:

Although Alyosha kept silent, he already understood his father quite completely. I repeat: This boy was by no means as naïve as everyone considered him.[172]

It will be remembered that the child in Ivan repeatedly appears immediately prior to his long speech about the suffering of innocent children. Much later, he cries out "with some kind of almost childish joy" at "catching" the devil on a point of logic in his famous hallucination;[173] and soon after that, he admits that Smerdyakov "hoodwinked" him "like a little boy."[174]

Silbajoris asserts that "Dmitri's childlike nature is clearly established throughout the narrative" and terms him "a living symbol of the metaphysical suffering Babe."[175] It is especially significant (as shown above) that Mitya becomes as a child when he sees the "meaning" of his dream about the "poor babe." Moreover, he is described as a "stubborn child" as the police search him[176] prior to this dream. Perhaps Mitya's most unusual manifestation of childlikeness occurs at his celebration when, brandishing banknotes and imbibing heavily, this violent man who has presumably just murdered his father empties another glass and

. . . it was as if something infant-like appeared in him.
. . . He seemed to have forgotten everything and surveyed everyone with delight, smiling like a child.[177]

Kalganov, who "believed fully in Mitya's guilt," cries for a long time when they take Mitya away, "as if he was still a little boy and not a twenty-year-old man already."[178] (Kalganov's childlike disillusionment closes Part Three of the novel and serves as a transition to the first book of Part Four: "The Boys.")

In sharp and curious contrast to the childlike, fallen Grushenka, righteous Katerina Ivanovna is surprisingly unlike a child; one can therefore conclude that Dostoevsky deemed childlikeness incompatible with one of her faults, pride. Typically, the childlike Alyosha brings out the novel's only two hints of the child in Katerina. At the "anguish-in-the-living-room" meeting, Ivan informs Katerina that he must go to Moscow the next day. She is shocked at first and then undergoes a strange transformation from girl in anguish to woman in full control. This change amazes Alyosha exceedingly.[179] The only other hint of childlikeness in Katerina is a scornful implication by Ivan to Alyosha that in her indecision as to how to testify in court she is like a baby who needs him, Ivan, to rock her cradle.[180]

The "villainous" old Fyodor Pavlovich, however, is decidedly childlike, despite his scarcely innocent pastimes. Alluding to a rumor that little old lecher cried "like a little child" at the death of his first wife, the narrator continues as follows:

> In most cases people, even villains, are far more naïve and ingenuous than we generally suppose. And we ourselves are, too.[181]

This passage ends the novel's first chapter and tends to keep Fyodor Pavlovich human despite the inhumanity he soon displays. And, in the opinion of Ivan, such "villains" are capable not only of being like children but even of liking them. "Mark this well," he says to Alyosha,

> cruel people, passionate and predatory ones, Karamazovs, sometimes love children very much.[182]

Thus, just as we have seen that the pious, childlike Alyosha is, nevertheless, a Karamazov, so we must now, it seems, be willing to discover the child — if the pun is pardoned — in the likes of Fyodor Pavlovich. S. I. Gessen has observed that the very same innate "carefree instinct" which surfaces in the voluptuary Fyodor Pavlovich as a "heedless '*carpe diem*'" can be discerned in Alyosha's "playful, childlike innocence."[183]

The range of adults likened to children in *The Brothers Karamazov* is truly astonishing. It encompasses the old Captain Snegiryov (twice described as childlike in Chapter One above) and Maksimov (who is described as a young man of no more than twenty who "sometimes speaks and looks like a child without the slightest inhibition, even when realizing it himself"[184]. It can even be construed to encompass, if briefly, such diverse individuals as Father Zosima (who excuses himself for babbling like a tiny infant [185]) and Smerdyakov (who admits to shuddering — as he prepares to murder his probable father — like an infant [186]). But surely, the most unexpected, if unserious such references in the entire novel are to Othello (described as possessing ''a soul as gentle and innocent as the soul of an infant'' [187]) and to Gogol — at Mitya's trial, the prosecutor forensically proffers the notion that compared to many contemporary voluptuaries, Fyodor Pavlovich is ''almost an innocent infant''; [188] he then suggests that Gogol finished Part One of *Dead Souls*

either in a paroxysm of infantly innocent purity of thought or simply afraid of the censors of his day.[189]

He is interrupted by applause. (The gathering storm of his point, of course, is that the contemporary man is capable of great evil and that Mitya is a typical contemporary man.)

Adult childlikeness is as significant in Dostoevsky's shorter creative works as in the major novels. The childlikeness of Blanche (*The Gambler*), for example, strikingly resembles that of Grushenka, Nastasya Filippovna, and Katerina Nikolaevna. Typically, the childlike Gambler (''Am I really, am I really such a tiny child!'' [190]) descries the child in Blanche (as did, in the above three, the childlike Alyosha, Myshkin, and Arkadi, respectively):

. . . with a bewitching smile, Mlle Blanche walked over to me *herself* . . . Her devilish face was able to change completely in a single second. At that instant, her face was sweet and pleading, smiling like a child's and even playful . . . she slyly winked at me, so that no one could see . . .[191]

Of still greater importance in *The Gambler* is the immortal, inimitable Grandmother's childlikeness. She is twice described in French as ''having fallen into infancy,'' [192] which adds a pleasant spice to the agonizing zest with which she gambles. Humorously enough, this delightfully outspoken creature disdains the kisses of her grandchildren because ''children slobber.'' [193] Humor also ensues when one of the men living with Mr. Prokharchin tells him he must recover and return to work because ''it is vile and shameful to get sick, and only little children do so.'' [194]

Of all Dostoevsky's shorter creative works, *The Little Hero* is the most replete with significant adult childlikeness. The two young women who unabashedly molest with caresses an "almost eleven-year-old" boy — much to his not entirely unpleasant embarrassment — are themselves repeatedly depicted as children. Ironically, it seems to be the innocent child in these women that seeks heedlessly to arouse the man in this boy. Theirs is a vicarious, childlike delight which tends strangely to beg the question of reponsibility for their actions. Moreover, both women are termed "exceedingly naïve." [195] "The blonde" is ". . . sprightly as a child, in spite of being married five years already." [196] She also "laughs like a child," [197] and she is twice termed a "schoolgirl" by the protagonist.[198]

Mme M. is also agile as a child,[199] laughs like a child,[200] blushes like a child,[201] and acts like a schoolchild.[202]

Of these two women, the blonde is the more repeatedly and remarkably described as childlike. One fascinating passage gives birth, by implication, to an entire roomful of hypothetical children. The Little Hero having reacted to the blonde's attentions with the exasperation she had apparently desired,

> . . . she ignored me and turned away as if nothing had happened — as if someone else and not she had been making mischief, just like some schoolchild who, no sooner has the teacher turned his back, has already succeeded in making mischief nearby, pinching some puny little boy and giving him a slap, kick, and elbow jab, and has instantly turned around again, straightened up, and buried himself in a book, starting to learn his lesson and thus pulling thick and unexpected wool over the eyes of his enraged teacher, who has swooped down, hawk-like, upon the commotion.[203]

The elaborate detail of this passage is perhaps slightly rivaled by a shorter description in *Polzunkov*. The hapless laughster of this name blurts out the words (soon to be returned in full) "April fool!" to Osip Mikhailych "like an idiot —

> that is, entirely like a little urchin who has furtively hidden himself behind his grandmother's armchair and then Yow!

right in her ear, at the top of his lungs — to make her jump.''[204]

(It is tempting to contend that in both the above passages, as so often happens in Gogol, various apparently irrelevant details evoke parallel suggestive connotations that strangely but persistently return to the point of departure — here, first like a homing pigeon and second, as an echo.)

Driven at last by the blonde's conduct to a state of gasping exasperation, the Little Hero upbraids her for telling "such a mean lie, like a little girl" in front of everyone.[205] (She has just slandered him as "a rival" of Mme M's husband — "in the woods.") The boy's moral superiority over his tormentors serves further to highlight the irony inherent in their strangely childlike seductiveness.

Also ironic and typical of the Dostoevskian childlike meek adult is the protagonist's uncle in *The Village of Stepanchikovo and Its Inhabitants*.

> His heart was pure as a child's. This was truly a child of forty years, highly effusive and always delighted, who took all people for angels and blamed himself for others' faults, exaggerating their good qualities without measure and even presuming them to exist where they obviously did not.[206]

As seen above, it is this man whom his fifteen-year-old daughter feels compelled to defend. He twice blushes like a child,[207] and even his servant Gavrila terms him "just like a tiny child compared to everyone else."[208] The rather fey Tatyana Ivanova, who often lives in her childhood memories as mentioned above, is "looked after" by everyone "like a child" prior to her death.[209]

It is also somewhat ironic that Aleksandra Mikhailovna — under whose aegis the almost thirteen-year-old Netochka becomes so childlike — is herself so much a child. She is first described as "a woman of about twenty-two . . ."

> Seriousness and severity were somehow incompatible with her clear, angelic features, like mourning clothes on an infant.[210]

Netochka later describes Aleksandra Mikhailovna's large, light blue
eyes as "clear as a child's" [211] and remarks that her "naïve, childish, baby-like eagerness to believe others" would have inspired an
artist to put her face on canvas.[212] But perhaps her husband Pyotr
Aleksandrovich most brings out the child in Aleksandra Mikhailovna,
and especially so through a Dostoevskian strange smile:

> Sometimes her husband would comply with all her wishes and
> even give her a condescending smile, as one smiles to a
> spoiled little child when one does not want to refuse its
> strange whim, fearing to confound its naïveté too early and
> too harshly. But — I know not why — this smile disturbed
> me to the depths of my soul . . . I would follow them with an
> infant's curiosity . . . He would often bless and make the
> sign of the Cross over her, as over a child . . .[213]

Typically, Dostoevsky works to advantage the two halves of contradiction. Netochka calls herself "a rebyonok" and then, on the
very next page, when stressing how much she understood of the adult
problems around her, "not a child [ne rebyonok]." [214]

When Netochka is seventeen, she asks forgiveness from Aleksandra Mikhailovna for being "such a bad child," whereupon:

> "We are all children," she said with a shy smile, "and
> I too am a child, worse, much worse than you," she added
> into my ear. . . . "I am even worse than a child." [215]

The "remaining" twenty-five pages of Netochka are fairly filled with
references to each of these two persons as children, made by themselves and also by the both hostile and sympathetic Pyotr Aleksandrovich.[216] This tendentious multitude of designations is set against a
background of "my dear child," "my sweet child," etc., which further emphasizes the unnatural (i.e., adult considered as child) references.

Dostoevsky can be seen to achieve adult childlikeness in two basic
ways. Either a person is deemed a child by sundry other characters,
and even by himself (for example, Devushkin in *Poor People* considers both himself [217] and Varenka [218] as children), or a person's

actions and appearance are described as childlike. The latter method often takes versatile shapes. For instance, Katerina (*The Landlady*) is first described as "a woman of about twenty" whose face has "child-tender and timid lines."[219] Typically in Dostoevsky, the strangeness of her smile parallels and even reflects this near contradiction in physical appearance:

A smile flashed for a moment upon her lips, but her face revealed traces of some kind of childlike fear and mysterious terror.[220]

Her features then evince "mysterious tender feeling and terror, washed with tears of delight or childlike repentance."[221] Soon she looks "with a child's astonished eyes," caressed "like a child" by Murin.[222]

Next it "seems" to the half-delirious Ordynov that she leans "with an infant's enthusiasm" upon his shoulder,[223] and again, she presses against him like a tiny child.[224] Quite appropriately, several of these descriptions seem to reflect the observations of Ordynov, who, in Murin's words, is "painfully young" and has a heart "hot as a young girl's."[225] In Dostoevsky's phrase, Ordynov's passion for science had long ago rendered him "an infant in the world around him."[226]

Perhaps the most unusual appellation effecting adult childlikeness in Dostoevsky is the Underground Man's apostrophe to "whoever first proclaimed" that man's vile and base actions result from ignorance of his true interests, the revelation of which would instantly cause his complete reform:

"O infant! O pure, innocent babe!"[227]

Finally, the prostitute Liza becomes quite childlike as she rushes after the Underground Man to show him a love letter she had received from a medical student:

Children look that way at those whom they love very much and whom they are asking for something.[228]

And, as she gives him the letter, the prostitute's childlikeness is signally emphasized:

> At that instant, her entire face was shining with an exceedingly naïve, almost childlike triumph. . . . When I finished reading, I met her warm, curious, and childishly impatient gaze . . .[229]

Notes

[1] F. M. Dostoevsky, *Collected Works* (Moscow, 1956–1958), III, 421.

[2] There is also Katya, who appears only in the novel's introduction, "an illegitimate child of about ten, a happy, pretty little girl," who is one of the prisoner's pupils after his release. In view of Dostoevsky's strange pursuit of such little girls, it is interesting that Goryanchikov, surprised while teaching Katya how to read, "got as flustered as if I had caught him committing some sort of crime" (*ibid.*, p. 392). More probably, however, the remark is intended to help fill out this eccentric's character, and the girl's primary importance certainly turns on her genesis of feelings when asked if she remembers Goryanchikov after his death.

> She looked at me in silence, turned her head towards the wall, and began to weep. Thus, it seems that this person could cause at least someone to love him (*ibid.*, p. 393).

[3] *Ibid.*, p. 403.

[4] *Ibid.*, p. 584.

[5] *Ibid.*, p. 429.

[6] *Ibid.*, p. 507.

[7] *Ibid.*, p. 544.

[8] *Ibid.*, p. 551.

[9] *Ibid.*, p. 629.

[10] *Ibid.*, p. 639.

[11] *Ibid.*, p. 648.

[12] All references, *ibid.*, pp. 452–53.

[13] *Ibid.*, p. 456.

[14] *Ibid.*, p. 552.

[15] *Ibid.*, p. 561.

[16] *Ibid.*, p. 434.

[17] *Ibid.*, p. 436.

[18] *Ibid.*, p. 446.

[19] *Ibid.*, p. 447.

[20] *Ibid.*, p. 499.

[21] *Ibid.*, p. 500.

[22] *Ibid.*, p. 516.

[23] *Ibid.*, p. 493.

[24] *Ibid.*, p. 526.

[25] *Ibid.*, p. 527.

[26] *Ibid.*, p. 528.

[27] They even sing Christmas songs about children (*ibid.*, p. 534).

[28] *Ibid.*, pp. 625–26.

[29] *Ibid.*, p. 554.

[30] *Ibid.*, p. 553.

[31] *Ibid.*, pp. 582–84.

[32] *Ibid.*, p. 398.

[33] *Ibid.*, p. 440.

[24] *Ibid.*, p. 437.

[35] *Ibid.*, p. 437.

[36] *Ibid.*, p. 596.

[37] *Ibid.*, p. 597.

[38] *Ibid.*, p. 461.

[39] *Ibid.*, p. 403.

[40] *Ibid.*, p. 622.

[41] *Ibid.*, p. 623.

[42] *Ibid.*, p. 427.

[43] *Ibid.*, p. 428.

[44] *Ibid.*, p. 26.

[45] *Ibid.*, p. 47.

[46] *Ibid.*, p. 52.

[47] *Ibid.*, p. 47.

[48] *Ibid.*, p. 53.

[49] *Ibid.*, p. 83.

[50] *Ibid.*, p. 29.

[51] *Ibid.*, p. 30.

[52] *Ibid.*, p. 91.

[53] This smile is foreshadowed several pages earlier (*ibid.*, p. 85).

[54] *Ibid.*, p. 253.

[55] *Ibid.*, p. 254.

[56] *Ibid.*, p. 261.

[57] *Ibid.*, p. 260.

[58] *Ibid.*, p. 209.

[59] *Ibid.*, p. 89.

[60] *Ibid.*, p. 264.

[61] *Ibid.*, p. 82.

[62] *Ibid.*, p. 338.

[63] *Ibid.*, p. 354.

[64] *Ibid.*, p. 292.

⁶⁵ Dostoevsky, *C. W.*, V, 363. It is thus somewhat ironical that Raskolnikov had looked down on his university comrades as if they were children (*ibid.*, p. 56).

⁶⁶ *Ibid.*, p. 86.

⁶⁷ *Ibid.*, p. 476.

⁶⁸ *Ibid.*, p. 549.

⁶⁹ *Ibid.*, p. 549.

⁷⁰ *Ibid.*, pp. 51–55.

⁷¹ *Ibid.*, p. 198.

⁷² *Ibid.*, p. 342. My italics.

⁷³ *Ibid.*, pp. 560, 563.

It is interesting to compare this deed of the killer with a statement made by the narrator of *The Possessed*. Having repeated Stepan Verkhovensky's pronouncement to the effect that everyone finds some pleasure in watching a fire, he adds that

> of course the very same admirer of a nocturnal fire will throw himself into the flames to save a burning child . . . (Dostoevsky, *C. W.*, VII, 537).

⁷⁴ Dostoevsky, *C. W.*, V, 77. My italics.

⁷⁵ *Ibid.*, p. 341.

⁷⁶ *Ibid.*, p. 337.

⁷⁷ *Ibid.*, p. 245.

⁷⁸ *Ibid.*, p. 247.

⁷⁹ *Ibid.*, p. 427.

⁸⁰ *Ibid.*, p. 428.

⁸¹ *Ibid.*, pp. 428–29.

⁸² *Ibid.*, p. 329.

⁸³ *Ibid.*, p. 343.

⁸⁴ *Ibid.*, p. 330.

⁸⁵ *Ibid.*, p. 330.

⁸⁶ *Ibid.*, p. 510.

⁸⁷ *Ibid.*, p. 377.

⁸⁸ *Ibid.*, p. 490.

⁸⁹ *Ibid.*, p. 147.

⁹⁰ *Ibid.*, p. 474.

⁹¹ In addition to the many instances discussed below, the reader is referred to Dostoevsky, *C. W.*, VI, 60, 195, 379, 412, 578, 610, 621, 625, and 675.

⁹² *Ibid.*, p. 189.

⁹³ *Ibid.*, p. 61.

⁹⁴ *Ibid.*, p. 61.

⁹⁵ *Ibid.*, p. 60.

[96] *Ibid.*, p. 59.
[97] *Ibid.*, p. 624.
[98] *Ibid.*, p. 86.
[99] *Ibid.*, p. 87.
[100] *Ibid.*, p. 88.
[101] *Ibid.*, p. 89.
[102] *Ibid.*, p. 66.
[103] *Ibid.*, p. 364.
[104] *Ibid.*, p. 338.
[105] *Ibid.*, p. 373.
[106] *Ibid.*, p. 595.
[107] *Ibid.*, p. 578.
[108] *Ibid.*, p. 127.
[109] *Ibid.*, p. 660.
[110] *Ibid.*, p. 667.
[111] *Ibid.*, p. 647.
[112] *Ibid.*, p. 648.
[113] *Ibid.*, p. 691.
[114] *Ibid.*, p. 692.
[115] *Ibid.*, p. 351.
[116] *Ibid.*, p. 143.
[117] *Ibid.*, p. 66.
[118] *Ibid.*, pp. 71–72.
[119] *Ibid.*, p. 337.
[120] *Ibid.*, p. 338.
[121] *Ibid.*, p. 229.
[122] *Ibid.*, p. 407.
[123] *Ibid.*, p. 491.
[124] *Ibid.*, p. 280.
[125] *Ibid.*, p. 489.
[126] *Ibid.*, p. 495.
[127] *Ibid.*, p. 626.
[128] Dostoevsky, *C. W.*, VII, 48.
[129] *Ibid.*, pp. 15, 26.
[130] *Ibid.*, p. 42. Yarmolinsky dubs him "a babe at fifty." (Avrahm Yarmolinsky, *Dostoevsky: His Life and Art* [New York, 1960], p. 288.)
[131] Dostoevsky, *C. W.*, VII, 67.
[132] *Ibid.*, p. 86.
[133] *Ibid.*, p. 129.

[134] *Ibid.*, p. 129.
[135] *Ibid.*, p. 216.
[136] *Ibid.*, p. 448.
[137] *Ibid.*, p. 165.
[138] *Ibid.*, p. 195.
[139] *Ibid.*, p. 288.
[140] See, for example, *ibid.*, pp. 81, 99, 133, 329, 330, and 530.
[141] *Ibid.*, p. 440.
[142] *Ibid.*, p. 441.
[143] *Ibid.*, p. 246.
[144] *Ibid.*, p. 250.
[145] *Ibid.*, p. 103.
[146] *Ibid.*, p. 122.
[147] *Ibid.*, pp. 700–02.
[148] *Ibid.*, p. 614.
[149] Dostoevsky, *C. W.*, VIII, 21.
[150] *Ibid.*, p. 448.
[151] *Ibid.*, p. 214.
[152] *Ibid.*, p. 137.
[153] *Ibid.*, p. 237.
[154] *Ibid.*, p. 351.
[155] *Ibid.*, p. 502.
[156] *Ibid.*, p. 594.
[157] *Ibid.*, p. 217.
[158] *Ibid.*, p. 320.
[159] Somewhat similarly, Myshkin is "unable to endure" and "fears" the face of Nastasya Filippovna (Dostoevsky, *C. W.*, VI, 659).
[160] Dostoevsky, *C. W.*, VIII, 275.
[161] *Ibid.*, p. 276.
[162] Dostoevsky, *C. W.*, IX, 189–90.
[163] *Ibid.*, p. 428.
[164] *Ibid.*, p. 442.
[165] *Ibid.*, p. 545.
[166] *Ibid.*, pp. 229–30.
[167] Rimvydas Silbajoris, "The Children in *The Brothers Karamazov*," *The Slavic and East European Journal*, VII, 1 (Spring, 1963), 31.
[168] N. K. Mikhailovsky, "Zhestoki talant," *F.M. Dostoevsky v russkoi kritike*, ed. A. A. Belkin (Moscow, 1956), p. 359.
[169] Edward Wasiolek, *Dostoevsky: The Major Fiction* (Cambridge, Mass., 1964), p. 186.

[170] M. A. Antonovich, "Mistiko-asketicheski roman," *F. M. Dostoevsky v russkoi kritike,* ed. Belkin, p. 260.

[171] Dostoevsky, *C. W.,* IX, 410.

[172] *Ibid.,* p. 44.

[173] Dostoevsky, *C. W.,* X, 173.

[174] *Ibid.,* p. 184.

[175] Silbajoris, p. 33. He also calls Dmitri "truly a child of the earth" (*ibid.,* p. 32).

[176] Dostoevsky, *C. W.,* IX, 602.

[177] *Ibid.,* p. 521.

[178] *Ibid.,* p. 634. Kalganov is called a "boy" twice by Grushenka and twice by Mitya (*ibid.,* pp. 539, 540, 548, 548); but then, Mitya thrice refers to the prosecutor, Nikolai Parfenovich, as a "boy" (*ibid.,* pp. 582, 583, 631).

[179] *Ibid.,* p. 239.

[180] Dostoevsky, *C. W.,* X, 116.

[181] Dostoevsky, *C. W.,* IX, 15.

[182] *Ibid.,* p. 298.

[183] S. I. Gessen, "Tragedia dobra v 'Brat' iakh Karamazovykh, Dostoevskogo," *O Dostoevskom: Stati* (Providence, R. I., 1966), p. 215. Vivas ventures to say that in Fyodor Pavlovich's "sinfulness" there is "something elemental which flows whence all life, whether good or evil, flows . . ." ("The Two Dimensions of Reality in *The Brothers Karamazov,*" *Dostoevsky: A Collection of Critical Essays,* ed. René Wellek [Englewood Cliffs, N. J.], 1962, p. 88).

[184] Dostoevsky, *C. W.,* IX, 523.

[185] *Ibid.,* p. 367.

[186] Dostoevsky, *C. W.,* X, 152.

[187] Dostoevsky, *C. W.,* IX, 474.

[188] Dostoevsky, *C. W.,* X, 236.

[189] *Ibid.,* p. 237.

[190] Dostoevsky, *C. W.,* IV, 432. The Russian reads *rebyonok.* See also *ibid.,* pp. 318–25.
    At one point, The Gambler tells of a French soldier who allegedly shot a ten-year-old boy merely to unload his rifle; the bullet creased the lad's cheek (*ibid.,* p. 288).

[191] *Ibid.,* p. 370.

[192] *Ibid.,* pp. 366 and 385.

[193] *Ibid.,* p. 348.

[194] Dostoevsky, *C. W.,* I, 407.

[195] Dostoevsky, *C. W.,* II, 249 and 259 ("the blonde," twice).

[196] *Ibid.,* p. 235.

[197] *Ibid.,* p. 260.

[198] *Ibid.,* pp. 256 and 261.

[199] *Ibid.,* p. 241.

[200] *Ibid.,* p. 248. (This is intensified by the phrase: "as she usually did.")

[201] *Ibid.,* p. 259.

[202] *Ibid.,* p. 250.

[203] *Ibid.,* p. 238.

[204] Dostoevsky, *C. W.,* I, 513.

[205] Dostoevsky, *C. W.,* II, 251.

[206] *Ibid.,* p. 426.

[207] *Ibid.,* pp. 461 and 591.

[208] *Ibid.,* pp. 510–11.

[209] *Ibid.,* p. 636.

[210] *Ibid.,* p. 173.

[211] *Ibid.,* p. 180.

[212] *Ibid.,* p. 181.

[213] *Ibid.,* pp. 177–78.

[214] *Ibid.,* pp. 183 and 184.

[215] *Ibid.,* p. 207.

[216] See especially *ibid.,* pp. 209, 214, 215, 216, and 229.

[217] Dostoevsky, C. W., I, 181.

[218] *Ibid.,* p. 90.

[219] *Ibid.,* p. 428.

[220] *Ibid.,* p. 429.

[221] *Ibid.,* p. 430.

[222] *Ibid.,* p. 446.

[223] *Ibid.,* p. 458.

[224] *Ibid.,* p. 459.

[225] *Ibid.,* p. 496.

[226] *Ibid.,* p. 425.

[227] Dostoevsky, *C. W.,* IV, 148.

[228] *Ibid.,* p. 221.

[229] *Ibid.,* pp. 221–22.

CHAPTER EIGHT

The Child in Descriptive Devices

Given Dostoevsky's somewhat sensationalistic tendencies, one is disposed to greet his relatively subtle narrational methods with a ready measure of relief. The rougher the fabric — albeit rich — the more responsible the stitching.

In all its protean appearances, the Dostoevskian child's is often a violent depiction. Alone, such shapes loom large and ominous, but beg for shading. Dostoevsky's ways of shading may be examined in terms of their effects.

Manipulation of apparent physical age often serves dramatic purpose. As has been shown, Dostoevsky constantly grades the ages of his children either up or down to intensify various aspects of their depiction — victimization, genesis of feelings, etc. The mechanics of such gradations are examined early in the present chapter.

As has also been shown, Dostoevsky often marshals the vividly typical to intensify the particular. He employs similar techniques of intensification as well. Just as vivid hypothetical or disturbingly typical children frequently intensify others (for example, the little beggar girl in *The Injured and The Insulted* foreshadows Nellie's future begging and vivifies her past), so the childhoods of Dostoevskian adults appropriately intensify (or mute) their childlikeness. Moreover, the language of childlike adults intensifies their childlikeness.

In addition to such gradations and intensifications, there are continual references, in Dostoevsky, to man in general as a child. Such general references (presumably accruing from the author's belief in God's parenthood) do provide a background that brings out the child-likeness of many Dostoevskian adults, but their mechanization and function are here held separate from his more specific metaphors and similes involving children and childhood. Their examination concludes the current chapter.

Age gradation has been seen above to play a supporting role in the depictions of Kolya Krasotkin, Ilyusha, Kolya Ivolgin, Nellie, and many others. The devices behind such gradations are numerous. Dostoevsky sometimes describes his characters' physical appearance as older or younger; at times, he deliberately manipulates their factual numerical age. Furthermore, the word *"rebyonok"* (which means both "child" and "baby" in Russian) is often conducive to such effects, as are the diminutives of many Russian words.

Perhaps most epitomically representative of these techniques is the description of a person Raskolnikov encounters early in *Crime and Punishment*. Wandering listlessly, as is his wont, along the streets of St. Petersburg, the nearly feverish, preoccupied hero "notices" vaguely ("about twenty paces ahead")

> . . . a walking woman, but at first he paid her no attention whatever . . .[1]

He is "accustomed," Dostoevsky explains, not to notice the things that "flash" before him. But there is something "so strange" about this "walking woman," we read, that Raskolnikov's attention at first reluctantly and even begrudgingly gains gradual focus:

> He suddenly began to wonder what exactly was so strange about this woman? First of all she was, surely, a very young girl . . .[2]

Thrice termed a "woman," the stranger becomes — as we see her through Raskolnikov's sharpening eyes — a girl by preemption, and, by supposition, a young girl at that. The word "so" and especially the question mark (which seems less self-conscious in the Russian) open descriptive doors through which the subjective judgment "surely" slips in virtually unnoticed. Most important, the more flexible (than in English) word order allows in Russian the phrase "girl very young" with a grace disarming to the undiscerning reader. Whether one is aware of it or not, this woman is, in the Russian, suddenly (as her "strangeness" makes natural this technique of descriptive inquiry to which the Russian language's flexibility so lends itself) a girl who is immediately extremely young. Extremely — because the word "young" (*molodaya*) is here employed in a form (*molo denkaya*) which carries some additional emphasis even apart from the word "very" (*ochen*).

The technique persists. After two sentences which seek the "woman's" strangeness in her clothing, we read: "To top it all off, the girl was walking unsteadily . . ." She is now without doubt a girl. Yet Dostoevsky must have her still younger. Having sowed the seeds of her youthful appearance, it is now an easy matter for the author to reap their harvest. Raskolnikov meets the oncoming "girl" opposite a public bench, upon which she collapses in apparent exhaustion. He even wonders if she is drunk (a descriptive technique used continually by Dostoevsky to render strange appearances credible [3]), and we now see her through his eyes at close range:

Before him was an exceedingly young little face of about sixteen, even, perhaps, only fifteen . . . The girl, it seemed, was aware of very little . . .[4]

She is now even more than "exceedingly" young, because again the diminutive form ("*molodenkoe*") is employed. Moreover, the diminutive of "face" (*lichiko*) loses a touch of its youngness in the English "little face." Most important, the girl's numerical age seems to decrease as, through Raskolnikov, we scrutinize her more closely.

But here Raskolnikov observes a "greasy," heavyset sensual-looking man of about thirty who has stopped nearby and who,

as everything indicated, wanted very much also to approach the *little girl* for a purpose of his own.[5]

The Russian word "*devochka*" (little girl) is incredibly far in meaning, considering that it follows so close — one page — in context upon the word "woman" (*zhenshchina*) used repeatedly above. The potential victim has thus a woman's desirability and a little girl's helplessness. But worse, insinuations of pedophilia are unmistakable, especially since Raskolnikov becomes "viciously enraged" even though the other man has made not a single move, and his intentions are thus far no more explicit than mere and slightly inspired conjecture.

Having driven away the alleged child molester, Raskolnikov "explains" the girl's situation to a policeman. (She has by now twice more been termed "little girl.") The policeman bends over her, and

. . . his features took on sincere compassion.
"What a terrible pity!" he said, shaking his head.
"Still exactly like a *child*. Been tricked, that's for sure." [6]

The word is "*rebyonok.*" Here, just as her victimization looms the most likely, this "woman" has finally reached the extreme of age gradation: part child, part baby. The entire transformation requires only two and one half pages.

The process continues. She is a "girl" (*devushka*) when the policeman asks where she lives, but a "little girl" (*devochka*) when she answers thickly in exclamations that strongly suggest her victimization.[7]

Once more the policeman expresses commiseration for the girl, whereupon Dostoevsky typically speculates that perhaps the man had had similar daughters (*dochki* — again, a diminutive) grow up at home.

The episode culminates with Raskolnikov imagining the girl's further victimization at home (her mother will find out, beat — perhaps even lash — the girl, and drive her into the streets; she'll end in the hospital, a cripple at seventeen, etc., etc.). This grim projection of the girl's future is touched off by three quick references to her as "little girl" (*devochka*), the last of which is Raskolnikov's exclamation: "Poor little girl!" [8]

This seemingly small incident has three large relations to the rest of the novel. As mentioned above, Raskolnikov's sympathy for this little girl victim and others serves to intensify his own childlikeness. (Also as seen above, the Dostoevskian child often experiences deep pity when others suffer, whereas the Dostoevskian adult typically and tendentiously feels an element of "undeniable pleasure."[9]) Second, the incident just discussed is also important in Dunya's depiction, because Raskolnikov ends by comparing her potential fate with that of the "little girl," projected. Furthermore, this little episode returns to haunt Raskolnikov later in the novel. (He has just hidden all the "ends" of his crime under a stone.) Smugly passing by the bench upon which the above victim had collapsed, he feels a sudden, horrible revulsion. As if to echo the effect of the girl's previous age gradation, she is now twice more termed "the little girl."[10]

The above techniques are often employed in the depiction of Dostoevskian children. As a child is victimized, its age abruptly becomes younger. But Dostoevsky typically derives persuasive effect from both halves of (strangely reconciled) contradiction. Despite the downward gradation of its age, a child victim remains old enough to think — to apprehend its plight. The Dostoevskian female pedophilia victim, for example, has almost invariably the sexual desirability of an older girl, the helplessness of a younger girl, and a near-woman's capacity for apprehending her victimization. Further persuasive factors (which often effect a strange reconciliation of such extremes) are the victim's suicides (insisting implicitly upon their capacity for mature suffering) and the victimizers' constant encomiums to "innocence" (the reader himself need be no Humbert to envision their vile delight).

Later in *Crime and Punishment*, Luzhin describes a female who apparently hung herself in the attic when Svidrigailov had finished with her. The description, under close analysis, seems purposely vague and mysterious, but its techniques — keen and clear. The victim, half-starved and "inhumanly" beaten by her aunt, is ". . . a deaf and dumb little girl [*devochka*] of about fifteen and even fourteen . . ."[11] one should note that this girl is set in "downward age motion" from the very first. (Similarly, the girl on the bench above was "sixteen, even, perhaps, only fifteen.") Yet the phrase here ("fifteen and even fourteen") does begin a (typically strange) reconciliation between "little girl" and "fifteen," although the task is not so great in the Russian: The diminutive *"devochka"* adds here a measure of pathos that is independent of lowering age, which "little girl" perhaps does not convey in English.

After the girl's suicide, the investigation revealed, says Luzhin,

. . . that *the rebyonok* had been — cruelly abused by Svidri-gailov.[12]

Just as the reader learns of the girl's double victimization (presumably, rape plus suicide), she is typically graded down to part child, part baby. Perhaps the rape's shock quality detracts from this extreme age gradation; perhaps pedophilia even justifies the girl's becoming a child; and perhaps words such as "mysterious," "it seems," and "all of this was unclear . . . all was couched in rumor" further obscure the victim's developmental duality. But the facts of Dostoevsky's descriptive technique are relatively clear. The victim's extremes (all strangely reconciled in context) are: age fifteen — baby; mature sexual attraction — immature innocence; and adult mental suffering — childlike helplessness.

It will be remembered that Nellie is described (at various stages of victimization) as potentially eleven, twelve, thirteen, fourteen, and fifteen. The Gentle Creature is similarly versatile. As her story begins, the protagonist purports to relate his "most important impression — the synthesis of everything":

> precisely that she was terribly young, so young that she seemed fourteen years old. And yet she was already only three months away from sixteen. However, that was not what I wished to say — the synthesis was not in that at all.[13]

The technique employed is that (examined above) of describing "by being wrong." Among its advantages here are (1) the factitious issue of synthesized impression detracts from age manipulation; (2) the girl seems both sixteen and fourteen (her real age, fifteen, has not even been mentioned); her subsequent victimization has thus the potential for sixteen-year-old apprehension of fourteen-year-old helplessness; and (3) the strange man's character attains a measure of development through his disturbed, self-conscious words.

But Dostoevsky must have the girl far younger before suicide. She is allied with children: tauntingly by the protagonist (who implies she could easily obtain work teaching tiny children[14]) and respectfully (he notices that an icon of the Mother of God with her baby is "dear" to the girl[15]). He observes "much of the child" in the girl's curiosity [16] and notes her "almost girlish open-heartedness." [17] He discovers that she had taught six tiny children at an aunt's, where "they had intended to sell her." [18] He derives strange pleasure from being twenty-five years her senior, and he purposely perverts (as seen above) her childhood memories, which she "would relate in her chatter (the charming chatter of innocence)." [19]

Just prior to the girl's suicide, she has a brief reconciliation with her husband — or, rather, he briefly ceases to torture her. She immediately laughs "with such a childlike laugh, a sweet one, just as before our marriage . . ." [20] She seems relieved, he concludes, that he will leave her alone.

> "I thought you were going to leave me alone" — that's what she told me then on Tuesday. Oh, idea of a little ten-year-old girl! [21]

These two passages immediately precede the man's renewed amorous advances and her suicide. Clutching the icon picturing Holy Virgin and babe, she jumps from a window to her death, as helpless as ten and as painfully aware of it, perhaps, as few sixteen-year-olds could be.[22]

In *The Brothers Karamazov*, Lise Khokhlakova's age gradation similarly highlights her abuse. Alyosha delivers a letter from Lise to Ivan which the latter scornfully shreds and scatters:

> "Not yet sixteen, I think, and she's already offering herself!" he said contemptuously . . .[23]

Ivan mentions the age of sixteen as if Lise were fifteen: one could easily infer that he has in mind her next birthday. (She is, of course, only fourteen.) But the raising of Lise's age at such a moment serves somehow to verify the authenticity of her credentials at no palpable loss to the situation's unseemliness. Helpless little fourteen-year-old girl or confused adolescent at the edge of womanhood — Lise is still greatly to be pitied.

Pressing this dramatic advantage, Dostoevsky immediately raises her age still further by insidious implication:

"What do you mean, offering herself?" exclaimed Alyosha.

"It's clear enough, how a lewd woman offers herself."

"Ivan, Ivan, what are you saying?" Alyosha sadly and hotly defended her. "She's a child, you're wronging a child!"[24]

The word is twice "rebyonok." Accused as a willful wanton woman, the girl is abused as a tiny helpless child. Seldom has even Dostoevsky reconciled such incompatible extremes with such dramatic diplomacy.

As seen above, Dostoevsky frequently employs the word "rebyonok" to effect intensive victimization. In *The Fir Tree and The Wedding,* for example, the governess's son is "a boy" at first, but "the rebyonok" (1) when he does not even dare to cry, "pummeled" by a bully and (2) when ordered by his mother not to "bother" the other children, who are playing nearby.[25] Similarly, when he pathetically tries to defend the eleven-year-old girl from Yulian Mastakovich, the "boy" is a "rebyonok": (1) when the man "strictly" tells him to return to the children he must not bother; and (2) when the man tries to "lash him out" from under a table with his "long handkerchief."[26]

The childhoods of Dostoevskian adult characters often serve symmetrically to balance their childlikeness in later life. Such childhoods appropriately intensify or minimize the child in its later adult.

Perhaps the most salient example of such effective correlation is The Raw Youth. As seen above, Arkadi's memories of his childhood serve as a series of vivid mirrors that reflect and intensify his somewhat distorted attitudes and apprehensions pervading the novel's present. In fact, as late as page 545 there begins a four-page flashback describing how Arkadi had been humiliated while receiving traveling money at a certain Prince V—sky's.

After ten minutes, a "lackey" brings the money "in his hands." When Arkadi flies into a rage, demanding to receive the funds from "the master," the servant disappears. Next, Arkadi is examined from afar through the imperious pince-nez of a haughty nobleman who smiles "viciously" and then vanishes. "Oh, these insulters begin as children!" exclaims Arkadi in the novel's present, "while still in their families, they are taught to insult by their own mothers!"[27] The same servant returns, now evincing aggressive disrespect, and re-hands Arkadi the money. "Trifles," concludes

Arkadi, "the tantrums of a baby — perhaps, but for me it was a wound — "

a wound which has not healed even yet . . .[28]

Indeed, the mere sight of this nobleman is later enough to "reopen" Arkadi's "wound." [29]

Besides the above incident and Arkadi's many childhood memories treated here in Chapter Three, there are two additional episodes which intensify his childlikeness.

Early in the novel, Arkadi is walking along the street, thinking how vile life can be, when:

> I met a little boy, so little that it seemed strange for him to be alone on the street at such an hour; he appeared to be lost; a woman stopped for a minute to listen to him, but, understanding nothing of what he said, threw up her hands and walked on, leaving him alone in the dark. I started over to him, but he got afraid for some reason and ran away.[30]

This entire passage can be construed as a microcosm of Arkadi's aloneness. The child is of the type described above as seeming almost artificially inserted into the text. Here, Arkadi's sympathy for the little boy is conveyed to the reader by a telling method of conscientious detail. Arkadi forgets his own problems and pities the child with an alacrity typical of the Dostoevskian childlike adult.

Such pity has far greater effect in the story of how Arkadi cares for an abandoned baby — a "three- or four-week-old whining little girl." [31] He manages to obtain the help of a couple who had recently lost a little baby girl, "the main thing — their only one, born after eight years of childless marriage . . ." Despite everyone's efforts, the baby becomes seriously ill, and Arkadi's description of her death suggests a genesis of feeling as young as any that one could imagine — even in Dostoevsky.

> . . . and she died towards evening, with her dear large dark eyes fixed on me *as if she already understood*. . . . I did not cry, I simply wailed that night . . .[32]

The Russian verb form *"ponimala"* (understood) stresses the action, implying protraction and/or repetition.

It is interesting that Dostoevsky similarly describes his own two baby daughters. In a letter to A. N. Maikov, he writes that Sonya "resembles me, even humorously, even strongly."

> The baby is just a month old . . . lies there — *as if composing a novel!* [33]

Nor does Dostoevsky fail to find advanced understanding in his second daughter; in another letter to A. N. Maikov:

> Lyuba is healthy and starting to *understand everything.*[34]

And again, to S. A. Ivanova:

> Lyuba is healthy and happy, a sweet, bright rebyonok, loves us, is beginning to talk, *understands everything,* and already walks across the room.[35]

Both Varenka (*Poor People*) and Nastenka (*White Nights*) recall their first feelings of love for a man. Both were fifteen at the time, and both blushed repeatedly, causing the objects of their awakening adoration to blush also.[36] Each past incident intensifies the sensitiveness, helplessness, and embarrassment that persists in its respective narrational present.

The childhoods of Mitya and Alyosha Karamazov are in several respects quite different from those of Ivan and Smerdyakov. All four childhoods are exceedingly instrumental in shaping the reader's reactions to these adults throughout the novel.

The two pages describing Mitya's childhood [37] seem calculated to engage one's sympathy and even indignation. The boy is called "Mitya" seven times, "little son" once, "boy" once, and "rebyonok" *nine* times, usually at moments of victimization or even ironic accusation. For example, Fyodor Pavlovich "abandoned his rebyonok," there was "no one to change the rebyonok's little shirt," and:

If his daddy had remembered about the boy, . . . he would have sent him off to the hut again, because the rebyonok might have interfered with his debauching.[38]

Alyosha is also called a rebyonok when sent off by his father to be brought up elsewhere.[39] Moreover, he is mockingly referred to as "the little girlie" (*devchonka*) by his schoolmates [40] and as "my angel" by his father, who "suddenly smiled his long, half-drunk, but not devoid of cunning and drunken slyness smile." [41]

Significantly, neither Ivan nor Smerdyakov are termed *"rebyonok"* when their childhoods are described.

Furthermore, Alyosha has a deeply positive and almost religious experience in childhood which develops him before the reader much as does the eight-year-old Father Zosima's first religious experience,[42] whereas Ivan precociously pens an article that "sets atheists applauding"[43] and Smerdyakov "loves very much to hang cats and bury them later, with ceremony."[44] At "about twelve," the boy Smerdyakov is quick to wonder where light came from on the first day if God created the sun, moon, and stars only on the fourth.[45] Despite earlier discouragement, he evinces a short-lived interest in reading at "about fifteen."[46]

Polzinsky devotes most of his study to Dostoevsky's views on education.[47] In a letter to "an unknown mother" dated March 27, 1878, Dostoevsky gives advice on how to bring up a child,[48] and in two other letters he gives detailed advice concerning what a child should read and at what age.[49]

It is well known that Dostoevsky held in great disfavor what he deemed to be artificial foreign influences on Russian life. In *The Diary* of 1876, he goes so far as to "daresay" that la bonne (who teaches the child French from its very first murmur) is in the moral sense precisely what masturbation is in the physical.[50]

In Dostoevsky's notes for a novel he never wrote, *The Life of a Great Sinner,* he plans as follows:

. . . A single, but detailed psychological analysis of how the writers, for instance. "The Hero of Our Time" (Lermontov), affect a child.[51]

One should note that Ivan's article prepares for and intensifies the presentation of his child victims and Grand Inquisitor scene, as does Smerdyakov's "astronomical" sophistry, his subsequent approval of renouncing God in order to save one's life in order to serve God better.[52] Also most significant throughout the novel is that Mitya alone, of the three sons of Fyodor Pavlovich, grew up expecting to be of independent means.[53]

As with Ivan and Smerdyakov, the childhoods of Stavrogin and Versilov tend appropriately to mute their adult childlikeness.

Raised by the "baby," Stepan Trofimovich, who often woke him up to cry upon his shoulder,[54] it is little wonder that Stavrogin reacted by developing an aloof armor of somewhat contemptuous, almost superhuman self-control. It is unlikely, we read, that the young Stavrogin loved his mother, who spoke few words to the boy but persuaded him with her gaze, which he "always and somehow diseasedly" felt fixed upon him.[55] Finally,

> When they sent him off to school at age fifteen, he was frail and pale, *strangely quiet and pensive.*[56]

All this seems a fitting prelude to Stavrogin's often bizarre and always unchildlike behavior throughout the novel.

Also enigmatic and unchildlike is Versilov, whose unchildlikeness similarly mirrors what little we know of his childhood. With a pensive smile, he tells Arkadi late in the novel that there are many pensive children — children who from early childhood brood about the problems of their family and environment. "I noticed these pensive ones while still at school," he continues,

> . . . I myself was a pensive child . . . Just like you, I never liked my friends.[57]

Just as adult childlikeness is often intensified by sympathy for and a rapport with children, so the childlike adult's words sometimes make for similar intensification. There can be little doubt concerning Dostoevsky's voracious interest in the language of children,[58] and it seems logical that he occasionally placed this language upon the lips of his childlike adults. The words of Lizaveta Prokofevna (*The Idiot*) and Marya Timofeevna (*The Possessed*) furnish persuasive examples.

A. V. Chicherin has noted that Lizaveta Prokofevna — whom Simmons calls "expertly drawn"[59] — evinces a child's honest eagerness[60] when she rather vehemently questions Myshkin about the nature of his feelings for Aglaya (at the end of part two of the novel).

> Lizaveta Prokofevna, the General's wife, expresses herself in bursts, seizing upon the strongest words . . .[61]

This is true enough: her third degree is choppy, repetitive, and childishly petulant.

When both Myshkin and the reader first meet Lizaveta Prokofevna, however, her mode of expression is perhaps even more suggestive of a child.[62] From the very beginning, she impetuously repeats capricious whims in choppy phrases.

For example, she employs the Russian "Ya khochu" (I want) seven times (with incremental rapidity: 1 — 2 — 4) on three consecutive pages.[63] Hers, here, is a child's naïve curiosity, humorously struggling against a lack of attention span. Her impatience to hear the Prince "tell something" shows typically through and in her words:

> "Why? What's strange here? Why shouldn't he tell? Has a tongue. I want to know how he talks. About anything."[64]

Her continual exclamatory interruptions reveal an impressionistic acquaintance with what the others say. Seizing suddenly upon individual words, she struggles bravely and tenaciously with their potential meanings. Even when she strives to express her own thoughts, the results are similar.[65]

All this is supported by Dostoevsky ("The General's wife questioned impatiently, rapidly, sharply . . ."[66]) and by Lizaveta Prokofevna herself, who compares herself to a child.[67]

Marya Timofeevna's language renders her childlike through its candid earnestness and (albeit disarming) simplicity. Vyacheslav Ivanov speaks of the "ineffable truths" that Marya "reveals to us," in a child's language and in symbols of her childlike clairvoyance.[68]

His reference is to the long passage ending with Marya's first mention of her "child" (discussed above).

Perhaps Dostoevsky's most unusual intensification device involving the child is exploited in *The Possessed*. It concerns the birth of Shatov's wife's child by Stavrogin. As Shatov listens from outside, the birth is strikingly described in terms of sound:

> Finally, there rang out from the room no longer groans but horrible, purely animal cries, unendurable, impossible. He started to cover his ears, but was unable . . . Now, at last, a new cry sounded, a cry at which Shatov shuddered and sprang from his knees, the cry of an infant, weak and discordant. . . . A wrinkled, horribly helpless little creature was crying . . . but crying and announcing itself as if it had some kind of fullest right to life . . . .[69]

These graphic sounds are twice carefully prefigured. First, early in the novel, one learns that Lyamshin — a master of mouthed imitations — would produce, when his friends were unusually bored, the sounds of "a pig, a thunderstorm, labor with a baby's first cry, etc., etc."[70] Secondly, Lyamshin is later described as a "rogue" who at Stepan Trofimovich's gatherings "would imitate upon demand various old Jews, the confession of a deaf peasant woman, or a baby's birth . . ."[71] These two descriptions comprise a strange but effective prelude to the passage cited above, wherein the sounds depicted seem vividly but almost disturbingly familiar in context. This is probably because these two unusual intensifications, prophetic accuracy notwithstanding, are both in a somewhat humorous vein that sits uneasily upon their subsequent realization and perhaps because the reader — formerly left to create the sounds in his own mind — feels subconsciously slightly in league with Lyamshin when the latter's tone is later proved so inappropriate.

Another such unusual intensification in Dostoevsky is a conversation between the "little tykes" (Nastya, age eight, and Kolya, seven) in *The Brothers Karamazov*. Baby-sitting, Kolya Krasotkin overhears their words, which presumably offer their interpretation of the fact that Katerina, a servant girl, has just "unexpectedly announced" that she "intends, towards morning, to give birth to a little baby." [72] The colloquy is marked by atypical Dostoevskian emotional control and narrational restraint, yet it evinces the author's typical rich insight into the thoughts and feelings of children:

> "I'll never, ever believe," Nastya heatedly babbled, "that the granny finds babies out in the vegetable garden, between the cabbage rows. 'Cause now it's winter, and there are no rows, so the granny couldn't bring Katerina a little baby girl."
>
> "Fooh!" Kolya whistled to himself.
>
> "Or here's what: they bring the babies from somewhere, but only if you're married."
>
> Kostya stared fixedly at Nastya, listening in deep contemplation.
>
> "Nastya, you stupe," he finally declared, firmly and coolly, "Katerina can't have any baby at all. She isn't even married."
>
> Nastya got horribly heated.
>
> "You don't understand anything," she snapped angrily, "maybe there was a husband, only he's in prison now, and here she's having a baby."
>
> "Has she really got a husband in prison?" Kostya inquired with grave respect.
>
> "Or else here's what," Nastya interrupted eagerly, completely rejecting and forgetting her former hypothesis, "she hasn't got a husband, you're right there, but she wanted to get married, so she started thinking about it, and she thought, and thought, and thought until a little baby came without any husband."
>
> "Well if that's it," agreed Kostya, completely de-defeated, "how was I supposed to know if you didn't say so before?"
>
> "Well kiddies," said Kolya, striding towards them into the room, "I see you're a dangerous lot!" [73]

If it is useful to consider that the relationship of Alyosha and Kolya "re-echoes in microcosm the tremendous issues of the book," [74] then it should perhaps be noted that several aspects of this relationship are subtly but effectively intensified by the combination of Kolya and the "tykes." One can find much of Alyosha's Kolya — precocious insights mixed with brazen naïveté and an aggressive independence that attempts to mask a vulnerable and vital desire for approbation — in Kolya's tykes. We are told, for example, that when Nastya usually won these sophisticated discussions, Kostya would appeal to Kolya Krasotkin, whose decision both parties regarded as absolute.[75] In fact, the above passage is prefaced by the remark that when the children saw Kolya stop to listen, "they continued their altercation even more heatedly." [76]

As stated above, there are sometimes references in Dostoevsky to man in general as a child, often with the implication of God's parenthood and, occasionally, purporting to establish a landowner as the father of his serfs.

Many of these have been discussed — for example, Alyosha's, Arkadi's, and Versilov's hope that man will become as a child and Myshkin's statement about God's rejoicing in man as in his own child. Further examples are Goryanchikov's reference to nobles as "fathers, in a certain sense," of the serfs,[77] and Foma Opiskin's eloquent, albeit hypocritical and self-glorifying, exhortation to Rostanev. "Be just and compassionate to your serfs," says Foma,

> These same people — are the image of God, young and entrusted to you . . . like children.[78]

The greatest concentration of such references is undoubtedly in *The Brothers Karamazov*, wherein they total twenty. Many of these are to be found in Father Zosima's Life or in the Grand Inquisitor scene, the most logical places, perhaps, to propound God's parenthood.

As stated above, these general references are here distinguished from more specific metaphors and similes involving children and childhood, many of which, especially similes, are discussed in Chapter Seven of the present study.

The Diary's most interesting such trope is probably what Dostoevsky writes of "publicity" in a critical article about Russian literature:

. . . we love publicity and fondle it like a newborn babe. We love this little imp, who has just cut his strong, healthy little teeth. He sometimes bites awry; he is still learning to bite. But we laugh at his pranks, his childish mistakes; we laugh lovingly, and why not? We forgive him because he is a child! . . . It's all healthy — all young juices, a young, inexperienced strength that gushes, bursting free like a fresh, clear spring! All good, healthy signs! [79]

The trope is indeed complex. Simile at once becomes metaphor, whereupon numerous and diverse implications, suddenly flushed, rise high upon the wing. For example, the "we" who love publicity here seem to do so because, having begotten it, they see a miniature of their own strengths and weaknesses, stumbling along delightfully, with incremental control and a tendency towards lovable misbehavior that is nearly evil.

The most unusual trope in Dostoevsky's *Collected Works* is probably one set forth early in *White Nights:*

There is something inexpressibly touching in our St. Petersburg nature when, with the coming of spring, it suddenly displays its entire might and all the powers given it from above, dresses up, primps, and splashes itself with flowers . . . It somehow involuntarily reminds me of a lame, consumptive girl you look upon with pity and sometimes, with a kind of compassionate love, or sometimes, you simply fail to notice her, but suddenly, in a single instant she somehow inadvertently becomes inexpressibly, miraculously lovely. Stunned and enraptured, you involuntarily ask yourself: What power could have caused these sad, thoughtful eyes to shine with such fire? What summoned the blood to these pale, emaciated cheeks? What splashed with passion the tender features of her face? Wherefore swells this breast? What so abruptly summoned life, strength, and beauty to this poor girl's face, set it shining with such a smile, revived it with such sparkling, glittering laughter? You look around, searching for someone; you conjecture . . . But the instant passes, and, perhaps, the very next day you will meet again the very same thoughtful, listless gaze as before, the very same pale face, the same submissiveness and

timidness of motion and even remorse, even traces of some
kind of morbid grief and vexation at a fleeting, heedless
passion . . . And you regret that evanescent beauty faded
so quickly, so irrevocably, that it flashed before you so de-
ceivingly and fruitlessly — you regret not having had time
even to fall fully in love . . .[80]

Although this passage presumably owes both its beauty and bad taste
to its protagonist's Romantic pen, one wonders whether it produced a
blush or two in the aging Dostoevsky. Its several Gogolian touches,
however, seem yet more savorable with age: for example, the fact that
St. Petersburg's glorious spring splendor is likened to a sickly girl,
who only four lines later justifies the comparison, while, in the mean-
time, one feels somewhat uneasy at "simply not noticing" the very
object which is under such careful and extravagant scrutiny. It is
similarly difficult to ignore the fact that "the instant" has a potentially disturbing antecedent, but even more disturbing is the strangely
reconciled suggestion (here, the techniques of Gogol and Dostoevsky
merge and perhaps overlap) that the girl feels remorse for the little
glory that was hers. Finally, the passage culminates in a pun which,
though compounded by attending ambiguity, superbly cements the
entire simile-again-become-metaphor. Since, in the Russian, both
"beauty" (*krasota*) and "girl" (*devushka*) are feminine in gender,
the phrase *"polyubit eyo"* (translated above as "to fall fully in
love") can refer first to the beauty of a St. Petersburg spring; second, to the girl's beauty; and third, to the beauty herself. Ambiguity
further ensues from the fact that *"polyubit"* ranges in potential
meaning from "come to like" to "love" and also from the versatility of *"naprasno"* (here rendered "fruitlessly"), which has connotations ranging from "to no avail" to "unjustly," both with a
slight flavor of "shouldn't."

There are a considerable number of references to children as
"little birdies" in Dostoevsky, although the comparison is perhaps
more natural in Russian than in English. Of these references, Prince
Myshkin's is certainly the most significant.

O God! When these sweet little birdies look at you, happy
and trusting, it is shameful to deceive them! I call them

little birdies because there is nothing better than a little birdie in the world.[81]

Children are also called birdies by Kolya Krasotkin,[82] Makar Ivanovich (thrice),[83] Svidrigailov (twice),[84] Mr. Golyadkin,[85] Polzunkov,[86] and Makar Devushkin (twice),[87] who compares a poor, cold, scared beggar boy to "a little birdie that has fallen from its broken nest."

Moreover, the childlike and helpless Varenka,[88] Katerina (*The Landlady*),[89] and Sonya Marmeladov[90] are all likened to little birds.

Finally, children are directly associated with birds in Dostoevsky. For example, Marya Aleksandrovna (*Uncle's Dream*) declares: ". . . bad is the child who soils his nest!"[91] The most striking such implied similarity is perhaps Father Zosima's evangelical exhortation:

Ask God, my friends, for joy. Be joyous as children, as the birds of heaven.[92]

Notes

[1] F. M. Dostoevsky, *Collected Works* (Moscow, 1956–1958), V, 51.

[2] *Ibid.,* p. 51.

[3] See, for example, Dostoevsky, *C. W.,* IV, 467 ff.; V, 82 ff.; 477; VII, 437; IX, 579.

[4] Dostoevsky, *C. W.,* V, 52.

[5] *Ibid.,* p. 52. My italics.

[6] *Ibid.,* p. 53. My italics.

[7] *Ibid.,* pp. 53 and 54, respectively.

[8] *Ibid.,* all on the lower half of p. 55.

[9] For example:

> Truly, man loves to see his best friend abased before him; for the most part, friendship is founded on abasement . . . (Dostoevsky, *C. W.,* IV, 426).

> . . . that indelicate derision, which sometimes reflects man's pleasure at his neighbor's misfortunes . . . (Dostoevsky, *C. W.,* VI, 6–7).

> There is always something in a person's every misfortune that cheers his neighbor's eye — and this is true no matter who you are (Dostoevsky, *C. W.,* VII, 345).

> . . . man is created physically incapable of loving his neighbor (Dostoevsky, *C. W.,* VIII, 237).

See especially the long such discussion: Dostoevsky, *C. W.,* VII, 537.

[10] Dostoevsky, *C. W.,* V, 115.

[11] *Ibid.,* p. 309.

[12] *Ibid.,* p. 309. My italics.

[13] Dostoevsky, *C. W.,* X, 381.

[14] *Ibid.,* p. 382.

[15] *Ibid.,* p. 383.

[16] *Ibid.,* p. 384.

[17] *Ibid.,* p. 398.

[18] *Ibid.,* pp. 385–86.

[19] *Ibid.,* p. 390.

[20] *Ibid.,* p. 414.

[21] *Ibid.,* p. 414.

[22] It is interesting that an ominous smile seems earlier to prophesy the girl's suicide: the protagonist suddenly sees upon her face

> a smile — distrustful, silent, and unpleasant. I led her into my house with this smile (*ibid.,* p. 391).

[23] *Ibid.*, p. 115.

[24] *Ibid.*, pp. 115–16.

[25] Dostoevsky, *C. W.*, I, 581–82.

[26] *Ibid.*, pp. 583–84.

[27] Dostoevsky, *C. W.*, VIII, 547.

[28] *Ibid.*, p. 548.

[29] *Ibid.*, p. 549.

[30] *Ibid.*, p. 84.

[31] *Ibid.*, pp. 105–07.

[32] *Ibid.*, p. 107. My italics.

[33] F. M. Dostoevsky, *Letters*, ed. A. S. Dolinin (Moscow, 1928–1959), II, 97. My italics. See also pp. 117 and 126.

[34] *Ibid.*, p. 227. My italics.

[35] *Ibid.*, p. 315. My italics.

[36] Dostoevsky, *C. W.*, I, 110 and II, 33.

[37] Dostoevsky, *C. W.*, IX, 15, middle — 17, middle.

[38] *Ibid.*, p. 15.

[39] *Ibid.*, p. 27.

[40] *Ibid.*, p. 29.

[41] *Ibid.*, p. 33.

[42] Both are described above, in Chapter Three and Chapter Five, respectively.

[43] Dostoevsky, *C. W.*, IX, 23–24.

[44] *Ibid.*, p. 158.

[45] *Ibid.*, p. 158.

[46] *Ibid.*, p. 159.

[47] P. S. Polzinsky, *Detski mir v proizvedeniakh Dostoevskago* (Ravel, 1891), pp. 22–85.

[48] Dostoevsky, *Letters*, IV, 11–13.

[49] *Ibid.*, pp. 195–97 and 221–22.

[50] F. M. Dostoevsky, *The Diary of a Writer:* 1873, 1876, 1877 (Paris, YMCA-Press), 1876, 304.

[51] F. M. Dostoevsky, "Plan of the Novel, 'The Life of a Great Sinner,' " trans. S. S. Koteliansky and Virginia Woolf, *The Criterion*, I (October, 1922), No. 1, 23.
All this concern notwithstanding, Dostoevsky seems interested in children's early exposures to sexually mature material — so interested, one can speculate, that his fascination with genesis of feeling sometimes induced him to explore the effects of inappropriate exposure. See, for example, the discussion of Nastenka's childhood reading (Dostoevsky, *C. W.*, II, 32–33) and the account of how Dostoevsky in real life allegedly exposed children to his memory of having raped a ten-year-old girl (F. M. Dostoevsky, *Letters of Fyodor*

Michailovitch Dostoevsky, trans. Ethel Colburn Mayne [New York, 1964], p. 326).

[52] Dostoevsky, *C. W.*, IX, 162–63.

[53] *Ibid.*, p. 17.

[54] Dostoevsky, *C. W.*, VII, 43.

[55] *Ibid.*, p. 43.

[56] *Ibid.*, p. 43. My italics.

[57] Dostoevsky, *C. W.*, VIII, 510–11.

[58] As has been noted (L. P. Grossman, "Problema realizma u Dostoevskogo, *Vestnik Evropy* [February, 1917], p. 76), Dostoevsky wrote to a teacher for "everything" the man knew about children, which he awaited "greedily" just prior to writing about the children in *The Brothers*. Among other things, he specifically requested typical "little words and phrases" (Dostoevsky, *Letters*, IV, 7).

Dostoevsky's continual interest in the language and behavior of children is also strikingly evident in two letters to Anna Grigorevna:

> You gave me great pleasure with your stories about the children. Write about them always. I feel revived and just as if they were with me (Dostoevsky, *Letters*, III, 66).

> How are the children? Write about them in as great detail as possible. . . . I think about the children ceaselessly (*ibid.*, p. 169).

Moreover, Mark Slonim has offered impressive evidence that Dostoevsky was always fond of, at home with, and instantly liked by children (Mark Slonim, *Tri lyubvi Dostoevskogo* [New York, 1953], p. 200).

[59] Simmons, p. 216.

[60] A. V. Chicherin, "Poeticheski stroi yazyka v romanakh Dostoevskogo," *Tvorchestvo F. M. Dostoevskogo*, ed. N. L. Stepanov (Moscow, 1959), p. 432.

[61] *Ibid.*, p. 433.

[62] Dostoevsky, *C. W.*, VI, 62–67.

[63] *Ibid.*, pp. 62–64.

[64] *Ibid.*, p. 64.

[65] See, for example, her humorous, childishly ingenuous usage of the word "good" (*ibid.*, pp. 65–66).

[66] *Ibid.*, p. 62.

[67] *Ibid.*, p. 66.

[68] Vyacheslav Ivanov, *Dostoevsky*, trans. Norman Cameron (New York, 1960), p. 42.

[69] Dostoevsky, *C. W.*, VII, 615–16.

[70] *Ibid.*, p. 37.

[71] *Ibid.*, p. 340.

[72] Dostoevsky, *C. W.*, X, 14.

[73] *Ibid.*, pp. 16–17.

[74] Rimvydas Silbajoris, "The Children in *The Brothers Karamazov," The Slavic and East European Journal,* VII, 1 (Spring, 1963), p. 36.

[75] Dostoevsky, *C. W.,* X, 16.

[76] *Ibid.,* p. 16.

[77] Dostoevsky, *C. W.,* III, 656.

[78] Dostoevsky, *C. W.,* II, 596. See also *The Diary* of 1873, pp. 135, 137–38, 143, 165; *The Diary* of 1876, p. 61; and *The Diary* of 1877, pp. 44, 588–91. See also a reference to people as "the sun's excellent children" in Versilov's idyllic dream (Dostoevsky, *C. W.,* VIII, 514).

[79] Dostoevsky, *The Diary* of 1873, p. 34.

[80] Dostoevsky, *C. W.,* II, 9.

[81] Dostoevsky, *C. W.,* VI, 78.

[82] Dostoevsky, *C. W.,* X, 18–19.

[83] Dostoevsky, *C. W.,* VIII, 431, 438.

[84] Dostoevsky, *C. W.,* V, 455, 506.

[85] Dostoevsky, *C. W.,* I, 364.

[86] *Ibid.,* p. 514.

[87] *Ibid.,* pp. 179, 180.

[88] *Ibid.,* p. 81.

[89] *Ibid.,* p. 483.

[90] Dostoevsky, *C. W.,* V, 330.

[91] Dostoevsky, *C. W.,* II, 288.

[92] Dostoevsky, *C. W.,* IX, 400. See also Dostoevsky, *C. W.,* VIII, 396.

Conclusion

Despite the plentitude of Dostoevskian child personages treated above, there is ample evidence to suggest that such children were accorded still greater prominence at various stages of their creation.

The Brothers Karamazov is perhaps the most striking example, notwithstanding this novel's multiplicity of significant children. Simmons comments that "references to children" in Dostoevsky's early notes for *The Brothers* "suggest that he had designed a more significant role for them than they have in the printed work."[1]

> Dostoevsky began *The Brothers Karamazov* as a novel about children; he visited pedagogical institutions; his first notes on the novel had to do with children.[2]

All this seems true enough. One is struck, for example — among Dostoevsky's spidery sketches of stained-glass windows — by the importance of Lise Khokhlakova in The Notes for the novel.[3] The Notes open with a "Momento" to find out whether one can lie between the tracks under a train passing at full speed.[4] This incident, of course, is a late and relatively minor event in the finished work.

According to Yarmolinsky, Dostoevsky's notes reveal he had "intended to make Dmitry Karamazov guilty of Stavrogin's crime."[5] And also Versilov (*A Raw Youth*)![6]

Both Grossman and Futrell stress the importance children were to have had in *A Raw Youth*.[7]

The same is true of *The Idiot*, the notes for which typically include a young girl's rape.[8]

As has been noted, Sonya (*Crime and Punishment*) is far more idealized than her characterization in The Notes suggests.[9] Her exceeding childlikeness could, in fact, reveal the Dostoevskian child's stubborn refusal to be excluded from the novel's final version.

As both Simmons and Grossman have noted, Netochka was to have had a "male counterpart."[10] Yarmolinsky points out that in the introduction to *The Little Hero*, "omitted from the final version," there is a "girl on the threshold of womanhood" to whom the story is told.[11]

Perhaps most interesting of all is the importance children were to enjoy in *The Life of a Great Sinner*.[12] A boy sees adults kissing,[13] a "lame girl" is constantly exposed to a man's "confessions,"[14] and, typically: "He wanted to shoot himself (a child was exposed at his door)."[15]

All this may significantly contribute to accounting for the Dostoevskian child's numerous other manifestations — as mental image and in descriptive devices. Denied one role, the child often enters disguised for another.

This in turn could perhaps suggest that the child was more a part of Dostoevsky's creative vision than even he would, or possibly could, have admitted.[16] Indeed, Dostoevsky saw children both ubiquitously and presciently. These children generally are not employed as foils; they are primary, not secondary characters.

The ironic and the grotesque frequently redeem, in Dostoevskian child drama, the otherwise sentimental and sensational. Similarly, the child's sweetness and goodness are often, unlike in Dickens, tempered by the impulsive, the corruptible, and even the perverse. At times, Dostoevsky's children are playfully or even vindictively malicious.

Despite such saving graces, the Dostoevskian child has been sharply criticized, primarily for its allegedly inordinate pensiveness[17] and for the factitious protraction of its suffering.[18] It is true that Dostoevsky endowed his children with vast potentials, which fact conduces to his child victims' pathos and his thinking children's pain. It is also true that Dostoevsky's own hypersensitivity and love for children often placed their suffering — as his powers allowed — in vivid, brooding focus. His undeniable sexual perception of children [19] adds a strange and mordant spice to their victimization and apprehension thereof. Whether the ensuing genesis of feeling is worth one's suspension of distaste is a matter which undoubtedly explains in part the divergence of views held by Dostoevsky's critics. But his dramatic examination of the child's potentials in confrontation with the adult world has surely prefigured and influenced much subsequent thinking.[20]

As has here been shown, there is evidence to suggest that Dostoevsky posited in the child an emotional mode of reasoning later displaced by relatively rational thought. This seems compatible with the child's vital role in a Dostoevskian love which (in Zenkovsky's phase) exceeds reason and extends even to communication with the dead. Also favorable to correlation is the Dostoevskian child's unambivalent pity (in Trubitsyn's words) occasioned by the misfortunes of others — a reaction both frequently and tendentiously denied in the Dostoevskian adult.

This is most important. Although, as mentioned above, Dostoevsky's children can be playfully or even vindictively malicious, they do not feel his adults' "evil-gladness" at the troubles of others. Dostoevsky is thus free to temper pathos with "easily vindicated" malice (either the child "knew no better" or had abundant justification); *yet Dostoevsky can still* successfully endow the child with a natural goodness almost invariably lacking in his adults.

The horror of Dostoevsky's most helpless and least pensive child victims assumes such metaphysical dimension as to arraign the very world in which they suffer.

A dual intensification frequently — and in *The Diary*, more explicitly — attends the depiction of such child victims. They are presented as factual and stressed as commonplace: a seemingly faithful journalistic style is laced with vivid detail and occasionally, with pronouncements that such instances are typical. The circumstances of such victimization frequently effect a dual assault upon the reader's sensibilities.

In most cases, however, the reader must imagine what transpires within the child, whose genesis of feelings is implied. Female pedophilia victims are numerous, and they are usually driven towards suicide, which fact still more impellingly presumes painful apprehension of victimization.

Endowing the child with vast potentials, Dostoevsky focuses upon the child's apprehension of its own experiences.

These experiences usually entail a confrontation between the child's potentials and the adult world, resulting in an abrupt and often painful genesis of feelings.

At times, Dostoevsky dwells upon adult ideas gone wild in the child's mind. He also explores the awakenings of family honor and social consciousness in the child. He examines at length the child's early development of perverseness, masochism, and hostility. And he lingers over the awakening of sexual love.

Dostoevskian childhood memories are both stronger and more influential than are any other memories.

Pleasant childhood memories provide an almost holy strength essential for enduring life's tribulations.

Conversely, unhappy childhood memories pursue one long thereafter, especially in dreams and with surprisingly manifold adverse consequences.

The powers of Dostoevskian pleasant childhood memories are most often released during periods of extreme depression and illness. Thus, Dostoevsky seems to illustrate that this inner strength is tapped when most needed.

Dostoevsky's negative and/or disturbed personages are deprived of — or even actively pervert — this power either in themselves or in others.

Aside from their obvious narrative advantages, Dostoevskian childhood memories serve as a background that develops the characters of his adult personages and intensifies their childlikeness.

Dostoevskian narration elusively vacillates between what is and what seems, and mental (or possibly mental) images of children serve to establish a rather tendentious tenuous relationship between illusion and reality.

Appearances by such children often reveal previous occurrences of child victimization returning — via the media of dreams, hallucinations, and illusions — to haunt the victimizer or the victim. Moreover, the child's frequent appearance via these media intensifies its importance to man's thoughts and emotions and perhaps hints at its almost supernatural, mystical significance.

Such media seem ideal for the plastic and vivid depiction of Dostoevskian intense childhood experiences.

So vivid can the unreal thus become that occasionally, the purportedly real is, by contrast, subject to doubt. Conversely, the after-experience of that which may or may not have actually occurred is at times disturbingly graphic and influential. Perhaps even more important, the stubborn after-image of such childhood experiences inevitably and indelibly affects the reader's "present" apprehension of the characters concerned.

The child is a natural and convenient vehicle for the conveyance of Dostoevsky's religious feelings.

Dostoevsky preferred Christ even to Truth and placed children closest to Christ.

Theirs is the Kingdom of Heaven, whereby man learns a dual lesson: To wrong a child is the greatest sin, and one's greatest hope for a harmonious existence and eternal salvation is to become as a child of God.

The Dostoevskian child is often the center of a super-rational love that frequently manifests itself in apparent communication between the living and the dead.

Dostoevsky had the power to imagine convincingly a world of rich details given a minimum of bare fact.

This rich detail is exceedingly rich in children. Numerous, diverse sets of circumstances seem to presume the existence of one or more children who "must be" involved, the feelings they "must experience," and the conclusions one "must draw."

The reality of such hypothesized children gains further dimension as they subtly merge and separate from the typical child and the child in general.

As they materialize both convincingly and abundantly, these children serve to intensify such Dostoevskian themes as child victimization, the genesis of feelings, and the child's impressionableness and vast potentials.

These children — hypothesized either by the author or by his characters — often provide emotional leverage in intense situations.

The child also appears constantly and significantly in the Dostoevskian adult. Indeed, adult childlikeness is distributed in Dostoevsky with catholic generosity.

Suggestive of natural goodness or at least of uncorruptedness, such childlikeness renders Dostoevsky's positive characters credible.

Moreover, it rounds his "villains" and infernal women, both of whom are astonishingly childlike, which fact in turn renders them worthy of credence, sympathy, and salvation. The "criminals" thus appear human, but too primitive to be "sophisticated." Significantly, statements combining children and religion belong both to Dostoevsky's most *and least* noble personages.

Dostoevskian positive characters — for example, Myshkin, Alyosha, and Marya Timofeevna — most often find and/or bring out the child in others. Their childlikeness seems to reinforce "positive goodness," as does their empathy with children. (Myshkin, Alyosha, and Sonya — all often likened to children — are liked by them, and vice versa.)

Least childlike are the law enforcers and persons with vast, unrealized potentials, both of whom understandably lack the natural spontaneity common to Dostoevskian childlike adults. Dostoevsky thus seems to censure those who deny the child either in others (by condemning, pursuing, and prosecuting them) or in themselves (by failing to develop their own potentials). A character's lack of childlikeness suggests the author's lack of sympathy and identification — for example, Katya (*The Brothers*) and "executioners" (*The House of The Dead*). Moreover, childlikeness seems incompatible with a person's appearing mysterious and fascinating (Stavrogin, Versilov). Conversely, childlikeness implies Dostoevsky's sympathy, solicits the reader's, and conduces to the latter's understanding of, and intimacy with, the character involved.

The two major works richest with childlike adults — one early, one late — reveal surviving emphasis but altered function. The wayward childlike adult, unheedful of responsibility (as depicted in *The Injured and The Insulted*), is replaced by the childlike adult who shares in the sufferings of all others (*The Brothers Karamazov*).

Dostoevsky had at his command several descriptive methods drawing directly upon the child. Such devices may be subdivided as gradations, intensifications, and tropes.

Dostoevsky often employs age gradation to calculated dramatic advantage. Children are typically "at their youngest" while being victimized and seem most mature when apprehending their plight. This is sometimes effected through the alteration of a character's apparent, or even factual numerical age. A similar device is the strategic usage of words (including diminutives) implying quite different ages to refer to the same character — also the potentially ambiguous word "rebyonok" (which means both "child" and "baby").

Often, such age manipulation suits nearly antinomical needs. For example, the female pedophilia victim has often a woman's sexual attraction, a child's helplessness, and a woman's awareness of her suffering.

Many seemingly minor or insignificant appearances of children and childhood in Dostoevsky's works actually serve to intensify his more obvious children. He studied extensively the language of children and used it effectively, even for his childlike adults (Lizaveta Prokofevna, Marya Timofeevna). He also considered the child's exposure to adult literature and was presumably interested in the attending genesis of feelings. Most important, the childhoods of Dostoevskian adults appropriately intensify (Arkadi, Varenka, Nastenka, Alyosha, and Mitya) or mute (Ivan, Smerdyakov, Stavrogin, and Versilov) their childlikeness in proportion as manifested in their later lives. Similarly, sympathy for and empathy with children (Raskolnikov, Arkadi, Myshkin, Alyosha, Ivan, and Mitya) intensifies adult childlikeness.

Dostoevsky's penchant for describing adults as children often joins forces with his belief in God's parenthood to produce references to man in general as a child (especially often in Father Zosima's Life and The Grand Inquisitor scene). Tropes involving the Dostoevskian child are at times exceedingly complex. Without question, children are most frequently compared in Dostoevsky to "little birdies."

The exceedingly numerous children in Dostoevsky's works, as well as his nearly inordinate preoccupation with the concept of childhood, in all their obvious and manifold extraordinary aspects, are thus an integral component of his artistic process and creative vision. Since his children are often adult-like and his adults often part children, Dostoevsky's creative vision seems almost inescapably to draw frequently and deeply upon the child.

Most important, Dostoevsky's little children often lead to his biggest ideas. As seen above, Dostoevsky's critics — for example, Shklovsky, Silbajoris, and Belkin — are quick to see his specific, individual children as typical, universal, and symbolic. As has also been seen, numerous Dostoevskian descriptive devices [21] contribute to this effect. The resulting universality of specific Dostoevskian-child instances thus serves both philosophically and stylistically to suggest and support his *Weltanschauung:* all are guilty for all, and man must become as a child before God, living by super-rational love and a belief in God's parenthood.

Notes

[1] Ernest J. Simmons, *Dostoevsky: The Making of a Novelist* (New York, 1962), p. 329.

[2] Edward Wasiolek, *Dostoevsky: The Major Fiction* (Cambridge, Mass., 1964), p. 186.

[3] F. M. Dostoevsky, "Teksty chernovykh zapisei k 'Bratyam Karamazovym,'" *F. M. Dostoevsky: Materialy i issledovania*, ed. A. S. Dolinin (Leningrad, 1935), pp. 111–20.

[4] *Ibid.*, p. 81.

[5] Avrahm Yarmolinsky, *Dostoevsky: His Life and Art* (New York, 1960), p. 302.

[6] *Ibid.*, p. 302.

[7] L. P. Grossman, "Dostoevsky — khudozhnik," *Tvorchestvo F. M. Dostoevskogo*, ed. N. L. Stepanov (Moscow, 1959), p. 407; Michael H. Futrell, "Dostoevsky and Dickens," *English Miscellany*, VII, 80.

[8] F. M. Dostoevsky, *Iz arkhiva F. M. Dostoevskogo: Idiot: Neizdannye materialy*, ed. P. N. Sakulin and N. F. Belchikov (Moscow, 1931), pp. 12, 211. See also R. Lord, "A Reconsideration of Dostoevsky's Novel *The Idiot*," *Slavic and East European Review*, XLV (January, 1967), 31; Simmons, p. 214; and Yarmolinsky, p. 246.

[9] Anaïs Nin, "The Id of Dostoevsky," *Saturday Review* (June 10, 1967), p. 35.

[10] Simmons, p. 42; Grossman, "Dostoevsky — khudozhnik," *Tvorchestvo F. M. Dostoevskogo*, ed. Stepanov, pp. 406–07.

[11] Yarmolinsky, p. 99.

[12] See especially F. M. Dostoevsky, "Plan of the novel, 'The Life of a Great Sinner,'" trans. S. S. Koteliansky and Virginia Woolf, *The Criterion*, I (October, 1922), No. 1, 23–27.

[13] *Ibid.*, p. 29.

[14] *Ibid.*, p. 23.

[15] *Ibid.*, p. 33. See also Yarmolinsky, pp. 268–69, 391.

[16] Twice in The Diary he defends vehemently his love for and deep interest in children. (F. M. Dostoevsky, *The Diary of a Writer*: 1873, 1876, 1877 [Paris: YMCA-Press, 1876], pp. 53–57; 1877, pp. 461–67.)

[17] See, for example, Simmons, p. 343; Maxim Gorky, "Eshchyo o 'Karamazovshchine,'" *F. M. Dostoevsky v russkoi kritike*, ed. A. A. Belkin (Moscow, 1956), p. 395; and Lyubimov (F. M. Dostoevsky, *Letters*, ed. A. S. Dolinin [Moscow, 1928–1959], IV, 410.) – all discussed above – and Trubetskoy, who says of Katya's (*Netochka*) perverse maturity that perhaps she was to become an "infernal woman" (N. S. Trubetskoy, "Tvorchestvo Dostoevskogo pered katorgoi," *The New Review* (March, 1965), No. 78, p. 266).

[18] "It is not without interest," remarks Leonid Grossman, that K. Pobedonostsev ends a letter of June 9, 1879 to Dostoevsky by calling the chapter containing Ivan's victims

> . . . a very strong chapter — but why have you so protracted the children's sufferings! (L. P. Grossman, "Dostoevsky i pravitelstvennye krugi 1870-ykh godov," *Literaturnoe nasledstvo*, No. 15 [Moscow, 1934], p. 90).

See also Ralph Harper, *The Seventh Solitude: Man's Isolation in Kierkegaard, Dostoevsky, and Nietzsche* (Baltimore, Md., 1965), p. 105.

Such considerations are undoubtedly among the causes of Nabokov's calling Dostoevsky "a much overrated, sentimental, and Gothic novelist" (Vladimir Nabokov, *Eugene Onegin: A Novel in Verse by Aleksandr Pushkin, Translated from the Russian, with a Commentary*, III [New York, 1964], 191]; as well as of Rexroth's rather unconscionable claims (Kenneth Rexroth, "The Brothers Karamazov," *Saturday Review* [December 3, 1966], p. 24).

But it must be remembered, as Lossky has noted, that the "huge positive significance" attributed by Dostoevsky to suffering has led certain of his critics to believe that he "nurtured a perverted love for suffering *per se*." (N. Lossky, *Dostoevsky i ego khristianskoe miroponimanie* [New York, 1953], p. 289.) This "positive significance," plus certain pronouncements by Dostoevsky's characters (for example, Ivan's persuasive words about the suffering of innocent children — F. M. Dostoevsky, *Collected Works*, IX [Moscow, 1956–1958], 298 — and the Underground Man's statement that suffering is the sole cause of consciousness — Dostoevsky, *C. W.*, IV, 161 — and even by Dostoevsky himself: "I think that the foremost and most deeply rooted spiritual need of the Russian people is the need to suffer — constantly, unrelievedly, everywhere, and in everything." — Dostoevsky, *The Diary* of 1873, p. 225) — all this, plus suffering's graphic depiction in the *Collected Works*, do easily give rise to suspicions of vicarious masochism and perhaps even of perversion. Distasteful as its manifestations may appear, however, suffering is a vital, inextricable part of Dostoevsky. Its treatment can be termed a literary vice, perhaps, but surely not a mere device.

[19] As shown above, there is evidence that Dostoevsky closely allied the end of childhood with the beginning of sex.

[20] "Fortunately," observes Mark Spilka,

> . . . we are beginning to study the child, in nineteenth century fiction, as *touchstone for sanity*, for secular and Christian love, for brotherhood and natural feeling, in the face of "growing up absurd." [17] (Mark Spilka, *Dickens and Kafka: A Mutual Interpretation* [London, 1963], pp. 265–66. My italics. His footnote seventeen praises "Peter Coveney's pioneer study" — Peter Coveney, *Poor Monkey: The Child in Literature* [Bungay, Suffolk, Great Britain, 1957] — but fails to comment on Dostoevsky's conspicuous absence therein.)

Fitzgerald has advised:

> Try and [sic] get something from a child's point of view as a contrast. It opens up another world. It lightens all the material. (Morley

Callaghan, "Fitzgerald's Paris," *Saturday Review* [March 11, 1967], p. 84.)

Recently, such statements are a legion. For example:

The child's mind has captured the imagination of our time. Children now play leading roles in novel after novel . . . (Virgilia Peterson, "Re-entry Into Childhood," *The New York Times Book Review* [June 26, 1966], p. 4).

The child seems significant even in the now fashionable philosophical cult of Zen:

Zen might be said to offer something in the nature of a return to the simple and direct view of life possible to a child, because children, like "the enlightened," live wholly in the present (Nancy Wilson Ross, *Three Ways of Asian Wisdom: Hinduism, Buddhism, Zen and Their Significance for The West* [New York, 1966], p. 181).

[21] For example, journalistic, factual narration laced with vivid detail; presentation of the particular as typical or representative; and intensifications, such as parallel instances, backgrounds, foreshadowings, and echoings. A device which contributes to the depiction of virtually all manifestations of the child in Dostoevsky is the unusual smile.

Index

Aglaya (*The Idiot*), 52, 179, 180–83

Akim (*The House of the Dead*), 165–66

Aleksandr (*The House of the Dead*), 166

Aley (*The House of the Dead*), 163–64

Almazov (*The House of the Dead*), 165

Alyosha (*The Idiot*), 125–26

Alyosha (*The Injured and the Insulted*), 80, 81, 170, 172–73

Antonovich, M. A., 189, 203n

Arkadi (*A Raw Youth*), 82, 84, 133, 149, 150, 187, 212–13

Barrie, J. M., 61n

Belinski, V. G., 43

Belkin, A. A., 137n, 235

Bem, A. L., 93, 95n

Berdyaev, 70n

Blackmur, R. P., 126–28, 137n

Brothers Karamazov, The, 3n, 4, 15, 32, 43, 50, 51, 76, 83

Bubnova, Madam (*The Injured and the Insulted*), 21–22, 25

Carroll, Lewis, 61n

Chicherin, A. V., 226n

Chizhevsky, Dmitri, 93, 114n

Christ, 119, 120, 127, 131, 174, 233

Christlike, 124, 178

Collected Works, xi, 221

Crime and Punishment, 11, 16, 61, 86, 93, 112, 148, 174, 175, 178, 206, 209, 230

Devushkin, Makar (*Poor People*), 66n, 78

Diary, The, ix, x, 5, 10, 11–13, 25, 26, 27, 42, 76; *of 1876,* xi, 27,

215; *of 1877 x,* 30n, 144; *of 1883,* 60n

Dickens, Charles, 46, 61n, 133
   The Old Curiosity Shop, 133
   Great Expectations, 23
   See also "Little Nell"

Doors of Perception, 98

Dowson, 61n

Dream of the Ridiculous Man, The, 94–95, 98, 120

Dreams, 95–97, 112, 139

Dunya (*Crime and Punishment*), 148, 177

Dzhunkovsky case, 7–10

Eliot, George, 61n

Eternal Husband, The, 14, 19, 109, 124, 125

Fir Tree and the Wedding, The, ix, 29n, 61, 130, 212

Fonvisin, Mme. N. D., 119

Ford, George, 68n

Frank, Joseph, 119, 136n

Futrell, Michael H., 46, 230

Gazin (*The House of the Dead*), 167–68

Gentle Creature, A, 61, 85

Gessen, S. I., 191, 203n

Gide, Andre, vii, xi, xii, 42, 120, 136, 143, 156n

"Glazyonki," 51

Gogol, Nikolai, 12, 150, 192, 194, 222
   The Overcoat, 153

Gogolian style, x, 151–53

Goryanchikov (*The House of the Dead*), 162–68

Grigori (*A Raw Youth*), 123

Grossman, L. P., viii, xin, 31, 39n, 43, 156n, 230, 236n

Grushenka (*The Brothers Karamazov*), 32, 65, 86, 111, 124, 188, 190

Heavenly Christmas Tree, The, 128, 140
House of the Dead, The, 50, 162–67, 234
Hundred-Year-Old Woman, The, 153
Huxley, Aldous, 46, 47, 68n

Idiot, The, 11, 32, 47, 52, 57, 87, 93, 97, 125, 128, 178, 216, 230
Ikhmenev (*The Injured and the Insulted*), 23–24n, 25, 63, 87–88, 110, 170, 171
Ilyusha (*The Brothers Karamazov*), 15, 45, 47, 48, 49, 50–51, 121–23
Injured and the Insulted, The, 15, 19, 23, 46, 49, 61, 78, 80, 81
Ippolit (*The Idiot*), 32n, 33
Ivanov, Vyacheslav, *vii*, 49n, 89n, 115n, 136n, 138n
Ivanova, S. A., 214

Karamazov, Alyosha (*The Brothers Karamazov*), 3, 4, 15, 43, 44–45, 48, 50, 51, 54, 55–59, 65, 75–76, 83, 86, 121–22, 124, 189, 190–91, 211, 219, 221
Karamazov, Dmitri (*The Brothers Karamazov*), 87, 124, 189, 214
Karamazov, Fyodor, (*The Brothers Karamazov*), 32, 111, 152, 191–92
Karamazov, Ivan (*The Brothers Karamazov*), 3–5, 107, 151, 189
Katerina (*The Landlady*), 196
Katya (*The Injured and the Insulted*), 62–64, 170–73
Katya (*Netochka Nezvanova*), 85
Kishensky, 26
Kolya (*The Brothers Karamazov*), 43, 44–45, 48, 49, 50, 53, 218–19
Kolya (*The Idiot*), 52–53
Kolya (*Crime and Punishment*), 27, 29

Kornilova case, 13n, 14, 35n, 143
Kroneberg case, 7, 9–10

Landlady, The, 36n, 61, 80, 95, 196
Leskov, N. S., 100, 115n, 154
Life of a Great Sinner, The, 215, 230
Lise (*The Brothers Karamazov*), 53–59, 63, 211
Little Hero, The, 64–65, 71n, 193, 230
"Little Nell" (Dickens), 46
Liza (*A Raw Youth*), 148
Lizaveta (*Crime and Punishment*), 176, 177
London, 146, 148
Lyubimov, N. A., *ix*, 44, 136n

Magarshack, David, *xi*
Maikov, A. N., 214
Makar, Ivanovich (*A Raw Youth*), 94, 133, 150
Maksim Ivanovich (*A Raw Youth*), 94–95
Maslennikov, K. I., 35n
Masloboev (*The Injured and the Insulted*), 22–23
Meier-Graefe, Julius, 66n, 72n
Mikhailovsky, N. K., 49n
Mitya. *See* Karamazov, Dmitri
Mochulsky, *xii*, 54n, 62, 70n
Modest Proposal, A, 12
Mortimer, Ruth, 81n, 90n, 93, 106, 108, 114n, 116n
Myshkin, Prince (*The Idiot*), 52, 57, 65, 87, 97, 98, 125–28, 134, 178, 179–83, 222

Nabokov, Vladimir, 70, 150, 157, 237n
Pale Fire, 70n
Natasha (*The Injured and the Insulted*), 23, 25, 80, 88, 170, 171
Natasya (*The Idiot*), 52, 134, 180–83

Netochka (*The Injured and the Insulted*), 47, 62–64, 101, 146
Netochka Nezvanova, 56, 85
Notes From the Underground, 146

Olya (*A Raw Youth*), 31
Orlov (*The House of the Dead*), 164
Othello, 192

Paris, 146, 148
Pavlovna, Tatyana (*A Raw Youth*), 149, 187
Peasant Marya, The, 77, 125
Pedophilia, ix, 15, 17n, 18, 25, 208, 235
Petya (*Poor People*), 66
Polenka (*Crime and Punishment*), 27–28n, 38n
Polzinsky, P. S., 225n
Poor People, 61, 66, 78, 145, 195, 214
Porfiri (*Crime and Punishment*), 174
Possessed, The, 94, 99, 111, 148, 184, 200n, 216
Pyotr (*Netochka Nezvanova*), 85

Raskolnikov (*Crime and Punishment*), 70n, 71n, 81, 96, 107–109, 112, 131, 175–77, 200n, 206–209
Raw Youth, A, 31, 65, 82, 83, 94, 102, 111, 123, 148, 186, 212, 229
"Rebyonok," 6, 7n, 8n, 9n, 16, 22, 23, 30, 50, 79, 84, 88, 98, 206, 208, 210, 212, 214–15, 234
Rogozhin (*The Idiot*), 127–28, 134, 180–81

St. Petersburg, 144, 206, 221
Seduro, Vladimir, 67n
Scklovsky, Viktor, 108, 116n, 235
Shatov (*The Possessed*), 99
Silbajoris, Rimvydas, 34n, 202n, 203n, 227n, 235
Simmons, Ernest J., xii, 39n, 41, 42, 46, 47, 50, 117n, 226n, 230n
Slonim, Mark, xii, 226n

Smiles, 77–78, 171, 176, 186, 192, 199n, 221; strange, 195, 196
Sonya (*Crime and Punishment*), 28, 86, 174–77, 230
Stavrogin (*The Possessed*), 99, 184, 185–86; confession of, 31, 61, 113
Steiner, George, 95, 114n
Suicide, 32n; child, 25, 31, 102–103, 209–11
Svidrigailov (*Crime and Punishment*), 11n, 17, 30, 61, 112–13, 177, 209

Teemofeevna, Marya (*The Possessed*), 99–100, 109, 184–85, 216–17
Tolstoy, Leo, 10, 31n
Childhood and Youth, 31n, 80
Torture, 84, 147, 166–67; of children, 5–11, 13n, 21, 27n, 59, 60; by Turks, 5–6n, 10n, 32–33
Trubitsyn, Nikolai, 27n, 29n, 30, 39n, 48, 52, 68n
Trusotsky (*Crime and Punishment*), 16n, 17, 18, 111

Unusual psychic states, x
"Uzhasno" (horrible), 21, 23, 30, 36n, 45, 54, 55–57n

Vanya (*The Injured and the Insulted*), 15, 19, 20–21n, 22–23n, 24, 78, 80, 81, 88, 94, 101, 110, 171, 172, 173
Varenka (*Poor People*), 78–79
Velchaninov (*The Eternal Husband*), 16, 17, 18, 19
Verhovensky, Stephan (*The Possessed*), 148
Versilov (*A Raw Youth*), 133, 145, 186
Vile Tale, A, 150
Village of Stepanchikovo and its Inhabitants, The, 7, 49–50, 85, 194
Voltaire, 43

Wasiolek, Edward, 236n
White Nights, 95, 214, 221

Winter Notes About Summer Impressions, 30, 146

Wordsworth, William, 100

Yantarevoy, R. A., 67*n*, 69*n*, 70*n*

Yarmolinsky, Avrahm, 201*n*, 236*n*

Zander, L. A., 115*n*

Zaslavski, D. I., 67*n*

Zenkovsky, V. V., 71*n*, 119–21

Zosima, Father (*The Brothers Karamazov*), 75, 122, 123, 134–35, 141, 155, 189, 191